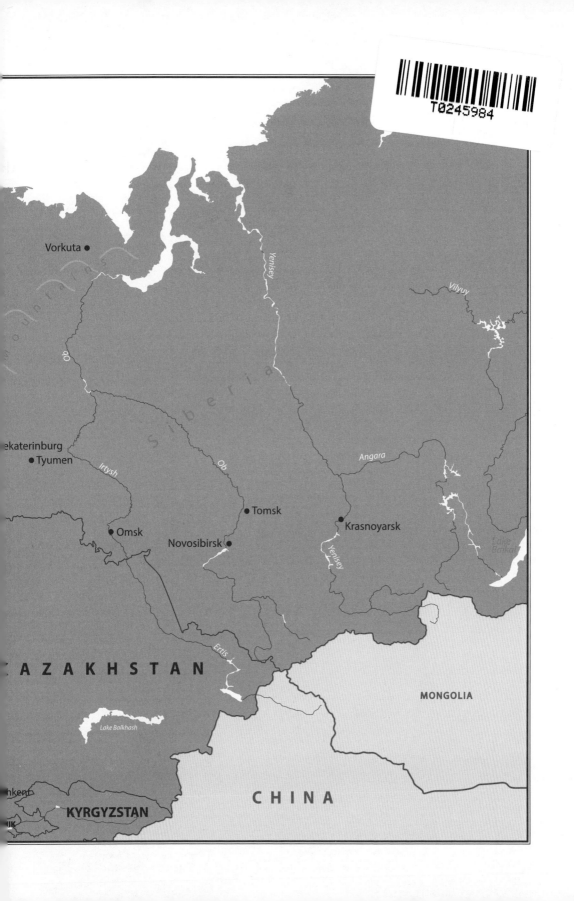

Vorkuta

Yenisey

Vilyuy

ekaterinburg
Tyumen

Irtysh

Ob

Angara

Siberia

Mountains

Tomsk

Omsk

Novosibirsk

Krasnoyarsk

Yenisey

Lake
Baikal

Ertis

KAZAKHSTAN

MONGOLIA

Lake Balkhash

hkent

KYRGYZSTAN

CHINA

SOVIET JEWRY REBORN

A Personal Journey

ASHER OSTRIN

gefen
publishing house
JERUSALEM ◆ NEW YORK
Est. 1981

On the cover:
Portrait of a kindergarten class, Kryvyi Rih, Ukraine, c.1929
(JDC ref. NY_43354).
A young girl studies Hebrew in St. Petersburg using JDC-distributed cards,
St. Petersburg, Russia, 1993 (JDC ref. NY_19041; photo by Searle Brajtman).

Editor: Debbie Ismailoff
Cover design: Leah Ben Avraham
Typesetting: Optume Technologies

ISBN: 978-965-7801-45-1

1 3 5 7 9 8 6 4 2

Gefen Publishing House Ltd.   Gefen Books
6 Hatzvi Street   c/o Baker & Taylor Publisher Services
Jerusalem 9438614   30 Amberwood Parkway
Israel   Ashland, Ohio 44805
972-2-538-0247   516-593-1234
orders@gefenpublishing.com   orders@gefenpublishing.com

www.gefenpublishing.com

Printed in Israel
Library of Congress Control Number: 2024935307

Contents

Preface

This book is about a specific period in Jewish history in a particular part of the globe and how the Jews of that time and place shaped that history. It is about a large number of Jews who were long thought to have been lost for eternity to the Jewish people but who, when a confluence of events made it possible for them to assert their identity, did so in a way that proved generations of experts wrong.

They – the Jews of the Soviet Union and of the independent states that emerged from that superpower's collapse – were not to be written off. In fact, they have experienced a renaissance and reconnection to Jewish life in numbers unprecedented in Jewish history. Many did so in the countries around the world to which they emigrated and where they continue to shape our people's present and future. Many remained in what, for want of a more elegant term, became known as the former Soviet Union (FSU) and there have worked to create exemplary Jewish communities.

The American Jewish Joint Distribution Committee, known as the JDC or, to generations of Jews around the world, more simply as the "Joint," has played a major role in this revival. I had the immense privilege of being entrusted to lead JDC's work in seeding that revival by helping the Jews of the FSU to cultivate it and bring it to fruition.

This book begins in the post-Soviet period. It is not a narrative that systematically examines the changes that the Soviet Union and then its successor states underwent. It does not attempt to explain why things developed the way that they did. Nor does it place the changes in this region in a broader geopolitical or economic context. It is a collection of experiences and reflections that I shared, in weekly email briefings, with people who had an interest in developments in the region during the early post-Soviet years.

These are reflections, registered in real time, based on my personal experiences. They are introductions to the people I met, the places I visited, the history I absorbed, and the experiences I had during the twenty-two years I worked in the Soviet Union and its successor states. I traveled several times a month during that period from my home in Jerusalem to somewhere in the region to observe, to plan, to evaluate, and to supervise our work there. Even after hundreds of trips, I was still captivated by the Jews I encountered.

The stories and analyses in this book should be read against the backdrop of the disintegration of a misconceived society and the totally unexpected rebirth of Jewish life that for generations appeared to be dormant – or worse. To frame the events each item describes in the time and context in which I experienced and described them, I provide the date when it was originally written. But they are not necessarily presented chronologically.

Rather, they are arranged into five chapters, each designed to highlight the themes that are identifiable within the narratives: the unprecedented reclamation of large numbers of Jews who, for decades, had been considered lost to the Jewish people; the possibility of building Jewish communal life where foundations for community had been obliterated; the efforts to instill the norms and the values of a Jewish community within a general environment fundamentally hostile to any expression of civic society and the rules by which it abides; and the broader role the Joint has played in shaping the direction of Jewish history since its founding in 1914, especially in these countries, during this period.

The book's first chapter is entitled "FSU", an abbreviation referring to the collection of states that emerged in the wake of the Soviet Union's demise. This chapter puts the contemporary Jewish revival in the context of the broader societies in which it was occurring. The "JDC" chapter relates how the work in this region, during this period, reflects the history, the values, and the mission of the Joint since its establishment in 1914. Chapters on "People" and "Places" are designed to provide insights into this remarkable Jewry and to demonstrate both its heterogeneity and what fundamentally unites it. The final chapter on "Identity" speaks to the efforts to reclaim these Jews for the Jewish people. Assimilation, we learn, can be reversed.

At the same time, each selection can be read alone, as each was originally written as a weekly update from the field during the time, between 1991 and

2012, when I was privileged to direct the JDC program in the region. The vantage point is from the ground up. Hopefully, it gives insight into what it meant, and means, to be a Jew in the former Soviet Union during this period, the last decade of the twentieth century and the first decades of the twenty-first.

I met Jews who had undergone incomprehensible suffering at the hands of the Nazis and the Soviets, and who then experienced the demise of a system that had promised them at least a social safety net in their twilight years. What few savings they had were wiped out by galloping inflation, state pensions were deliberately set below the poverty line, and access to supposedly free medical care in fact required "gifts for service" that were well beyond their reach. There was so much pain and suffering in the course of this life.

I write about Jews I met who sacrificed lucrative careers or opportunities to emigrate in order to take part in the enterprise of reestablishing Jewish communities in places where they had been suppressed for generations. Among these are communities that will flourish and make contributions to Jewish life and scholarship, to the Jewish people, and to the Jewish state.

I write about Jews who relocated from large cities with renascent Jewish life to far-flung regions to teach young Jews in isolated villages that are often inaccessible for large parts of the year due to harsh weather conditions. About Jews who, under fire in the midst of a civil insurrection in part of a city that had become a war zone, risked their lives to ensure that elderly members of the community who lived there would not feel abandoned and have to manage alone. I write about Jews who have watched their community's Jewish population slowly disappear, but who have resolved to remain in the community for as long as it has the critical mass to function as such. And there are many who stay beyond that point, to support the remaining few Jews who need support and have nowhere else to turn.

These pages relate stories of the last Jews in towns that in previous generations produced Jewish scholars and scholarship, where Hebrew poets and artists argued and studied with rabbis and revolutionaries. I write of Jews who live in FSU countries still ruled by dictators and despots, Jews who live in a Buddhist region in Russia, and Jews who live in walking distance from a border with Iran. Their stories are here.

Victoria was a retired nurse. In the early 1990s, during one of my visits to Leningrad, our staff told me that they had learned of her physical deterioration and invited me to join them when they brought her a wheelchair to enable her to be at least somewhat mobile.

We knocked on her door, but initially she would not let us in. The elderly were often victims of crimes, and Victoria was suspicious of us.

When she finally opened the door, she refused to accept the wheelchair. It was totally inconceivable to this woman, a product of the Soviet system, that anyone would give her something and not demand something in return. She asked, "Why are you giving this to me? What do you really want?"

Why *had* we come to her? What *did* we want? Our explanation was composed of simple words, but they represent the profound mission of JDC since its founding: "You are a Jew in need. Our mission is to help Jews in need without regard for what they believe or how they identify."

It is that simple statement that has determined the course of JDC's operations throughout its history, and it is what motivated us in our work every day in the USSR and its successor states, and indeed wherever JDC works in the world.

This book is about the Jews of the region once known as the Soviet Union: how they lived during those dramatic first decades that followed the collapse of the Soviet regime and the dismantling of its sprawling empire. It is about their struggles, their aspirations, and their motivations. It is about what set them apart from their neighbors and about how they have found their way back to the Jewish people.

It is about them, and about me. It is a book about my own personal journey among these people. In my encounter with them, I have come to understand the value and the content of identity and community in new and unexpected ways. For that I will always be indebted to them, and to the Joint, the organization that has enabled this extraordinary enterprise.

The JDC's board of directors never wavered in its commitment to JDC's vision for FSU Jewry, and its philanthropic partners facilitated the vision's fulfilment through their generous support. Many of these extraordinary individuals became valued advisors and counselors.

A driving force in my career has been the friendship and assistance of my JDC colleagues. There are too many names to mention individually. Together they are what makes the Joint the organization that it is. They have continued to enrich an organizational culture that gives practical expression to the values of a tradition all of us treasure. We are a collection of Jews from different places, with different backgrounds, with different understandings of Judaism and Jewish life. But we share a fundamental and unwavering commitment to the Jewish people.

I hope this book does justice to the hard-earned reputation of the Joint and what it represents to generations of Jews who have benefited from its support and to the dedicated staff who have made it all possible.

Ralph Goldman was a teacher and a mentor. It was a privilege to work with him and to come to know this man who, for so many of us, served as a model of commitment to the Jewish people.

This book is dedicated to my three children, Avishai, Yael, and Nadav, who spent so much time without Abba at home during their formative years. Through their sacrifice, they were full partners in my endeavors. I hope and pray that they see in my work the translation of the values that my wife, Ruth, and I tried to instill in them, supreme among them *ahavat Yisrael*.

Finally, a gratitude that knows no bounds to Ruth, my life partner. She is always there for me with wise counsel and boundless love and support. This book, like my career, is as much hers as it is mine.

"איש ואשה – שכינה ביניהם – זכו"

Asher Ostrin
Jerusalem 2024

A Personal Journey

I came to the Soviet Union twice for the first time.

In 1977, I was sent to the USSR for two weeks to meet with Jews whose applications to emigrate had been refused by the authorities. It was part of an effort by Israel to encourage these refuseniks and to keep them apprised of developments in international support for their struggle.

Two weeks in the Soviet Union of that time confirmed all that I, an American raised during the height of the Cold War, had been told about it in school and in the media: it was a powerful superpower that aspired to direct virtually every aspect of the lives of its citizens. It curbed their access to the outside world. Newspapers and magazines from the West were confiscated at border crossings; local newspapers, television, and radio were wholly controlled by the government; mail was subject to censorship; international phone calls were limited and monitored; police were stationed outside hotels to ensure that locals had no contacts with tourists. In sum, its population was sealed off from contact with the outside world to a degree that is difficult for us to imagine given the world that has developed since then. In the preparatory briefing for our visit, we were told that if the Soviet authorities had any suspicion about us during our stay, we would be followed, harassed, and – in a worst-case scenario, but one for which we had to be prepared – perhaps even detained and subjected to physical and psychological abuse.

We succeeded during the two-week visit in meeting with twelve refuseniks in four cities. Those meetings changed my life.

I was raised in a traditional Jewish home. My parents were active in Jewish communal life. It was important to them that their children have a Jewish education, that we care deeply about the fate of Israel and the Jewish people, that our Jewish identity play a significant role in who we are. The cost of all this? Tuition fees, time away from favorite activities, occasional scheduling inconveniences.

During those two weeks in Soviet cities, I met Jews who were not raised in Jewish environments, whose Jewish identities were not nurtured in their families, who had no exposure to a Jewish community. They were Jews who did not take any aspect of their newfound Jewish identity for granted. They risked paying an unfathomable price for the slightest identification with the Jewish people: to gather in a local park to commemorate the Holocaust, meet once a week in someone's home to learn to read Hebrew, or write an academic paper on Jewish life in Baku a hundred years earlier, you risked being fired from your job, arrested, and forcibly separated from your loved ones for an indeterminate length of time. Your children could be subject to daily acts of derision in school and in the schoolyard, and more.

Until that trip to the USSR, I knew that I was a Jew, but I wasn't particularly conscious of the fact on an ongoing basis. It was one of a multiplicity of identities that comprised who I was. Day to day, I gave it little thought. And identifying as a Jew certainly entailed few risks.

During that two-week trip, I sat in the kitchens and living rooms of people who were supremely aware that they were Jews. They had consciously chosen to endure the risks that this identification involved. The very notion that an identity could put a person at risk was foreign to me – and existential to them.

I was profoundly moved and fundamentally changed by these encounters. And while I had no way of knowing this at the time, they determined the course of my professional life and, ultimately, my Jewish identity.

Twelve years later, in the fall of 1989, I came back to the USSR. This was the second of my "first-time visits," because the conditions and circumstances of this second visit were so different from those I experienced in the Soviet Union of 1977. The names of the cities on the map were the same. The buildings were unchanged. The border agents and police wore the same uniforms. But the country was almost unrecognizable.

My 1977 visit was marked by fear and a total lack of hope. Yes, I was inspired by the commitment of the refuseniks. But they represented a tiny minority of the millions of Jews in the USSR at the time. The courage of these few Jews in defying the regime was remarkable, but the regime was generally perceived as all-powerful and invincible. The refuseniks were glimmers of light in a context infused with darkness and gloom. In 1977, it was evident that six decades of Soviet efforts at obliterating Jewish community and erasing Jewish identity had clearly been effective. Jewish life in the USSR had no future. The few who wished to might eventually leave, but most Soviet Jews were effectively lost to the Jewish people.

The USSR of 1989 was a different country. It was no longer ruled by an all-powerful government. By that time, many of its Warsaw Pact allies had repudiated their Communist allegiances and made demonstrative progress toward new political and economic systems, leading in turn to new geopolitical alliances. The Soviet Union was crumbling internally; the nationalities and nations that comprised it were talking openly of a new, different relationship with the Kremlin, the periphery newly empowered at the expense of Moscow's dominance. Mikhail Gorbachev's glasnost and perestroika tentatively – and in some cases unintentionally – introduced new freedoms in the political and economic realms. The sense of absolute control, the oppressive atmosphere that one felt walking the streets of Moscow in 1977 had lifted and been replaced by an excitement of the unknown and the now-possible. This was a radical departure from the predictability of Soviet life and the omnipotent regime of the previous decades. Society was changing on an almost daily basis. No one at the time could predict where all of this would lead.

My perspective on these differences was also very much the result of an evolution I had personally undergone during that period. The lens through which I viewed the Soviet Union in those two visits was not the same.

Between the trips, in 1986, I was offered an opportunity to make a direct contribution to the Jewish world. I was recruited to become the director of the Vienna office of the American Jewish Joint Distribution Committee. I knew of the JDC's legendary history as a key player in events affecting Jews worldwide since its founding in 1914. In addition to programs from Israel to Latin America to Europe and Africa, JDC's connection to Soviet Jewry was historic and significant. It operated overtly in the Soviet Union from shortly after the Communist Revolution until it was expelled and its leadership exiled or killed by Stalin in the late 1930s. Toward the end of Stalin's life in the early 1950s, he singled out the Joint as the operating arm of a world

Jewish conspiracy designed to undermine Soviet authority. Jewish artists and doctors were accused of being Joint operatives. That charge was sufficiently serious to justify their executions.

The Joint's Vienna office, which I now directed, had traditionally been the first transit point for Jews fleeing oppressive regimes on their way to resettlement in Israel or the West. Many Jewish refugees in the immediate aftermath of the Second World War transited through Vienna and the JDC office there, followed by Hungarian Jews, Polish Jews, Czech Jews, and a trickle of Jews from other Eastern European countries who were either let out or escaped in the ensuing decades. In 1986, the office dealt primarily with young Jews smuggled out of Iran and Soviet Jews in transit to a new life in the West.

When I arrived in July 1986, Vienna was hosting a multiyear conference of diplomats from European countries who were charged with negotiating the destiny of a Europe divided between East and West. That conference turned out to be a kind of harbinger, coinciding as it did with the dramatic changes in Eastern Europe at the time. At social events, we would hear a British diplomat speak of off-the-record conversations with Bulgarian counterparts who, quite unexpectedly, criticized a long-standing Communist economic policy. An Austrian friend, a delegate from his country's foreign service, related the day's highlight from the conference, when a Hungarian diplomat publicly challenged an "outdated Kremlin policy" on censorship. A French arms-control expert told how a Polish envoy spoke of the Warsaw Pact as anachronistic and entirely ineffective and, more significantly, as an unnecessary vestige of a Cold War created by Soviet imperialism. Countries that for decades had been virtually indistinguishable politically from the Soviet Union were exercising a degree of independence that was astounding. Change was in the air.

No one knew how far this would go. The Soviet satellites were rebelling. But the real question focused on the USSR. Would it react violently to the changes in the direction of its satellites, as it had so often in the past? And if it let the other countries go their own way, what would this mean for the USSR itself? And what would it all mean for Soviet Jews?

JDC did not wait for the answer to these questions. Given these developments and recognizing an opening to play a more central role with Jewish communities in the Eastern Bloc, I was asked to lead an effort to expand our involvement in Hungary, the largest Jewish community accessible to us in Eastern Europe at the time. JDC's leadership was quite explicit in its goal: "As we begin to work with populations and program areas in Hungary previously closed off to us, like youth, young families, and Jewish education, be cautious. The Soviets will undoubtedly be watching. Do not *do* or *say* anything that would someday discourage them from inviting JDC back into the Soviet Union." It was a weighty warning, couched as advice, without much detail. It was not at all clear what would constitute activities that would be perceived as problematic to the Soviet government and thereby endanger a possible return for JDC to the USSR. "Go in. Push the boundaries. But don't go too far." I didn't find the advice particularly helpful. Even less so in retrospect.

The problem was exacerbated by the chaos that marked Soviet life at the time. From sources we developed, we learned that the line between acceptable and forbidden behavior for an organization like ours in the USSR was not only unclear, it was also highly fluid and constantly changing. What was forbidden one day was encouraged the next. And there was no guarantee that it would not, in short order, revert back to being illegal. For what seemed like good reason, Soviet bureaucrats charged with executing policy were often afraid to actualize more permissive legislation endorsed by the newly democratic Duma (parliament), lest it be reversed shortly thereafter as the political winds changed. Not acting was generally seen as less threatening to one's career than possibly being held responsible for steps that might later be perceived as unacceptable.

Ironically, the opening in the Eastern Bloc posed another risk for JDC. The Hungarian government was pushing us to go far beyond what had ever been permitted in our work with Hungarian Jewry. They were doing so in part to demonstrate their independence from their Soviet overlord and to prove that they had thrown off Soviet shackles. "Invest in our Jewish schools. Build a Jewish summer camp exclusively for Jewish children. Create Jewish cultural festivals showcasing Jewish tradition and culture." In essence, our Hungarian interlocutors were encouraging us to move into areas that had been forbidden for decades in accordance with Soviet policy. JDC was a convenient tool for the Hungarians to demonstrate their new reality and to convey to the Soviets that they would chart their own path henceforth.

Therein lay a trap for JDC. By taking maximum advantage of new opportunities for Eastern European Jewry, JDC could be creating the conditions for further alienating the Soviets, thereby postponing, perhaps for decades, the chance to work with Soviet Jewry. The delay in a JDC return to work in the USSR might give even more time for the Soviets to carry out their intentions to wipe out any vestige of Jewish identity.

That was the context in which we began our first, tentative forays into the USSR some fifty-plus years after our ignominious expulsion. As it turned out, our expanded efforts with Hungarian Jewry did not present a problem. Prolonged negotiations with the Soviet government in the late 1980s finally yielded an official invitation for JDC operatives to reconnect with Soviet Jewry. The goals, the strategies, the programs – all of that would have to wait for some later date. We were told, "For now, you are welcome to make connections in our country."

JDC put together a team of six veteran staff members to do what could generously be described as "fact finding." Winston Churchill's famous characterization of Russia as "a riddle, wrapped in a mystery, inside an enigma," was as true in 1989 as it had been in 1939 when he first said it. It was a small source of comfort that Churchill, with extensive Western intelligence sources available to him, had been as perplexed about this country as we were.

During many of my early trips, I was debriefed by officers at the American embassy in Moscow. At the time, this single embassy covered all the Soviet empire's constituent republics. These would soon become independent, each with a US embassy in its own capital.

We found that the American diplomats, too, were flummoxed by the USSR in 1989. Since the country had long been the target of intensive Western intelligence gathering, a great deal of information was available about Soviet positions on geopolitical issues, on the USSR's macroeconomic challenges, on the state of agriculture and crop yields, and even on demography. Much less was known about the lives of individual Soviet citizens.

Constrained by bilateral diplomatic agreements, these diplomats could not travel freely. Moreover, both Soviet law and American security concerns generally prevented them even from entering the homes of local citizens.

As a result, they had little idea about the fine grain of life in the country. How did ordinary people make ends meet with inadequate salaries? How did they manage in an environment of chronic shortages of essential products? What was day-to-day life like for a teacher in Vinnytsia, for an engineer in Dushanbe, or for a longshoreman in Murmansk? The Jews among them were the people we met. We were in their homes. We were invited to their birthday celebrations. We heard their stories and answered their questions about a world from which they were cut off, and about the Jewish world they had heard about from their grandparents and often knew only through the vilification by Soviet media.

I remember several instances in which things that I described left the American diplomats speechless. They were largely unaware of the depth of the poverty we witnessed outside the large cities. They had heard rumors, but few had witnessed the reality themselves. They knew only in the most general terms of the primitive conditions in which people in peripheral areas often lived.

In countless towns and villages, residents drew water from wells and, in winter, used latrines far from their dwellings – best described as hovels – with temperatures hovering around minus 30 degrees (the number is in Fahrenheit, but it doesn't really matter – however you count it, when you get to those temperatures, it's really cold). Refrigerators in the homes of Jews who hosted us often had a few moldy potatoes and a cabbage or two, which comprised a week's menu.

Many medical and educational institutions throughout the USSR were in advanced stages of collapse. Antibiotics were frequently unavailable; syringes were reused without being properly sterilized. Schools were often unheated in the dead of winter, and textbooks were too expensive to purchase.

We would see much more. As lingering restrictions fell away, we traveled the length and breadth of the country and were stunned by the living conditions we encountered. But we were also moved by how Jews everywhere were undergoing a collective awakening. It gradually dawned on us that Soviet efforts to wipe out Jewish life and erase any vestige of Jewish identity had not, in fact, been as successful as was widely believed. Jews were learning and teaching Hebrew. Educational frameworks for children were established. Welfare societies were organized. Groups of volunteers were collecting money and goods to distribute to indigent Jews. Jewish doctors were seeing elderly Jewish patients and waiving their fees. Jewish electricians repaired radios and television sets for the homebound. Choirs were established with Jewish repertoires, including the latest Israeli songs.

In Tyumen, a regional capital in the far reaches of Siberia, a large banner was unfurled in December over the city's main entrance welcoming visitors to "Tyumen's Chanukah Festival Week," organized by two Jewish medical students who had been granted an unprecedented leave for a semester to plan the events. This in a town none of us could locate on a map. Similar things were happening across the vast expanse of the USSR, in large metropolises and in small villages. If there were a few dozen Jewish residents in a city, there was inevitably some Jewish activity. It was extraordinary to witness. Soviet Jewry was experiencing a rebirth.

We gradually realized that we stood on the cusp of one of the great challenges to face the Joint and indeed the Jewish world in our generation. For years, world Jewry united in a struggle against a cruel and apparently invincible foe to "free Soviet Jewry." It appeared that this phase of the struggle was over. Soviet Jewry was free. It was free to leave – or to stay and recreate Jewish communities.

It was clear that many Jews would not stay. Once emigration became an option open to almost all, many would take advantage of the opportunity. While never on this scale, there had been periods of liberalization in the USSR before. All were followed at some point by a crackdown and a reversion to the status quo ante. That was a threat that constantly hovered over this whole enterprise in the early years. There was no time for individuals to pause and observe, to consider the direction the changes were taking and their implications. The opportunity presented itself, and if you even considered emigration an option, you would likely leave. One never knew when the tide might turn back to the repression that was so familiar.

What made this situation unique was that emigration was no longer the only option for Jews who yearned to have a Jewish life. For the first time in Soviet history, it appeared to be possible to remain and, in this new environment, rebuild Jewish life and community.

The political situation continued to change at an incredible pace. Discussions on formalizing the liberalization proceeded. Real elections were held, with multiple candidates competing for a limited number of positions. An attempted coup d'état in August 1991 to reassert central control over the empire lasted all of four days. The *putschists* were confronted with large-scale protests, and the revolt collapsed. Individual republics began to declare independence, and at the end of December 1991, the red flag with a hammer and sickle was lowered from the Kremlin for the last time. The Union of Soviet Socialist Republics, a nuclear superpower, imploded with nary a whimper.

CHAPTER 1

FSU

How Is This Night Different? (March 30, 2012)

Passover is in many ways *the* holiday of the Jews of the former Soviet Union (FSU). Its message resonates for the Jews in that part of the world unlike anywhere else. The themes of slavery and freedom, of the promise of spring after a long winter of misery and oppression, mean much more to those who experienced life behind the Iron Curtain and then witnessed the USSR's collapse than to those who have known freedom all of their lives. Even today, we hear older Jews tell of what matzah meant to them in the dark years when it was, often inexplicably, available: of waiting patiently in lines outside local synagogues with other Jews to get their kilo of matzah; of actually tasting the bread of affliction, closing their eyes as they did so, and imagining how perhaps one day they too would experience redemption. Older Jews in the FSU often speak with tears in their eyes of how, by touching the matzah and then tasting it during those few days each year, they were reconnected to their roots and to memories of Seders with their grandparents. And, of course, they were supremely aware that their fellow Jews around the world were, at that very moment, sharing this very experience. Eating matzah was one of the few demonstrable Jewish acts that were not expressly forbidden, and it bound each of them to the Jewish people worldwide.

Here is a vignette of Passover in our early days of FSU work: As Jews began to identify, we knew that holiday celebrations were particularly meaningful to them. If the Jewish libraries and books that JDC was providing appealed to their intellect, and as our nascent welfare services began to address their physical needs, we were constantly on the lookout for things that would encourage them to nurture their Jewish identities through experience. Reclaiming the Jewish calendar became a priority for them, and therefore for JDC. We sent chanukiot and shofarot, groggers and candles. And in the early years we sent in people who could help plan community-wide holiday celebrations.

Passover Seders were the highlight of those first communal celebrations. They were not elaborate affairs – a hall was rented, volunteers prepared food, and children learned songs – but the turnouts were massive. Elderly Jews who still remembered sitting at their grandparents' Seders came together with the next two generations of their families to rediscover a common heritage.

Jewish university students embodied all that was special about FSU Jewry during this period. They were enthusiastic, creative, and determined. While many of their parents made only tentative moves into communal Jewish life, attending an occasional program and often educating themselves in the privacy of their own homes, younger people had no such inhibitions. They were not ashamed of what they didn't know; that was only a motivation to learn more. When it came to Jewish life, they may not have been familiar with the fine points of ritual or the proper pronunciation of the liturgy, but those were minor details. To be a Jew was to live as a Jew; it was something to experience, and not just to observe and learn about. Mobilizing them (instead of foreigners) to organize and lead communal Seders did not intimidate them at all. Instead, it was a challenge. They were prepared to devote their time and energy to learn how to do it, and then to create the environment appropriate for the event in each city, town, and village where they were welcome.

Sasha and Luda, two students in Ukraine, accepted the task of creating and running a Seder in a small town in the northern part of the country. As members of Hillel, the Jewish student organization that JDC helped introduce to the FSU, they attended two weeklong seminars to prepare them, and they were ready to roll. Whatever they lacked in knowledge they made up for in enthusiasm.

Luda had been to her first Seder the previous year. She was raised knowing that she was a Jew, but the term was essentially devoid of any significance for her. Other than a stamp notation on her internal passport (an identity card required of all Soviet citizens; the personal data it contained included the notorious "Fifth Line" identifying the bearer's nationality, in this case, "Jew"), nothing distinguished her from her neighbors. She came to her city's Hillel for the first time by accident – literally. She fell on the street in front of the rented hall where Hillel was holding an event and was brought inside to sit down and catch her breath. A few questions later she was smitten, and Hillel became a central part of her life.

Sasha had never been to a Seder. In fact, he was first told that he was a Jew when he was nineteen years old. His parents were hesitant about identifying publicly as Jews, as they were still skeptical that the post-Soviet openness, then in its infancy, would endure. Somehow, he became aware of his roots, made a connection, and volunteered with Luda to run one of the communal Seders.

Four days before Seder night, they came to the chosen town, which was home to an estimated 700 Jews. Sasha and Luda hoped to attract between 150 and 175 Jews to the Seder. The pair was told they were overly optimistic, but they were undeterred. They came with some money to rent a hall and buy some Seder staples, and they brought along about 150 Haggadot in Hebrew and Russian. The first order of business was to rent space to accommodate a crowd.

In the center of the town was a local art school. It was a large building with a basement hall that was perfect for the Seder; it was also equipped with tables and chairs. One of the school's staff explained to them that the building had been the local Communist Party headquarters just four years earlier, which was why it was outfitted so well. When the Soviet Union disbanded, the Rada, the Ukrainian Parliament, outlawed the Communist Party. That accounted for the building's transformation.

Sasha and Luda worked hard to prepare. They hung posters advertising the event and inviting local Jews. They taught some children Passover songs. They decorated the hall.

The advertisements promised the event would begin at 7:00 p.m. on Seder night. By 6:15, the 168 seats were taken. And people kept coming. And coming. By 7:00, there were more than three hundred people squeezed into the hall and disappointed people in the hallways throughout the building (fire regulations were viewed as advisory rather than compulsory).

The two students began the Seder, and only paused to breathe. During their explanations there was not a sound in the room. The silence was punctuated with boisterous singing, mostly without words, which were unfamiliar anyway. Wine, questions, eggs, salt water, matzah – all went off without a hitch.

The meal itself was modest, but no one had come for the food. When they finished eating, Sasha gave a short explanation of the fifth cup of wine, known as the cup of Elijah. He explained its folk derivation, and how Elijah was to be the harbinger of the messianic era. He spoke a bit about the Jewish notion of that time, and about Jewish history as a linear concept always moving toward a better end, in contrast to the circular, repetitive concept of history favored by the Greeks.

When he finished, there was a stirring in the back of the room. An older man stood up, pointed his finger at Sasha, and began to speak to him in a very agitated way. Under different circumstances the others would have quieted him, but his jacket was full of medals. He was clearly a war hero and therefore entitled to a modicum of respect, despite his rude interruption.

Wagging his finger, he said to Sasha, "Now you've lost us. You've simply gone too far. Until now, this whole evening brought back wonderful memories to me. I closed my eyes every few minutes and remembered the Seders of my childhood. My grandfather led it in Hebrew and explained it all to us in Yiddish. I remember the melodies and the smells. It's been almost eighty years, but it was like yesterday. And your explanations were wonderful. Slavery. Freedom. Spring. All wonderful. But what is this nonsense about a Messiah? And a 'messianic' era? You've gone too far. You can't prove any of that. It's all a bunch of nonsense. Made up. Fantasy. You've lost me. And I bet you've lost a lot of others here. Stick to history and tradition. Leave out the make-believe."

Again, silence in the room. I would expect that most people felt sorry for these two young people, who clearly had invested so much in making the evening memorable. In one moment, the goodwill and positive feelings hung in the balance. This was a test, and a patently unfair one. Sasha's and Luda's youth and inexperience were working against them, as was the setting: All eyes were now fixed on them. After a slight pause, Sasha spoke, slowly and respectfully.

"You're right. This business about the Messiah and the messianic era can't be empirically proven. And yes, it does require a leap of faith, or at least imagination, to embrace it. But I want to ask you about another fantasy, another leap of faith. One that perhaps for you and me was even more far-fetched than this one.

"Imagine that you and I had walked down this street together five years ago, when the USSR was still intact. We would have passed this building, the most prominent building in town. And covering the facade of the top floor is a large stone circle with a hammer and sickle at its center. You and I would have stopped to admire the building. And then I would have said to you: 'I know this will be hard to believe, but five years from now, in the basement of this building, in this Communist Party headquarters, our community will hold a public Seder. A Seder! *Our Jewish community*. It will be publicized so that everyone in town will know that it's going to happen. And hundreds of Jews are going to come out. And two young Jews will lead the Seder. And Jewish children will sing. And families will learn together and experience Jewish tradition. Not secretly and in a rush, but proudly, in a public place. And not *any* public place, but in the building that represented our oppressors, the great and powerful Soviet Union."

Sasha paused a moment to let it all sink in. And then he continued, still in a very respectful manner, looking straight at his challenger:

"Now I ask you: Between that scenario and the scenario about the messianic era – which strikes you as more outlandish and improbable?"

There was absolute silence. The Seder concluded with the singing of *Am Yisrael Chai*, a kind of anthem of the Soviet Jewry protest movement that speaks to the eternity of the Jewish people.

We risk taking the wonder of this enterprise for granted. Passover is the time to remember that we should not.

Secret Cities (May 30, 2003)

Anyone with experience of life in the USSR has myriad anecdotes about how the flow of information was stymied: there was the need to order international calls three days in advance, the confiscation of *Time* and *Newsweek* magazines on entry into the country, and so on. I had a close friend who lived in Leningrad, and when we first were introduced, he told me that his professional training was in "theoretical computing." I was unfamiliar with the field and asked him to elaborate. "We can't afford computers," he said, "and the government considers them a potential political risk, so we can't own them, or even generally have access to them. So my work in computers is theoretical."

When things began to change in Eastern Europe in the late 1980s, a small number of NGOs looked for ways to encourage and effect further change in various aspects of life there. Numerous paths were chosen, some creative, others less so. Looking back, one can point to many initiatives that nudged societies in the direction that was necessary to replace what had been with a new reality. One such initiative that took place several years before the changes in the USSR occurred sticks in my mind as particularly innovative in that it addressed a core problem at its root. Ultimately, it had both a symbolic and a very real impact that is difficult to comprehend, even in retrospect. The Open Society Foundation flooded Eastern Europe with photocopy machines.

In the early period of our work in the USSR, one needed official permission to photocopy a piece of paper. Access to copiers was strictly controlled as a way of ensuring that only officially sanctioned information could be disseminated. To secure permission, one needed a good reason to copy the item, forms filled out in triplicate, and an official stamp on a document to authorize the (one) copy. Needless to say, an enormous amount of discretionary time was required to get this done, and one attempted to complete the process only for things that were absolutely essential.

Limited transparency and access to information were essential for the regime's stability, but as with everything else, the USSR took things to an extreme. Certain types of information were deemed critical to the security of the state. This led to the creation of a new concept: the secret city.

These cities appeared on no maps, and there was no public access to them. In many cases, the cities didn't even have names. And of course, no outsider could visit them – because, after all, they did not exist!

The cities generally fell into two categories: cities with major military installations and cities engaged in top-secret work related to nuclear energy. The residents of the latter were generally highly educated and well paid. Jews were resident in disproportionate numbers because of their disproportionate representation in the sciences and engineering, even though there was a quota at work in many of these locales that limited the numbers of Jews.

Merit generally took a back seat to ideological concerns. A mediocre scientist with impeccable political credentials was often preferred over a colleague who was not a member of the party, even if the task at hand was of supreme national importance and required the better mind. Jews who were drawn to live in these places were generally highly assimilated and certainly had no desire to put their positions at risk by exhibiting undesirable behavior – for example, by identifying publicly as Jews.

With the collapse of the USSR and the ensuing economic crisis, many secret cities and their residents fell on hard times. Government budgets were cut back, and things like pensions did not top the list of urgent government expenditures. Once attracted by material advantages such as luxury items sold at a discount, exotic foods unavailable elsewhere in the USSR, and the availability of housing, which was very limited elsewhere, many older Jews were now stranded in these out-of-the-way regions, with limited possibilities for bettering their plight. Many were even left without the right to emigrate, as residents of these cities often had high-level security clearances that required a "cooling off" period, essentially preventing them from leaving for up to ten years after the end of their employment.

JDC serviced Jews in eleven of the twenty-six secret cities in Russia. We, of course, couldn't work with them directly, as we were not allowed access. Getting the job done meant working through local organizations.

In one such city, Novouralsk, its Jewish population of some 150 souls had created a community structure with which we could partner. A representative of the community would come every two months to our office in Ekaterinburg, the regional capital with a substantial Jewish community, to coordinate the delivery of JDC welfare services to thirteen elderly members of the Novouralsk community.

The assistance was provided by the Ekaterinburg Hesed but brought to Novouralsk by a member of their own community. In addition to receiving food packages, this assistance also included a medical equipment lending program and a volunteer doctor who provided medical care. The newborn community ran biweekly social programs, including youth and family clubs that were established with JDC input.

That's how we brought a full menu of services to Jews living in a place that officially does not exist!

Pravda (August 13, 2002)

During the Soviet period, the newspaper *Pravda* ("Truth") was the mouthpiece of the regime. If an individual or a national or ethnic group fell out of favor, a denunciation on the pages of *Pravda* was generally the first official indication that trouble was to follow.

In December 1952, a group of doctors was accused on the paper's front page of being part of a plot to kill Stalin. They were agents of an international imperialist organization determined to undermine the USSR – the Joint. The fact that most of the accused had identifiably Jewish names made it clear that Jews were now in Stalin's crosshairs. Only his death in March 1953 aborted his plans.

Today's *Pravda* has little in common with its predecessor. For your reading pleasure, a piece from *Pravda*, dated January 6, 2004:

Ten of the Most Stupid Laws in the Former USSR

Not only the USA has funny laws; there are plenty of them in the new independent states of the former USSR:

- In Kazakhstan, it is prohibited to address state officials in foreign languages. If you say "sir" to the official, you will have to pay a $10 fine at once.
- In Turkmenistan, if you are a Turkmen citizen and come to the country's capital, Ashkhabad, it is your obligation to visit the square in front of the presidential palace. This is a recent law because the construction of the complex of monuments and fountains was completed only several months ago. Few real ancient monuments have been preserved in Ashkhabad up to now.
- By law, all citizens of Turkmenistan must acknowledge that Turkmen President Niyazov is a good-humored person.
- Laws prohibit stepping on Turkmen coins and bills because national heroes are depicted on them.
- In Tajikistan, women are not allowed to drink more than one glass of wine in bars and restaurants. Lawmakers believe that a large amount of alcohol makes a woman "morally and sexually unstable." Breaking this law results in a big fine and provides valid grounds for divorce.

- In Kyrgyzstan, traffic policemen are obliged to report to their bosses all bribes they received during the working day.
- In Russia, surprisingly, nobody canceled the Soviet law forbidding the placement of advertising boards at road curbs. This same law further forbids constructing apartment and public buildings and warehouses in proximity to a road and does not provide any further specifications of its context.
- The Administrative Code adopted in 1948 is still valid in Russia. As a reminder, this code was adopted at the height of the power and influence of one of the worst dictators of the twentieth century. According to this code, we all violate the law, which provides a justification for incarceration or more serious punishment. For example, according to point 3 of Article 164, people must pay a fine for "contacting foreign citizens with the purpose of purchasing some items." It is difficult to understand this in light of how importers in contemporary Russia make their living.
- These are minor things when compared to the authority the government has according to the Russian Federation law "On requisition and confiscation of property," adopted on March 28, 1927. This law has not been canceled so far. Article 17 of this law allows the state to confiscate the property of the persons "who left the territory of the Republic and did not return by the moment of confiscation." This means that if you go abroad, all your property can be confiscated if you do not return by the time the procurator sets.
- Article 152 of the Russian Administrative Code strictly prohibits purchasing bread from a bakery for feeding cattle and poultry.

Stability (November 28, 2003)

I began my JDC career working in Vienna in the mid-1980s. At that time Vienna was a transit point for Eastern European Jews on their way to freedom in the West, which it had been since the mid-1950s. By the time I arrived, in the immediate aftermath of the Brezhnev period, known as a "period of stagnation," the USSR had turned inward (unbeknownst to us at the time, it was in the midst of its death throes), and emigration was almost completely choked off.

However, concurrent with the pause in Soviet migration, Jewish emigration from Iran was burgeoning. Hundreds of refugees became thousands during that period. Reaching Vienna was not easy, and it was the culmination of an arduous journey, the details of which will someday make a great screenplay.

During the first year or two of this exodus, we often asked the newly arrived Jews what had caused them to flee. Many would pull aside corners of their clothing to reveal scars from beatings. Most, though, would whisper one word: Khomeini. For them the name of the ayatollah summed it all up: the persecution, the beatings, and the lack of prospects for improvement in a retrograde society.

I write now because of a change that gradually occurred about a year and a half into my tenure in Vienna. First occasionally, and then with some degree of frequency, the response to the same question, "Why leave now?" was diametrically opposite: "Because Khomeini might die." The ayatollah was sick, and they were increasingly concerned about what would follow in the aftermath of his demise. First, they feared him, then they feared a situation in which he was no longer there.

I was reminded of this by events that occurred in the former Soviet Republic and now-independent nation of Georgia, which resulted in the ouster of its president, former Soviet foreign minister Eduard Shevardnadze. From the time he assumed the presidency after the breakup of the USSR, his government was frequently accused of corruption. Demonstrations spread and grew until he had to vacate his office.

It was interesting to follow the stance of the local Jewish community as disenchantment with the regime grew. Despite being Stalin's birthplace, Georgia has traditionally been a warm host to its Jews. That said, the Jewish community was not prominent in the efforts to throw out Shevardnadze's corrupt regime. As a minority, the Jews would have been wise to keep their heads down and out of the fray, and to remain neutral as all waited to see how things developed.

But that's not what happened. The Jews were solidly lined up behind Shevardnadze. While they suffered no less than their neighbors from the corruption and lawlessness that had taken hold in Georgia on his watch, they nonetheless backed him.

It's important to understand why, and the "why" is connected to the Iran story above. The most important thing for this community, above all else, was stability. Jewish communities in places like this fear upheaval and political change. Sudden shifts and the unknown strike fear in their hearts. Ferment in society often leaves its vulnerable exposed to radical forces.

Traditionally, Jews learn to adapt to all kinds of societies and regimes. While Georgia is the most prominent example of the volatility that followed the Soviet Union's breakup, there are many others. Take Azerbaijan, where the president rigged an election after appointing his son to be his party's only candidate, essentially anointing the son as his successor. There were protests…and the Jews, by and large, stayed home. The devil you know simply trumps the one who is unknown, especially when you are a part of a traditionally vulnerable minority with a long history of victimization.

Dysfunction (May 1, 2009)

What follows is a personal experience that is indicative of the situation in Ukraine. I could write about unemployment figures, rises in prices, or government torpor, but one small anecdote illustrates the dysfunction pervading the whole country.

We stayed in a small hotel with twenty rooms and a small restaurant attached to it. In order to avoid taxes and engagement with a byzantine and unwieldy legal system, businesses have come up with all sorts of methods to circumvent the bureaucracy. As a result, the hotel has five different owners – not "partners" in the sense that we normally understand, but individual owners. Which owner you paid depended on which room you occupied. One owner supplied the food in the restaurant, another provided liquor, a third provided soft drinks, and yet another was responsible for coffee and tea.

When you checked out, if you wanted to pay by credit card, you were faced with separate bills from each of the above. During my two-day stay in that hotel, my credit card was charged for six different transactions. All I did was sleep there and eat breakfast.

Now multiply that by all the businesses in an entire country, and you begin to understand the predicament of post-Soviet Ukraine!

The Medical System (April 29, 2002)

When our enthusiasm for the strides we'd made got the better of us, there would be reminders of where we were operating. One of our staff in Moscow went to a hospital to visit a colleague who was hospitalized with pneumonia. He was asked by the attending physician to give blood on behalf of the hospitalized colleague.

That alone is bizarre. I have no pretensions of knowing proper medical procedure. Suggesting a transfusion for pneumonia seems a bit off, but not yet noteworthy. This staff member went to the nearest blood-donor clinic and was interviewed by a professor in one of Moscow's medical schools who was moonlighting at the clinic. He refused our colleague's request to give blood because he wears eyeglasses.

Voluntarism (January 31, 2003)

In the USSR, voluntarism was generally an exception to societal norms. One example of how ironic Soviet ideology was: Every year on Lenin's birthday, citizens were forced to "volunteer" to engage in public works. It is no wonder that real "voluntarism" carried with it a stigma. The concept of "forced voluntarism" contributed to a cynicism that developed around many aspects of civic society, which made instilling a notion of shared responsibility – the basis of any Jewish community, and indeed of civic society itself – that much more challenging. And that makes this example even more moving.

It's told in a note from our translator in Kostroma, a city in the Volga region of Russia, whose mother was a Hesed volunteer:

> My mother is doing better and is almost recuperated from the course of treatment for her heart arrhythmia. I suspect that she overloaded herself for her age with her volunteer work – for the last four months she made two hospital visits each day. After one of the ladies got home, my mom had to climb the stairs to the fourth floor to visit her; there was no elevator. All the while, she was worried about having to confront the patient's neighbor when

she reached the correct landing. He has a drinking problem and called my mother nasty antisemitic names each time she appeared. He threatened her with an axe and locked her in the patient's apartment twice as punishment for visiting.

Also, in that period my mother took five trips to Ivanovo [over eighty miles away] to accompany an elderly couple to a cardio center for consultations and an operation. There were no local municipal services to assist them.

She also had to deal with the bureaucracy here for two months to get documents for a young Jewish psychiatric patient who was homeless and ill. He was found alone in an attic, moaning in pain. The bureaucracy demanded all sorts of certificates to excuse him from military service, even though he was hospitalized in an asylum.

But even after all this, and her own illness, my mother cannot wait to return to her Hesed responsibilities.

Russian Jewish Congress (February 3, 2006)

Over the last few months, several developments occurred in the Jewish political scene in Russia that warrant explanation, specifically with respect to changes in the Russian Jewish Congress (henceforth referred to by the initials of its Russian name, REK, an acronym that can also be read phonetically as an appropriate description of the organization in its early years). This background provides a window into the earliest expressions of Jewish philanthropy in the post-Soviet system.

First, a bit of history. When the Iron Curtain began to disintegrate, there was a rush for the gates, with Jewish traffic running two ways. The exit gate was crowded during the massive waves of emigration but, at the same time, Western Jewry was pushing through the "in" door. Anxious to reconnect with this enormous pool of Jews, numerous organizations trekked to Moscow and points beyond to establish a presence and begin to carve out a niche for themselves. This included, of course, JDC and the Jewish Agency for Israel, but also dozens of smaller organizations and movements across the religious spectrum, Jewish "defense" organizations, and numerous other communal bodies.

It was clear to most that, in order to function effectively, one needed a local partner. This could be a person or a Jewish organization from among the many that mushroomed during the heyday of perestroika.

Among local Jews there was a desire to institute some control over the process. At a founding congress in 1989, a collection of newly established Jewish cultural organizations from around the USSR formed "Vaad," which was to be…well, it actually was not entirely clear what it was to be. Depending on who was speaking, it was either a coordinating body for local organizations, or an association that spoke for Soviet Jewry to the West, or one that represented Soviet Jewry to the authorities in Moscow. And these are only the descriptions given by those positively disposed toward Vaad.

For Western Jewry, Vaad was a convenient representative body. By working with it, one could hopefully refute charges of imperialism, which were regularly leveled at foreign organizations.

This is not the place for an evaluation of why Vaad unraveled. Suffice it to say that the collapse of the USSR had an impact on the unity of Jewish communities from the various states. Just as the Baltic states chafed under centralized rule from distant and alien Moscow, Jewish communities also moved toward decentralization and a rejection of anybody purporting to speak or act on their behalf.

That was how a group of Jewish oligarchs came to establish REK. The organization's goals were manifold, but the primary one was to raise money for Jewish causes. It was really the first initiative of local Jews to raise "local" money – the beginnings, as it were, of Jewish philanthropy in Russia. I use the term "beginnings" for convenience. Russian Jewry once had tremendous philanthropic enterprises, but all of that was eradicated in the Soviet era.

There was never really an administrative structure to REK. Instead, it was an organization built around the personality of its leader. From across Russia, newly-wealthy Jews affiliated with REK, as the founding oligarchs had excellent connections with the regime and, where needed, provided access commensurate with the level of contribution to REK.

The agenda of REK at the time was not clear. Emphasis was put on raising funds; little attention was paid to allocations. Instead of giving directly, most wealthy Jews who were interested in donating to some Jewish cause funneled their Jewish charity through REK, with instructions indicating where their money was to go. But there was no effort to assess needs or to create an allocations process – or a fundraising campaign, for that matter.

Because they are not accountable to the community, REK's choices of projects to support through the years have sometimes seemed quite strange. To give one example, enormous sums of money went into the construction of a new synagogue at the site of the official Russian World War II Memorial in Moscow, alongside a new church and mosque at the same site.

It is easy in hindsight to criticize this allocation. After all, in this region, many Jews end the month without food or medicine due to inadequate government pensions, numerous Jewish children have needs that can be easily addressed by money that no one provides, and so on.

But there were extenuating circumstances at the time. In this instance, the statement made by having a synagogue at an official government site, alongside other houses of worship, was important to a Jewish community just emerging from years of persecution and isolation.

REK leadership eventually ran afoul of the Kremlin. They were targeted not because of their involvement in the Jewish community, but because their business interests and growing political involvement violated what was understood to be an agreement with Kremlin satraps. In quick succession, REK presidents came and went. Gradually, REK's influence waned as it became a victim of political trends beyond its narrow focus. It had, though, blazed a trail, enabling Jewish philanthropy in Russia to take on its next iteration.

Conception Day (August 17, 2007)

The Associated Press reported yesterday that a Russian region has found a novel way to fight the nation's declining birthrate: It has declared September 12 "Conception Day" and is giving couples time off from work to procreate! The hope is for a big brood of babies nine months later, on Russia's national day. Couples who "give birth to a potential patriot" during the June 12 festivities are eligible to win money, cars, refrigerators, and other prizes.

Ulyanovsk, a region on the Volga River about 550 miles east of Moscow, began holding similar contests in 2005. Since then, the number of participants in the contest, and the number of babies born to them, has been on the rise.

Now you may wonder what connection this may have to you readers. I am pleased to inform you that, after extensive negotiations, we have closed a deal that makes members of the JDC board sitting on any one of JDC's four FSU committees eligible to participate in the contest! Kudos to our staff who, in the best JDC tradition, spotted an opportunity and have found a way to capitalize on it so that JDC benefits (through board engagement, if you'll excuse the term) and the Russian people will potentially benefit from a large number of superior-quality new patriots!

The downside is that the only prize for which you are eligible is a Russian-made refrigerator.

The Economy (February 6, 2009)

I am going to start this update with a kind of executive summary. For those of you who are too busy to read the entire document but who are interested in the bottom line, in a moment I will sum up the content of this briefing in one sentence.

First, the subject: I am just back from a short visit to Kyiv. The purpose of the visit was to get a better understanding of the current economic situation in Ukraine, and how it is affecting our programs and clients. The picture the experts paint of Ukraine's situation is not a pretty one, but there is no substitute for being on the ground, seeing what is happening, and speaking with professionals and lay people. The anecdotes illustrate the cold statistics and make the situation understandable.

Our first meeting was with a woman representing the municipal administration's welfare department, who told me of a recent decree by the mayor that sums up the scope of the problems facing Ukraine today: "As of next Monday, the city is imposing a cemetery tax, to be levied on all visitors for each visit to a cemetery in the city of Kyiv."

As they say, "All the rest is commentary." That one decree tells the whole story: the desperation of the authorities to raise revenue by any possible means, the manner in which the current crisis affects the population in totally unanticipated ways, and that the emotionally and materially needy are the primary victims. Rather than raise taxes to generate real income to address very serious challenges, they nickel-and-dime the population, exploiting the citizenry at a time of emotional vulnerability.

As a state, Ukraine is in an advanced stage of decline. It has not had a functioning government for a generation, and there is no political coalition prepared to grapple with its problems. On top of that, the economy has collapsed. Ukraine's currency, the hryvna, is in free fall. Markets for the few goods the country produces, such as steel and chemicals, have constricted considerably with the worldwide economic slowdown, and demand for one of its major exports – people to work in Europe's construction industries – has also almost completely stopped as construction grinds to a halt on the continent due to the credit crunch. It is almost impossible to get a seat on a flight from Kyiv to western Ukraine. That region, bordering on Poland, once supplied enormous numbers of construction workers for the EU. As these workers flock back home due to the halt in construction, they return via Kyiv before flying on to their final destinations. Tickets for the connecting flights are booked weeks in advance.

Official unemployment figures have remained steady over the past few months. At first blush, this is counterintuitive, until one learns further that labor laws make firings very difficult. Therefore, employees are sent on months-long unpaid leave. Factories operate only three days a week. Their employment rolls remain at their previous numbers, but output has been reduced by more than 50 percent, and salaries have been reduced commensurately.

In the Kyiv region, requests for support from the Jewish Family Service for mothers giving birth and for food for their neonates are up 31 percent. Parents are still employed, but their incomes are halved, or worse.

Pensions have traditionally been calculated based on the average salary during the last three years of employment. Those salaries begin with a base to which all sorts of additions accrue. One gets extra money for being a World War II veteran, for having a college degree, or for attendance at specialty training sessions throughout one's career. All those extras have now been eliminated; pensions throughout the country are now calculated only on the salary base, often retroactively eliminating those components that gave an added buffer and made the pensions reasonable. Pensions are once again below the poverty line.

If we had hoped that more recent retirees might not be as dependent on Hesed services as those who preceded them, that hope is evaporating for now. Pensions are not being adjusted to keep pace with inflation. In real terms, the elderly who are dependent on this (generally inadequate) money each month are faced with challenging price increases with which they lack the means to cope.

It is becoming increasingly difficult to conduct competitive bidding processes. Inflation renders prices meaningless after a few days – previously reliable contractors often change their bids after being selected because of the unstable prices of essential materials. Entire lines of products are unavailable. Diapers for seniors must be imported, and therefore cannot be purchased. To conserve hard currency, imports are limited, even if they are necessary. Examples abound, but perhaps the most painful is medicine. Ukraine is not a major manufacturer of medicine, and our elderly clients are major consumers.

Vaccinations have been postponed. In the current climate, that is a synonym for *canceled*. Children are not vaccinated. Period.

Prices of commodities are rising faster than inflation. In the last month, the cost of bread rose 28 percent, milk 15 percent, and pasta 35 percent. The cost of electricity and home heating has risen in four out of the last six months. The social workers with whom we spoke returned repeatedly to the subject of the difficult choices the elderly must make each month, such as whether to buy medicine or food. Purchasing enough of both is simply out of the question in the current economic climate. These kinds of dilemmas had virtually disappeared in the region during the last few years but have now returned.

We met with the director of a hospital, who is also a member of the Hesed's board of directors. According to law, all medical services are free. In practice, however, that is not the situation.

The hospital director illustrated his problem with the following example. He employs about a thousand people in his hospital, a number that includes the entire staff – doctors and nurses as well as custodial and administrative help. He was given 720,000 hryvna to pay salaries in the month of January. It was his to divvy up as needed. That is an average of about 700 hryvna per person. During our visit the hryvna/dollar exchange rate was 8.2 hryvna to one US dollar. The average pension in Ukraine is about 490 hryvna per person.

Thus, he had an average of less than one hundred dollars per employee per month for his 350-bed hospital, including physicians and all kinds of specialists.

As if all of that were not sobering enough, he referenced the shocking fact that the life expectancy of a Ukrainian male in the early years of the millennium is 58.2 years. This life expectancy will diminish as the current crisis worsens.

Finally, a personal note: It was inspiring to meet with JDC field professionals and members of local Jewish communities, and to hear from them how they are coping in this situation. So much around them is collapsing, and their challenges are breathtaking. They persevere and flourish, all the while maintaining an infectious optimism, an unwavering commitment to assist the Jewish elderly who rely on them.

I note this because it runs counter to what is generally perceived to be the situation with the citizens of former Soviet states. Sociologists in the region often refer to *Homo sovieticus,* by which they mean that the perverse values and polluted morality of the Soviet state were inculcated so deeply in the psyches of its citizens that this dire situation remained even after the Soviet Union imploded. The lack of civic bonds, the damaged social fabric, and the corruption are all so endemic to these societies that it will take generations to correct them.

This may be true of vast swaths of Ukrainian society, but it has not been our experience with those who have chosen to rebuild their Jewish communities. Quite the contrary. And given that this is the context in which this rebuilding is taking place, it is all the more remarkable.

The Police (February 27, 2009)

From time to time we are reminded that while the countries of the FSU are very different places now than they were in the time of the USSR, there still remain some unpleasant similarities to that time. Are they vestiges of the old regime that will fade away with time? Or do today's governments still see them as necessary in order to ensure their survival?

The following is a verbatim report we received from our security personnel in one of the countries where we work. The only change in the report is the obfuscation of the name of the city, so as not to cause us any problems in the future.

Today I received a report of a man who was observing the comings and goings at the Jewish community center. He seemed particularly interested in who was entering the building. He was clearly a local and I was not concerned about terrorism. I watched him for about thirty minutes. I wanted to observe whether he had partners or was working alone. I did not see anyone else.

At the end of that time, I approached him and introduced myself as responsible for security at the JCC. I asked him what he was doing there, and what his interest was in the JCC. The man told me that, apparently, he had made a mistake, and started to walk away.

I called after him and told him that he could not do that without an explanation. If he left, I would follow him and would inform the police. I also told him that I was armed and would not hesitate to use my weapon if I needed to.

At that point he took out his wallet and showed me a card identifying him as an agent of the local security police.

I phoned an associate of mine who works for that agency, explained to him the circumstances, and gave him the identifying information of that man. My friend asked me to hand the telephone to this man, and they had a brief conversation. Afterwards, my friend confirmed his identity. I agreed with the man to meet later that evening at a neutral place.

We met, and he told me the following: He had been observing the JCC for about three hours when I accosted him. There are elections soon to be held in the country and there are political activists (local Jews) who frequent the JCC. They come in various capacities: to drop off or pick up their children, or to participate themselves in some of the activities. They represent a wide range of political affiliations, and some of them are active in movements that oppose the current government. Moreover, next to the JCC is the office of a "quite radical political party that opposes the government and is supported by the American embassy." It was necessary to determine if this was just a coincidence, or if there is a connection between the JCC and the party.

This interaction was relatively benign. But imagine, for a moment, what this represents on a larger scale. The political systems may have changed in FSU countries, but in many places the security services are still functioning and performing functions more suited to our notions of the USSR.

Philanthropy (April 3, 2009)

Enormous amounts of ink have been spilled in studies of philanthropy over the last few years. Universities have established departments to investigate the issue from an academic perspective. Studies have been commissioned, books written, and lectures given. And it all keeps coming.

The focus in most of these instances is on philanthropy in Western countries, and to a large extent, in the US. But what about philanthropy in the FSU? What characterizes it? How is it developing? What are its limitations and its potential?

A conference on these issues was held recently in Moscow, attended by activists, scholars, and officialdom. The purpose was to look at the state of charitable giving and volunteerism in Russia. There was no particular Jewish focus at the conference, although we can assume that its findings apply equally to the evolving Jewish and non-Jewish philanthropic environment in Russia, and it is therefore valuable to us as we ratchet up our efforts at increasing local giving.

What follows are some of the key findings of the conference, and my comments:

1. Russian philanthropy is currently dominated by a few wealthy and ultra-wealthy Russians. The notion of an obligation to give has not yet percolated down to the middle class. The few big players also dominate the philanthropic agenda, which is considerably narrower than it might be if the responsibility for giving were shared among a broader spectrum of people. To a large extent, these wealthy givers are cut off from broader Russian society. They live in closed-off areas, among their own kind, and they shop, vacation, and educate their children with others just like them. As media is government controlled and focused on a positive spin at the first sign of a problem, they are rarely exposed to the life of the common man or woman.

Therefore, decisions concerning support are often made within narrow contexts and with limited information and experience

2. Russians as a community know little or nothing about the charitable activities of the large foundations the big players establish. One recent poll revealed that the only foundation most Russians could name was George Soros's Open Society Foundation. This is particularly troubling because that organization closed its Russian office and discontinued its presence there several years ago. In the eyes of most Russians there is no third sector. There are no models for giving because charitable giving in general is unknown. The notion of charity as a responsibility of those who have resources is alien.

3. Most Russian philanthropy is conducted in nontransparent ways. If you are interested in finding out more about the activities of specific foundations, there is no way to do so. These organizations are not accountable to the population at large, whose lives they may impact in significant ways. There is little legislation governing foundation practice, which fosters further suspicion.

4. Russians generally do not trust philanthropic groups to distribute money properly, and consequently, nearly half the population surveyed in a recent study said that they were not prepared to contribute time and money to charitable groups. They were, however, prepared to give charity directly to those who most needed it. In a sense, they see foundations in the same light that they view government – corrupt, unaccountable, and driven by a desire for self-enrichment on the part of those who run them.

5. Russian philanthropic giving is highly focused. Four sectors – education, culture, orphans, and hospitals – get 99 percent of the money disbursed. Only one ruble in a hundred is spent on all other things *combined*. Neglected populations include the elderly and the poor. The areas not addressed are seen as the proper purview of government, and philanthropic giving, to the extent that it relieves government of its obligations, at least in the minds of the population at large, simply allows government bureaucrats to abscond with more government funds.

From a Western viewpoint, two subjects were noticeably missing from the discussions on philanthropy. The first was the church. The Orthodox Church plays an increasingly dominant role in Russian civic life. Politicians strive to be associated with the church, which has official status in Russia and often takes positions on the social issues of the day. And yet, unlike the religious sector in Western countries, it is not at all associated in the public's mind with charity. People surveyed were hard-pressed to name philanthropic endeavors backed by the church.

The second system conspicuously missing is the government. Or perhaps the fact that it is unnamed points to its ubiquity; its presence is so dominant in the philanthropic sector that it need not be mentioned. The primary issues mentioned above – culture, education, orphans, and hospitals – are arenas in which government responsibility is thought to be primary.

Many of the foundations in today's Russia are endowed by businessmen who reached their lofty positions through connections with government officials. In return, the foundations become a kind of slush fund by which businessmen repay their patrons. In effect, they function as extensions of the government.

The Kremlin reclaimed many Russian treasures for sale on world markets by encouraging foundations to purchase them and donate them to Russian institutions. An orphanage run by a relative or friend of a powerful politician will benefit from the largesse of the local business community. The quid pro quo is obvious. The politician who solicited the donation is seen as having the interests of his constituents at heart, and in return for donating a percentage of his or her profits, the businessperson will get the sought-after license, access to the formulators of legislation, tax breaks, etc.

The situation is problematic, to be sure, but there is no reason to despair. The first step in creating a culture of philanthropy is to understand its current state.

A piece of JDC lore related to the charity as "middleman": This is not unique to the FSU. In his recent book of memoirs, *From Couscous to Kasha*,[1] former colleague Dr. Seymour Epstein (aka Epi) tells the following story:

---

[1]   Seymour Epstein, *From Couscous to Kasha: Reporting from the Field of Jewish Community Work* (Jerusalem: Urim, 2009).

It seems that a penniless Jew landed in New York, and he was concerned that he would not be able to celebrate Passover properly because of his poverty. He decided to write a letter to God asking for help: "Dear God, please send me 100 dollars to celebrate Pesach as required by Your law." He addressed it to God and dropped it into the nearest mailbox. By wondrous luck it fell into the hands of a Jewish postal employee, who sent it to the JDC headquarters. The workers at JDC were not sure what to do with it, but the director instructed them to send the fellow 50 dollars. After receiving the money and using it to celebrate a fine Passover, our friend decided to write a letter of thanks: "Dear God, Thank You very much for the money You sent. It was used well over the holiday. Only, next time please don't send via the Joint, since they deducted fifty percent."

Professional Courtesy (December 27, 2002)

Since the collapse of the USSR, Georgia has gradually deteriorated into a social cesspool. So many attempts have been made on the life of its president that the press has stopped counting. Kidnapping for ransom is part of the price that local businesspeople pay for doing business.

Much of the Georgian mafia moved to Moscow in the mid-nineties. One can assume it was market forces at work – that's where the money is. As part of President Putin's cleanup campaign of Russian society, he put in place several "disincentives" for them to pursue their career choices in Moscow (to phrase it delicately), prompting them to reopen some of their "franchises" in several peripheral cities in Georgia.

In one of those cities, a significant amount of money passes through the Hesed operation to purchase goods and services. These gentlemen decided to target the Hesed and aggressively approached the director and let him know that they expected their share of the Hesed "profits" (for that is how they saw the budget). They further generously outlined for him, in graphic terms, what the consequences of his refusal would be.

We arranged to spirit the director and his family out of the country several days before their deadline expired, and were forced to find alternative ways to service needy elderly in the city.

That incident reminded me of an experience we had, with a slightly different outcome, when we opened our office in Kyiv shortly after we re-entered the USSR. Hours after the official opening, three men presented themselves at the office and, in a most polished and diplomatic way, "recommended" that we enter into an agreement with them that amounted to paying protection money. As the conversation progressed, they proceeded to spell out, in great detail, what would transpire if the money was not forthcoming. Not that they, of course, would be involved in any way in the damage that would be done to staff, equipment, and the office itself. But we needed to understand that without this agreement, they would not be available to ensure that this scenario would not come to pass. They "politely" requested an answer within two weeks.

I need not describe the tension during that period. There was no recourse to a legal system, and the security apparatus basically did not function. The payment demanded, while modest in its initial stages, would undoubtedly escalate. We were, after all, transferring into Ukraine fantastic sums of money to assist the needy throughout the country. That we were an NGO and not a business was not of particular interest to our new friends.

After consulting numerous "experts" about how exactly to proceed, and with the deadline soon to expire, I had a serendipitous meeting with a local Jew whom I knew to be very well connected throughout the city. I raised the issue in a desperate hope that perhaps he had an idea. He was neither surprised nor terribly troubled. "No problem. Call Yasha at this number. He will help you."

Yasha was friendly and reassuring, and he dealt with the issue. I later learned that he was connected with a similar racket in another district of the city. It turned out that his aunt was a client of our welfare program. He contacted his "colleagues" and told them to leave us alone, which they did. A kind of "professional courtesy."

Renaissance (October 8, 2010)

What is it like to be a young person in a small town in the FSU?

I can cite all sorts of data on the impact of the rising cost of living and growing unemployment. I can reference statistics that point to poor opportunities for education and the deterioration of the social fabric, as reflected in crime statistics. We can look at rising infant mortality and the collapse of the comprehensive medical system, and much more. It is not a pretty picture. But none of these has the same impact as the following description by a young man named Artyom. Twenty years old, he is a resident of Sumy, in northeast Ukraine, about which a bit of background will be forthcoming.

Artyom was asked to describe life for his contemporaries in Sumy, and his words are absolutely haunting. As he speaks, his slumping body gives added emphasis to his words: "You wake up and you go to work, if you are fortunate enough to have a job. In the evening, the only entertainment available is drinking. Nobody reads anymore. Nobody is interested in self-education or self-development; all that is outside of our grasp. There is nothing to do in this town for fun or socialization. No high culture, or even low. This place is empty. There is nothing to do here, and we are stuck. We don't have the money or connections to move anywhere else."

Clearly, not everyone feels this way in Sumy or in other small towns. But this description resonates with our staff. As we travel around the FSU and meet with people in these cities (both Jews and non-Jews), many speak in terms similar to Artyom's.

Sumy is about a four-hour drive northeast of Kyiv. It is an industrial center known for its production of chemicals, fertilizers, and automobiles, and for its sugar-refining factories. As in most other regions in the FSU, the factories have swollen overheads and have had little investment in production, and as a consequence were hard-hit when the global economic downturn happened. Massive layoffs caused ballooning unemployment rates.

The subject of this update is not the life of the general population of Sumy. Rather, we want to explore how the opportunities and options for the Jewish community differ from those for the population at large.

Jewish life in Sumy can be traced back to the mid-nineteenth century, but because Sumy was on the border of the traditional Pale of Settlement, the Jewish population never burgeoned there as it did elsewhere. There were synagogues and some other communal institutions, but all on a very modest scale.

During the early Soviet years, several of the Jewish institutions were closed and their property confiscated. What remained lasted until the Nazi invasion, at which point any remnant of Jewish life in the city was obliterated. There are now an estimated two thousand Jews in Sumy, out of a total population of 280,000.

There is a narrative that runs counter to the malaise that permeates society in Sumy. That narrative is rooted in the Jewish community and the renaissance it is undergoing. There are daily programs in the Jewish community center that target all age groups among the Jews living there: a Sunday school for families, a host of adult education programs each week, a lending library that runs book clubs for all ages, a robust volunteer program for teenagers, Shabbat programming, and much more.

This list of activities is not unique to cities in the FSU, nor is it by itself all that impressive. Its real value is to be understood in the context of Artyom's remarks above. Culture and community, as concepts, have not been high priorities for minority communities in the post-Soviet reality. The reason is not a lack of tradition in these areas. Rather, these things have been assigned a lower priority in municipal and regional budgets due to severe economic conditions. Amid efforts to rebuild a sclerotic medical system and refashion schools, an emphasis on the spiritual side of the citizen has been lost.

Against this background, JDC has provided modest funding and intensive training for a select group of young people, who in turn have applied their imagination and enthusiasm to the creation of a vibrant Jewish community, which is unique in this environment.

For now, in Sumy as in many other places in the FSU, the Jewish community is the best show in town.

Weather Conditions (February 10, 2012)

There has been a great deal of attention in the media over the last two weeks about the cold snap in Europe. The JDC response in places like Bulgaria and Ukraine was rapid and comprehensive. Unquestionably, lives are being saved.

During this time, I was in St. Petersburg, Moscow, and Minsk. On my return to Israel, people who heard I had been there stopped me in the street and asked what it's like to be in that kind of cold. They hear about the temperatures of minus 18 degrees Celsius and shake their heads in wonder. They remark how they have personally been dealing with unseasonably low (!) temperatures in Israel and then ask what it's like to be in places where it is colder than that to an unfathomable extent. I was uncomfortable describing it, but

I was not sure why. After giving it much thought, I think that I now understand the reason.

Simply put, in order to really understand what it means to experience this intensity of cold, one must understand the general conditions in which many of these people live. The bitter cold was difficult even for me to cope with; at minus 18 degrees, no amount of insulation keeps you warm if any part of your body is directly exposed to the elements. At a minimum, your eyes burn. It is difficult to walk on the sheets of ice that cover all outdoor surfaces. The transition from a warm building or car to the outside shocks your system and generates some perspiration, which freezes on contact with the air outside the moment you step out the door. Ice forms on your face. When you speak outdoors, your teeth literally feel the piercing cold, which is exacerbated by the wind. The cold is, in a word, unpleasant.

But the elderly in the FSU and Eastern Europe live in circumstances that make this cold spell not simply unpleasant, but life threatening. So yes, I found it very cold in the FSU this week and last. But we need to be aware that this is a relative condition. In the same temperature, my cold was not theirs.

Tractor Factory (November 15, 2007)

We recently held meetings in Ekaterinburg in the region of the Ural Mountains, near the border of European and Asian Russia. Ekaterinburg is known to many as the place where the last czar and his family were executed on Lenin's orders, but it has further significance for Jews: The name of the city was changed by the Soviets to Sverdlovsk, after a hero of the revolution, Yakov Sverdlov. This made it one of the few cities in the world – perhaps the only one – outside of Israel named after a Jew.

This region was the location of the Soviet industrial belt. When we conjure up images of Soviet heavy industry with its large factories, this is where much of it was based. Steel factories, airplane factories, and truck factories employed tens of thousands in the region.

One of our visits in a nearby city was to the museum of the "Chelyabinsk Tractor Factory." The museum has three rooms. The walls are covered with Soviet-era posters of "ideal workers," tractors that won special prizes, Communist Party slogans, etc. The color red, associated with the Soviet Union, is ubiquitous. There is a row of medals won by factory workers for outstanding levels of output. There are models of tractors and plane engines, for which the factory was converted during the war. There is a video of a television program dedicated to modern tractor equipment, which was prime-time viewing in the USSR.

The director who showed us around wore medals won in a war fought more than sixty years ago. The past glory of this factory, so important in the Soviet era, has not diminished one iota for him with the passage of time. The fact that the factory is a shadow of its former self, with a customer base that long ago looked elsewhere, was not relevant to him. The Great Patriotic War happened yesterday, and he was proud of the factory's contribution to the great victory over the Fascists.

Visiting there was like being in a time warp. We had gone back decades, to a country in which the individual had no intrinsic value; all was for the collective. The pride of the nation stemmed from achievement on the battle-field and in the factories and mines. Social progress was of secondary concern.

Why "waste" our time in a museum like this? Because this is the milieu in which so many of the Jews with whom we work spent their formative years. In order to understand them, to address their needs and concerns, and to appreciate their anxieties, we need to have knowledge of the societies in which they were educated and socialized, the norms and values of those societies, how they defined success, and so on. They may not identify with these societies; in fact, they may be dedicated to correcting or altering much of what they were taught. But it is critical to understand the foundation of their identity in order to partner with them.

The thing that made the biggest impression on me in this museum experience is the gift we, as VIP visitors, were each given as we left. It was a small box made from the green stone malachite found throughout the Urals. However, etched in the bottom of the box is the name of the place from which this particular box came. This gift, from a museum dedicated to the greatness of the USSR, carved from a type of stone for which the region is famous, was manufactured in the Congo!

It seemed like a final insult to those who had grown up in the Soviet era and now were engaged in trying to create civic societies from the ashes of that empire. When we recount how much our older volunteers have lived through – the war and Nazi occupation, the Communist regime and its disdain for Jews – we tend to concentrate on the macro, geopolitical developments. These Jews also lived through the collapse of the society of which they were part a few short years ago. Much of what they valued and took to be true was discredited almost overnight. This surely contributed to their own worldview and helped to shape the people they are today.

Belarus (May 7, 2010)

Belarus is a funny place. Home to an estimated fifty-five thousand Jews, it has a rich Jewish past. But because it's fundamentally a quirk of history, few associate the specifics of that past with Belarus. During short spells in the last several hundred years it was independent. At other times it was an integral part of Lithuania, then Poland, and later the USSR. It has its own language, but one that even its political leadership does not speak well. In fact, we attended a cultural program led by a local woman who speaks only Belarusian – as an act of dissidence! Of how many countries can it be said that speaking the national language is a form of protest?

Belarus has no national heroes and no national literature to speak of. It has museums dedicated to famous artists who lived in the region, but none of these contains a single work by any of them, the entire oeuvre located elsewhere.

Khatin is a memorial to the Belarusian victims of the Second World War (not to be confused with Katyn, on Russian soil, where Stalin ordered the KGB to kill the entire upper echelon of the Polish Army in 1940). It is a large outdoor memorial, covering several acres, on the site of a rural village that fell victim to a Nazi reprisal raid. It is hours away from the nearest city. The current borders of Belarus contained a population of eight million on the eve of the war. Two million Belarusians fell victim to the Nazis, among them some eight hundred thousand Jews.

So, the war was a defining event for this country, and Khatin is the national memorial. We found it extraordinarily moving, but something appeared to be missing. It was only several days later that I realized what it was. Understanding it, I found that the memorial offered tremendous insight into today's Belarus and significant parts of the states once bound together in the USSR.

If one views Yad Vashem in Jerusalem as the Jewish people's analogue to Khatin, one cannot help but be struck by the contrast. Yad Vashem has an element that is absent from Khatin. Both memorials are profoundly moving, but the Yad Vashem experience ends on a patio that looks out over Jerusalem. The goal is not to provide a vista of natural beauty; it is to draw attention to a vibrant city and to the ultimate triumph over the events described in the museum which the visitor has just emerged from.

Khatin, as moving as the Yad Vashem museum in its own way, lacks any postscript. When your visit is complete, you climb into your bus and return to the highway. The memorial is surrounded by fields and forests. The enormous catastrophe the citizenry suffered is what defines them as a people; there is nothing that emerged from those ashes. That explains much of the Belarusian population's apparent resignation to a political and economic malaise that sets them apart from the rest of Europe, and even from most of the former USSR. There has been little privatization, elections are one-dimensional and of one party, and there is little sense of excitement. Instead, wherever one goes, one feels heaviness and drudgery, a kind of internalization of victimhood that haunts Belarus to this day, decades after its defining moment.

The day after the trip to Khatin, I visited Leppel, a small town about two and a half hours north of Minsk. Actually, to call it a "town" is to exaggerate. It is what we learned to refer to as a shtetl. Before the war, 70 percent of the residents were Jewish. Now there are about ten thousand residents, among them eleven elderly Jews.

Leppel is located on a river, which was essential for the Jewish woodcutters, who used the river to transport their lumber to the mills downstream. There is still an intact Jewish cemetery, where gravestones bear Hebrew inscriptions from Stalinist times, something quite rare in the FSU. The town has mostly wooden houses and unpaved roads.

Water is still drawn from public wells, and the house I visited does not have indoor plumbing. The eighty-one-year-old Jewish babushka living inside has an outhouse on her property, some ten yards away from her door. The physical conditions are abominable, and the poverty is heart-wrenching, but two things stood out from my visit to her home, crowded with the Jews of the town.

The first was the singing and laughter of the participants. They told stories in Yiddish, smiled throughout, and bragged of their new winter coats (from the Hesed), of the fact that they had enough wood for their stoves in the winter (courtesy of the Hesed), and that their neighbors are all much younger, as their non-Jewish contemporaries all predeceased them (which they attributed to food, medicine, and home care from the Hesed). That they could still smile was extraordinary.

The second striking thing in this home came from the context. I associate this kind of poverty with – and excuse me for being politically incorrect – the peasantry. That is, uneducated, simple people who are the salt of the earth. They work hard to support their families and have little connection with the larger world. But the hostess in the home we visited, which was impoverished by any standard, had a wall full of books in her bedroom. I looked through them while the others sang. A collection of the works of Tolstoy and Thomas Mann were closest to her bed, and I opened them to find them annotated in what I later learned was her handwriting. Those, she told me, were her favorites. Throughout her adult life, after a day's work as a seamstress, she returned home and immersed herself in these kinds of classics. She lamented the fact that there were few in her town with whom she could discuss what she read, with the exception of several other Jews. With some of them, she enjoyed discussing Tolstoy – in Yiddish!

Tapuz (February 12, 2010)

On picking up the phone in the Moscow JDC office, this is what the JDC staffer heard: "This is Arkady. I am calling from the Presidential Administration. I want to speak with the director of Tapuz."

In these three sentences one can learn a tremendous amount about the state of Jewish life in Russia, the position of JDC in Moscow, relations between the Russian government and its citizens, and more.

Let's begin with the lexicon. The "Presidential Administration" is better known by its colloquial name: the Kremlin. The caller was an aide to Russian President Dmitry Medvedev.

The other piece to clarify is "Tapuz." Tapuz is Hebrew for "orange" (the fruit). It's also the name of the preschool program in Nikitskaya, JDC's Moscow JCC.

This is the third year of the preschool, which was begun as an anchor program in the JCC. From the beginning, several factors were meant to distinguish it from other Jewish preschools in Moscow and around the FSU. Its target population was the emerging Jewish middle class in Moscow, and young Jewish families who had begun to acquire significant personal assets would be attracted to this program for their children. Second, the program was thoroughly infused with Jewish content: the children learned Jewish songs and basic Hebrew words, celebrated holidays, decorated the school with posters of Israel, etc. And finally, the preschool was located in Nikitskaya and served as a magnet to expose these families to other Jewish programming. Family camps, Jewish cultural events, and more would be on their radar.

That was the plan. The preschool currently runs at capacity – 102 children, with a significant waiting list. When *Forbes Russia* listed the top ten preschools in Moscow, Tapuz was in the top five!

That is all relevant background to this phone call. Note that there are no niceties. One dispenses with the formalities and gets right down to business. This is the prerogative of someone calling from the top.

One more short digression, to ponder what these three sentences would have meant in another era: A call from the office at the head of the Soviet establishment wanting to talk to the person in charge of a Jewish program for children. Those of us with JDC experience in Eastern Europe before the wall(s) fell remember the fear of Jews there when they heard from government officials. The latter were quick to establish the rules of the encounter: "We speak, and you do as we say." The dread felt by Jews – and indeed by most Soviet citizens – in these circumstances was visceral and palpable. If you were contacted directly by a government official, it was generally not for a good reason.

That was an earlier time. This call was entirely different. The presidential aide went on to request intervention by the director of Tapuz. Apparently, someone in the president's office had applied to have his daughter admitted to Tapuz but did so too late and the application was denied. This call, from the Kremlin, was to ask that the decision be reconsidered. With the weight of the president of Russia behind the request, could this girl be admitted to Tapuz?

From this three-sentence phone call we learn that:

1. The Kremlin, at least occasionally, asks and doesn't dictate.
2. Nikitskaya, a Jewish community center, and now its kindergarten, is known to them. In a previous era, the KGB would deal with "Jewish programming."
3. A Jew can travel in Kremlin circles without the need to dissemble about his or her identity, and in fact can call on Kremlin officialdom for help in a personal Jewish issue.

CHAPTER 2

JDC

What's in a Name? (July 29, 2005)

Recently a donor who has worked in this arena with JDC in other parts of the world approached us with an offer to start an interest-free loan fund for small businesses in an FSU Jewish community.

While we talk about self-sustaining communities, this is an area in which, for a whole host of reasons, we have not gotten involved: It is generally not considered a core competency of the FSU team; the economic climate in the FSU is incredibly unstable; and there are legal obstacles too numerous to mention. Thus, this was outside of our strategic plan.

On further consideration, though, there were reasons to consider an experiment in this field: It does represent a potential exit strategy for young families currently benefiting from the children-in-need initiative due to unemployment. And the donor fully understood the risks involved.

But the issue of the strategy still nagged. Is a strategy document so pliable that an opportunity with intuitive appeal takes precedence over the strategy? Can a strategy be altered to fit any opportunity, as opposed to serving as a guide in determining whether an opportunity is indeed appropriate? I am aware that this is an oversimplification of the dilemma, but it is real nonetheless.

And then I came across a lecture given recently by Professor Yehuda Bauer, the doyen of scholars of the Shoah, and not incidentally the unofficial historian of JDC's early period. It was a talk he gave to JDC staff based on his research on the JDC's establishment. The element relevant to the issue I raise here, small loans, comes in a paragraph at the very end of the excerpt. What precedes this part is a bit long, but it is full of fascinating material, which arguably justifies the length.

This is the transcript of the talk; it was not presented as a written piece. There is minimal editing.

The JDC started with Henry Morgenthau Sr., the American ambassador in Constantinople in 1914, appealing to his friends who were American Jews of German origin and belonged to the economic and social elite of American Jewry at that time, because he saw a threat to the survival of the Jewish settlement in Eretz Yisrael [the Land of Israel]. I want to remind you that this was in 1914, after Ottoman Turkey entered [the First World War] in August on the side of the Kaiser's Germany and the Austro-Hungarian Empire. The US was neutral at the time.

Historians have just discovered some fascinating things about 1914. We knew for a long time that, in the autumn of 1914, most Jews of Palestine were expelled to Egypt. Generally, it is not clear from textbooks why exactly this was so, how, and so on. What has recently surfaced is that there must have been a plan for mass murder of all Jews in Eretz Yisrael by the Ottoman regime, using the very same methods that were used shortly afterwards against the Armenians. First, weapons were collected. Not simply collected, but each settlement received a quota for the number of weapons it must deliver, whether it had any or not. If it did not have any, it had to buy the required quantity and hand it in.

Then they arrested all the men, and what was to happen next was clear. Each step along the way is an almost exact parallel to what happened later to the Armenians.

On the way to this solution, there was apparently an intervention by the Germans, who thought that it was not a good idea for the Young Turks to murder the Jews in Eretz Yisrael because this might cause problems for the Kaiser's Germany with the neutral US. They did not want them to alienate the American Jewish community, who might in turn press the American government to join the Allies, as indeed happened three years later. For the time being this was averted. Instead of killing the Jews in Eretz Yisrael, they placed male Jews from Jaffa and the coast in two ships, one American and the other Italian, and took them to Egypt.

The Jewish community that remained behind was impoverished, its situation worsened with so many young workers now in exile.

This is where the JDC started, in a very typical Jewish way, because Jews never can agree among themselves regarding what to do, when, and how. At the time, three competing Jewish organizations – one made up of Jews of German origin, the rich ones, the elite; another made up of Orthodox Jews; and the third one made up of socialists – joined efforts to create the JDC (hence the name "Joint"). They raised money in response to the plea of the American ambassador in Constantinople to help this population. He was a prominent German Jew from among their New York social circle. The three groups then came together to establish this organization, to distribute the funds that would be raised, first of all to Eretz Yisrael, and then to other places. And thus, the word "distribution" becomes part of the name – the American Jewish Joint Distribution Committee.

"Joint," then, has a certain meaning in America, but a completely different one for an impoverished Jew who lived in Poland between the two World Wars. If this Jew needed to get a loan, he went to the Joint. What did he care about the meaning of the word – the main thing was to get the money. What the Joint did between the two wars did not cost a lot of money; American Jewry at the time was not particularly generous. With very modest sums, they tried to do the maximum possible to extricate European Jews from the financial and social problems that emerged between the wars, and to reduce the dire poverty in which these Jews and their communities languished.

All this is by way of background to a special operation launched by a Russian Jewish Social Democrat who emigrated to the US in the beginning of the twentieth century, whose name was Joseph Rosen, an agronomist by profession, together with one of the Jewish American millionaires of the time, James Rosenberg. The two of them were philosophical opposites – one was a socialist and the other an American capitalist who was an avowed conservative. Nonetheless, they built an alliance and Rosen set off to help the Soviet Jews, who had considerable problems in the young Soviet Union. Many had backgrounds in small businesses and as free-standing artisans, and as such were labeled "capitalists," a distinctly pejorative term in the new Soviet setting. They had no right to engage in business of any kind, nor did they did have the right to send their children to school. They were social pariahs. They were not entitled to any health-care services because they were capital-ists. If an impoverished Jewish shoemaker had an apprentice, he was considered a capitalist, regardless of his income; so the major-ity of Soviet Jews in the post-revolution period were capitalists, and doomed to live on the edge of society without reasonable hope of eking out a decent living.

In Russian they were called *lishentsy*, i.e., people deprived of rights. So what could be done now? These people could be settled on land and maybe organized into some kind of collective teams of artisans in order to escape the tag of *lishentsy*, and in order to enable them to survive. Rosen and Rosenberg established an orga-nization called the Agro-Joint within the framework of the Joint. The Agro-Joint started to settle Jews on land in southern Ukraine and Crimea and to train them to be farmers. Among the settlers were Jews who came back from Palestine, many of whom were Communists, who did not like Zionist capitalism in Eretz Yisrael. They returned to the USSR and established settlements there with Russian names like "Fountain" and "Hope."

The agricultural collectivization achieved in the early Soviet period was made possible to a large extent by agricultural machin-ery first imported by the JDC. In fact, according to Soviet archival records from the time, the Joint was the first importer of tractors to the USSR.

But by the thirties, all of this was over. Rosen managed to escape to the United States. Not a single person among the Joint activists in the Soviet Union of that period survived Stalin's "Great Terror."

They were all taken to the Siberian Gulag camps in 1936–38, and they were killed there, and not one of them lived to tell his story. There was, of course, a lot of criticism of the Joint at the time: "You have invested all that money for the good of the Jews in the Soviet Union only to have them all killed." But there is, of course, a different opinion: that this project helped many Jews escape from an impossible social and economic situation and reach the maximum advancement that could be reached in the Soviet Union, which became a stepping stone for careers in industry. Many of these same Jews used their training to advance to central positions in Soviet society as it industrialized. So the Jews got out of that bad situation and achieved a high economic status compared to other populations in the Soviet Union.

In other places in Europe, the JDC established small centers to best distribute the funds it raised. The main objective was to establish lending organizations. This was actually an ancient, traditionally Jewish phenomenon: charitable lending organizations, often referred to as "free loan societies." These societies made numerous interest-free loans. A Polish Jew would come and say that his horse had died, and he had made a living off this horse, because with this horse he had traveled from one village to another selling his merchandise; without the horse, there was no money to buy food and support his family. They would give him the money to buy a horse, and he would commit to returning the money within a certain period of time, without interest, so that subsequently another Jew would be able to buy a horse. I am describing it here in a figurative way, but, of course, it was not only about horses. It was also for artisans – carpenters, blacksmiths, shoemakers, tailors, and the like. During the first decades of its existence, the JDC did these kinds of things mainly in Poland, Romania, eastern Czechoslovakia, and to a smaller extent in a host of other countries.

So ends this part of Professor Bauer's talk. As for loan funds, not only is there historical precedent for JDC's involvement in this, but it was a key part of what our organization did in the early years. Precedent alone is not a justification for entering a program area, but it is a factor.

Agro-Joint (February 4, 2005)

At the foot of the Matterhorn there is a cemetery. The graves are those of individuals who died trying to reach the top. I recently read a first-person account of a visit to the site. Very moving. But upon reflection, I couldn't help but wonder, *for what?* To die and then to have engraved on your tombstone that you died trying to scale this mountain?

There is clearly a lot to reflect on here. I was reminded of this cemetery this week while reading an e-mail that was quite jarring. The e-mail notified staff of a decision to create a place of honor in the JDC Israel building for members of staff who had been martyred in the service of JDC. The numbers were stunning to me – there are enough people in this category to warrant the creation of a space memorializing them. What follows is the story of one man who worked in the same region to which we had now returned:

Samuel Lubarsky was born in Ukraine in 1878. He trained as an agronomist and was arrested periodically for involvement in antigovernment affairs while a student during the czarist regime. In a letter to his daughter later in life, he acknowledges that he was not a Zionist, nor was he religious, but he was "committed to normalizing the status of Jews in Russia by teaching them productive labor." His first job was in a Jewish agricultural school, concentrating on practical skills like field crop cultivation, dairy and poultry farming, vine growing, and horticulture.

While he welcomed the overthrow of the czar, his family suffered terribly in the post-revolution period. His wife was murdered during the Ukrainian uprising in the wake of the revolution and the subsequent unrest in Ukraine. Ukrainian nationalists were not prepared to accept Moscow's hegemony and conducted guerilla warfare for several years to undermine Moscow's authority. Many of these groups were rabidly antisemitic and victimized Jews, who were viewed as the Bolshevik elite and therefore considered legitimate targets, even if they had no military connections. Lubarsky's parents and two siblings were killed in a pogrom a short time later.

In 1922, Lubarsky hosted Joseph Rosen in his home in Mykolaiv, Ukraine. Rosen was a world-class agronomist, but more important to this story, he was the JDC representative in the region. Rosen's proposal was for Lubarsky to take an active role in assisting Jewish settlements in Ukraine that had been attacked during pogroms and whose members were victims of the famine that occurred in the aftermath of the civil unrest. In accepting the offer, Lubarsky established an agronomy department in the JDC regional office in Kharkiv.

As the Bolsheviks consolidated their power, they eliminated small businesses, in which Jews were disproportionately represented. Lubarsky believed that material and financial assistance given without charge had a demoralizing effect on Jews who had been impoverished by these policies. To boost morale and motivation, he issued them loans "payable against the future harvest." The NKVD (the forerunner of the KGB) took issue with this approach, claiming (as Marxists would) that taking loans against future crops is a form of indentured servitude. Lubarsky's efforts were undermined, and he searched for alternative ways to be of assistance.

In 1924, JDC established Agro-Joint. It represented JDC's post-revolution presence in the USSR and was charged with helping train Jews for a life as agricultural workers, which would spare them the punishments meted out by authorities to shopkeepers and other businessmen who occupied a social status that was anathema to the new Soviet regime. Agricultural work, as part of a cooperative, was ideologically acceptable, and Agro-Joint engaged in setting up these cooperatives for Jews and training them to work the land. There were large numbers of Jews in need in the region, and the Joint, established in the previous decade by American Jews, felt a responsibility to assist them. It defined its role as an effort to help Jews become productive members of the newly established empire.

It was not an easy decision to reach or implement, as we shall see later. The relationship of an American organization with a regime still not recognized as legitimate by the United States was not simple. But JDC convinced the American government that its investment was humanitarian, and the State Department granted it permission to proceed.

To address the plight of large numbers of newly unemployed Jews, Agro-Joint signed an agreement with the Soviet government to establish Jewish collective farms in Ukraine and in Crimea, a peninsula contiguous with Ukraine that was conducive to farming. The government provided the land,

and Agro-Joint provided the training. The indigenous Tatar population was none too happy about the resettlement of massive numbers of Jews in their midst. As a result, by 1926, almost a quarter of the JDC funds transferred to Agro-Joint were being used for what are characterized today as nonsectarian projects, to soften the Tatar opposition by making them co-beneficiaries of the aid. Jews were the primary recipients of assistance, but the general population benefitted as well.

By this time, Lubarsky had assumed the position of JDC director for Ukraine. The program was managed out of Moscow for political reasons, and he brought his family there and began working in the JDC building that remains there today (although under different ownership).

Lubarsky's position enabled him to be involved in all aspects of life in the villages supported by JDC. The JDC representative was expected to weigh in regarding land allocation, construction, acceptance of new members, cattle breeding, crop rotation, decisions about establishing factories, and more. It was not a case of cash transfers to the indigent; it was technical assistance by experts in each field designed to ensure that, eventually, the village and its members could be self-sustaining, a goal that became the hallmark of much of JDC's work with Jewish communities in the decades that followed.

An estimated three hundred thousand Soviet Jews moved to the colonies established by Agro-Joint in the Soviet Union. Hundreds of collective farms were built. The total Agro-Joint investment for the duration of the program was $16 million, equivalent to more than $250 million in 2021 dollars.

Lubarsky was arrested for the first time in 1930 on trumped-up charges of absconding with government money. He was convicted but got the relatively light sentence of being forbidden to reside in the USSR's twelve largest cities. He was undaunted and remained committed to the Jews he had met and begun to assist. He moved to Kursk in the Russian interior. A letter to his daughter survives from that period:

> It is the eve of Yom Kippur. You know that I do not believe, but I went to the synagogue last week to be with my fellow Jews on Rosh Hashanah. The men's section was completely full – more than five hundred participants. You can see that the traditions are strong, even now [i.e., after years of Soviet efforts to weaken Jewish identity – AO].

After eighteen months, Lubarsky was allowed to return to Moscow, only to find that many of the Agro-Joint colonies were being disbanded as younger people entered the professions and gravitated to the cities. But there were still a substantial number of collective farms, and Lubarsky was determined to enable them to flourish. He was not convinced that the Soviet push for industrialization would render the farms irrelevant.

From its founding in the 1920s, Agro-Joint was the only foreign organization that had firsthand knowledge of developments in the Soviet Union's rural areas. It was a major partner of the American Relief Administration (ARA), which was headed by a businessman who would later be elected president of the United States – Herbert Hoover. It should be noted that Agro-Joint and the ARA were providing humanitarian assistance well before the US established diplomatic relations with the USSR. The Joint is credited in early Soviet histories with major contributions to modernizing farming in the region.

But there were political developments in the USSR that overshadowed the JDC's contributions. Stalin's repression of real and imagined enemies traumatized Soviet society for generations, and as part of that program, the NKVD was empowered to arrest "anti-Soviet elements" and oversee their punishment. Agro-Joint employees were prime suspects due to the organization's apolitical – that is, not explicitly pro-Soviet – ideology and its international funding and connections, and gradually all of them were expelled, internally exiled, or shot.

Lubarsky was one of the last to be arrested. He was taken in on March 27, 1938, and accused of having been a German spy since 1925 and an American spy since 1926, and of recruiting Agro-Joint employees to work in his spy network.

It took investigators three months to compel Lubarsky to write a confession that Rosen had recruited him to spy against the USSR. He was further accused of gathering intelligence to aid in an assassination attempt against Lazar Kaganovitch, Stalin's right-hand man, and of "sabotaging the Ukrainian agricultural system and providing financial assistance to Zionists and clandestine rabbis adhering to anti-Soviet positions."

Lubarsky pleaded guilty to the trumped-up charges, presumably as a result of torture. He was tried on September 1, 1938, *in camera* and without counsel. Recently uncovered documents from the NKVD's files show that the entire proceeding, from the opening of the court to sentencing, took fifteen minutes. He was executed that night.

THE OFFICIAL PROTOCOL OF THE LUBARSKY TRIAL

Lubarsky's File (Central FSB Archive)

Document 1

P. 13.
To the NKVD Investigator Gorelkin
From the prisoner Samuil Efimovich Lubarsky

Statement

I was the deputy-director of the Agro-Joint since November 1926, and in December 1926 the Agro-Joint director I.B. Rosen draw me to the espionage activity against the Soviet Union. For this activity I used the agronomists A.E. Zaichik, V.K. Redkin and M.F. Itkin, who were the Agro-Joint representative in Crimea. I will give details of my espionage work and my other unlawful work later.

June 24, 1938.

Signature
S. Lubarsky.

Document 2.
pp. 7-8.
Protocol of the Closed Session of the Military Collegium of the High
Court of the USSR

September 1, 1938　　　　　　　　　　　　　　　　Moscow

Chairman of the Court is.. Matulevich

The session started at 18:00

The accused has been brought to the court. No witnesses were invited.
...
On the question of the Chairman, whether the accused admitted his guilt, the accused answered "Yes."
The court investigation is closed, and the accused is given his last word. In his last word the accused is asking the court to be merciful and not to deprive him of his life.
　　　The court has left for consultations. On its return the court gives its verdict.
The session is over in 18:15.

A translation of the NKVD file on the trial of Samuil Lubarsky, deputy director of Agro-Joint. From 1938.

Lubarsky was partially "rehabilitated" in 1959, in a process that cleared the names of many "criminals against the state" from the Stalin era. This was part of a de-Stalinization program begun by Nikita Khrushchev at around that time. An associate of his wrote to Lubarsky's daughter upon learning of his rehabilitation, "Your father had much love for the people, and he sacrificed his entire bright and spirited life for the sake of the people." It is noteworthy that the reference to "the people" here is intended to mean the Jewish people, but the writer feared noting that in case his letter was intercepted.

Lubarsky's full "rehabilitation" came only in 1989, during the Gorbachev era.

The Cossack Dilemma (September 3, 2010)

In this week's update, I will share two policy dilemmas that are among the most wrenching JDC staff and lay people were ever forced to address. Unfortunately, these very same dilemmas have resurfaced periodically throughout JDC's ten decades of operation, each time in some different guise. As a treat, we will close a discussion of the USSR era with a photograph that documents the presence of a well-known person at a JDC-sponsored orphanage where he taught. But that is getting ahead of our story.

In the wake of the Russian Revolution in 1917, there was an enormous amount of upheaval in the new empire. After the Bolsheviks assumed power, various regions within Russia and its immediate surroundings continued to experience prolonged periods of civil unrest and war. Soviet power was not consolidated in the area for a number of years. In fact, in many areas, there was little in the way of central control by any government.

But there were a lot of Jews in this territory. They were concentrated in high numbers in the region that until 1917 had been the Pale of Settlement, to which the czarist government restricted Jewish residency. In the immediate post-revolution period, this was the scene of enormous turmoil in which the Mensheviks battled the Bolsheviks, Ukrainian nationalists fought Russians, and, as the Tom Lehrer song goes, "everybody hates the Jews." The number of factions fighting each other and persecuting the Jews was almost unlimited and the bloodletting severe. Enter JDC, established in the United States less than a decade earlier.

JDC regional operations at the time were overseen out of its office in Warsaw. The reports that streamed in from numerous sources were appalling. In 1920, two JDC staff were dispatched to what is now western Ukraine, and as a result of their findings, an emergency allocation of $1.5 million was granted to open a new office closer to the conflict zone to assist the rebuilding of Jewish infrastructure – hospitals, schools, housing, and a small-loan program to start cottage industries. A further investigation yielded an even more horrific report of the damage inflicted by the fighting: *ten thousand* Jewish orphans in Kyiv alone, living in what were described as subhuman conditions.

The year is now 1920. JDC has just negotiated an arrangement with the Soviet government to set up a local public committee to assist "pogrom victims." This term was considered politically correct, as it did not indict any one of the numerous protagonists, all of whom were guilty of crimes against Jews. Shortly after the memorandum was signed, a vicious famine struck southern Ukraine and the Volga region (east of Moscow). The United States, which until that point did not grant diplomatic recognition to what it considered the illegitimate Soviet government in Moscow, nonetheless decided that it had a responsibility to respond to the humanitarian crisis in the USSR. It channeled its assistance through Herbert Hoover's American Relief Administration. Originally established by the US government, by this time the ARA was a fully independent nongovernmental agency that united other American relief initiatives under its umbrella, JDC primary among them.

For a host of reasons, it was in JDC's interest to be associated with this broader relief effort, although its primary interest was the Jewish population, and within that group, its primary focus was children. A JDC employee of the era visited a Jewish orphanage in what is now the Ukrainian city of Dnipro, an area hard hit by the famine. He describes his visit in 1921:

> The first orphanage we visited was a two-story cement structure with about fifty Jewish orphans, near the ARA headquarters in the city. Windows were broken, and the facility lacked a basic sanitation infrastructure. It was a dreary looking place, with almost no equipment or furniture. Most of the children were between the ages of 8-10 and were dressed in rags or were stark naked.

The children were emaciated, some of them unbelievably thin and gaunt, with skin drawn tight over their jaws and cheekbones, and with deep, sunken eyes. Their faces looked like skeleton heads. They had vertical creases between their eyebrows, which I later learned was typical of starving children. There were a few who were even in a more advanced stage of starvation, with bloated stomachs and swollen legs. They all slept three or four to a mattress. The two Jewish women in charge of the children's home were deeply ashamed of the condition of the house and of their charges, although there was little they could do.

And here we encounter our first dilemma. As noted at the beginning of this piece, JDC worked under the umbrella of the ARA. To do so, it had to forgo – at least officially, and to a large degree in practice as well – its sectarian approach. That is, while JDC could target its funds (to a certain extent) to a particular region, which may have had a high concentration of Jews, it could not earmark funds exclusively for Jews. Fair enough. JDC did this and does so quite often in similar circumstances. But here the situation takes on a moral dimension. A staff member sent by headquarters to report back on the use of JDC funds in the region frames the dilemma:

> To what extent must we be bound to ARA policy in this region? Is it conceivable that, in order to pacify the ARA, JDC funds will be used in eastern Ukraine to support the general population, including suffering Cossacks who are undoubtedly in need, but who just yesterday engaged in the wanton slaughter of Jews? Is our money going to be used to keep alive people who showed no mercy for our women and children? Worse, are we going to feed these bandits so that they can be kept alive to kill us at a later date?

To those who would answer this question today by speaking about the lessons learned from the rehabilitation of American enemies after World War II with the Marshall Plan, remember that this assistance in Ukraine in the early 1920s came without any efforts at rehabilitation. It was an effort to feed starving people, but not more than that.

The dilemma: How to proceed if, in order to help Jews, you must support antisemites as well? These were not ordinary antisemites who had merely made ill-advised comments about Jews. These were perpetrators of pogroms. The orphans to whom JDC assistance was directed had in fact been orphaned by these same Cossacks.

While I labeled this a dilemma at the outset, it was not considered one by JDC leadership at the time. The questions raised in the report were treated as rhetorical; if, in order to save Jews, humanitarian assistance had to be extended to the enemies of the Jews as well, it was clear how JDC was to act. This was a painful but acceptable price to be paid. Of course, this dilemma surfaces in a more acute form when support needed to sustain Jews and Jewish communities must be funneled through odious governments that will use it to strengthen their hold on power. But that is not the case here. It is a challenge that has surfaced repeatedly throughout JDC's century-plus of operations, with respect to despots like Saddam Hussein, Nicolae Ceaușescu, and others.

It is interesting, and probably not a coincidence, that the question of supporting the Cossacks was raised by the JDC staff member who had arrived from headquarters in Warsaw. The local staff is not in the least troubled by the prospect of extending humanitarian aid to suffering human beings, with no consideration of their ideology or prior behavior. The local JDC response is very clear: "As Jews, we cannot say that we do not care for the anguish of the Christian mother holding fast to her breast her dying child. Her ideology and the past behavior of her compatriots are of no concern to us. There is no dilemma here: The support to mother and suckling child is humanitarian and rooted in Jewish values, and therefore must be given."

The ARA withdrew from the Soviet Union in 1923. At the same time, JDC signed a separate agreement with the Soviet authorities to remain behind to help the Jews in a wide range of areas. JDC's concern was now children. The fledgling Soviet state proclaimed that the care of destitute children was its responsibility and set about to organize orphanages. The first ones were located in the confiscated former residences of the nobility, so they were certainly adequate in terms of size and fixtures. But gradually the situation deteriorated. Operating funds were scarce, and health problems were rife. So the government hit upon a scheme of sponsorship: army units, trade unions, and large factories adopted children's homes and took financial responsibility for them. Jewish homes, though, could find no patrons. JDC assumed this responsibility.

At one point in time, JDC provided support to more than seventy-three thousand Jewish children in more than 913 institutions. Support spanned Russia, Ukraine, what is now Belarus, and the Caucasus. The first priority was food, then clothing, heating supplies for the winter, and so on. According to an internal report for 1924, JDC supplied forty-two thousand pairs of shoes and sixty thousand items of clothing for Jewish children in the homes in that year alone. All of which brings us to the orphanage in Malachovka, a Moscow suburb, where we will encounter a second dilemma, and our photograph.

Malachovka was a suburb of Moscow that through the early 1920s had a very large Jewish population. A report from 1919 indicated that at the time there were five Jewish orphanages in the area. The orphanages were initially divided up on the basis of ideology; they were either Orthodox or Zionist. Once the Soviet regime was ensconced in the region it decided that it could brook no competition with its ideology. The orphanages could remain Jewish, and thereby continue to enjoy the support of JDC, but the residents were to be educated to be loyal Soviet citizens. To that end, a well-known Jewish educator with impeccable Communist credentials was sent to oversee the operations in the region. His charge – the stated goal of the orphanages' education program, by order of the Education Ministry – was to make loyal Soviet citizens and good Communists of these children. This meant they were to be "educated" – in its Soviet meaning, more akin to "forcibly acculturated" – to deny any loyalty or connection to a specific religious or ethnic community. Each child was raw material to be molded in accordance with the ideology of the state.

Which brings us to our second dilemma: At what point does JDC decide that it is being used? It is clear that the Jewish orphans had physical needs and that these were being addressed by JDC as the patron of the orphanage in lieu of the government. Freed from its responsibility to provide basic support, the government was using the funds it had thereby saved to educate students (where possible) in a way that would drive them further from the Jewish people. Would JDC wish to maintain, even at this cost, a connection to the orphans? Is access what is ultimately important? Given its limited resources, at what point does JDC decide that it is colluding in a situation that harms the interests of the Jewish people? Should JDC resources be used to perpetuate a situation that provides for the physical comfort of these young Jews, while at the same time creating an environment conducive to socializing these children to reject Jewish life? In the ensuing decades, there would be myriad applications of this question to our work in various states.

What was decided in the end? We do know that JDC's relationship with most of the orphanages ended by the mid-1920s, although we don't know exactly when. Nor do we know why: Did JDC decide to pull the plug for the considerations above, or were we simply banished, as happened later on a large scale in the USSR in the 1930s?

There is one very interesting artifact that remains from the period during which JDC provided resources to Jewish orphanages, although it is not known what ideological positions were imposed on this particular institution. And that is this picture:

Photo credit: JDC

The director of the orphanage pictured here (not one of those referred to above) was particularly progressive. During that period, and certainly in that environment, a child's education was primarily utilitarian. A child learned a trade as soon as he or she was able to do so. The Soviets added another component to education – deep immersion in Marxist ideology. In this case, the child's ability to grasp the concepts was not particularly relevant. All were subject to this indoctrination.

The director of this orphanage had a distinctly different outlook. In addition to the basic government requirements for the curriculum, he believed that a child should be encouraged to develop intellectually and emotionally in an educational setting. For him, the orphanage was not only a place within which to provide for the basic needs of its young residents. It was also a place to develop the child into a productive, independent human being. To that end, prior to the Soviet authorities' asserting total control over the institution, he introduced subjects like art and sports into the school curriculum.

The picture attached, from the early 1920s, is of the orphanage's staff. The progressive director is in the middle foreground, wearing a suit. Seated in the first row to the right is a budding young art teacher from a small shtetl in what is now Belarus. This art teacher wrote in his autobiography about the time he spent teaching the orphans in this JDC-sponsored institution: "I taught them art. I loved them. They drew. They pounced on paints like beasts on meat."

This teacher was in the employ of JDC, teaching these orphans for about a year and a half. At the end of that period, he applied for a position as the designer of sets at the Bolshoi and was accepted. From there, he began to paint scenes from his native village, which caught the eye of an art dealer who encouraged him to pursue this line in his career.

And Marc Chagall went on to world renown.

There is a footnote to this story, a Chagall connection to JDC several years later. Eventually he moved to Paris, where he integrated into the French art world. Following the German invasion of the country in 1940, Chagall fled from France and in 1941 arrived in the United States. During that escape he was assisted by JDC, the very organization with which he had started his art career years before.

Ideology versus Assistance (January 27, 2012)

This update is dedicated to the memory of Yehezkel Groyer, a colleague of ours in JDC. The connection between him and the story below will become clear further on.

Irina Groyer has been a client of the JDC welfare program for the elderly since 2002. She receives medicine and medical assistance, ten hours a week of home care, and food supplements on a monthly basis. She was one of two girls born to a middle-class Jewish family in Petrograd (later Leningrad) in 1914. She now lives in what was once a prestigious area in Moscow, in an apartment that has seen better days. She is intelligent and alert, with all her wits still about her. Her memory is prodigious. She lives alone and has been widowed for many years. At ninety-seven years old, she has witnessed and lived through the history of Soviet Jewry; her personal story paralleled that of many of her contemporaries, most of whom are no longer alive.

Irina graduated from Moscow University in 1933. After earning her master's degree, she began working in her chosen field, chemistry. But she soon realized that her advancement would be limited without a PhD, so she returned to the university and her chemistry studies, in pursuit of a doctorate. In her last year, shortly before completing her dissertation, she was expelled from the program. Her father had been "repressed" several years earlier by the Stalinist regime and, as the daughter of "an enemy of the people," she could not advance professionally in the scientific world. She took a position as a teacher, teaching chemistry at a level well below her capabilities. She married and had a son, who is still alive. He is a pensioner and struggles to make ends meet.

Like most of her contemporaries, Irina has little access to medical care, which is available primarily to those who can pay under the table. As she ages and her physical condition deteriorates, she has no prospect of leaving her apartment for a more suitable setting; assisted-living facilities simply do not exist.

What sets her apart from most of the people in the Jewish community's welfare system is her family history and the fact that, in giving her support, JDC is closing a circle, fulfilling a debt to someone who served JDC loyally for many years…and paid for that service with his life. This is his story.

Yehezkel Groyer was born in 1886 to a middle-class family in Ekaterinoslavl, today Dnipro, Ukraine. In 1905, there were pogroms in the region and his parents decided to emigrate to Palestine. By that time, he had already graduated high school and fallen in love and his love interest caused him to refuse to accompany his parents. Irina is quick to point out that her mother had another suitor at the time, a young Jew by the name of David Gruen. The woman chose Yehezkel and Gruen left the area and went to Palestine, where he changed his name to Ben-Gurion.

After they married, the young couple moved to Petrograd, where Groyer studied in the law faculty. Due to the numerus clauses in place at the time, he was one of the few Jews who were admitted. He was exceptionally accomplished in his studies. Upon graduating he was offered a position on the faculty, with the proviso that he first convert to Christianity. While he was not a religious Jew by his own reckoning, his sense of his identity was strong enough for him to refuse the offer.

In 1923, he was appointed as legal adviser to JDC in the USSR and shortly thereafter he was transferred to the newly-created Agro-Joint.

Groyer was apparently admired within the organization, and he was promoted to the position of deputy director in 1932. He was, in effect, the number two in the JDC USSR office. As part of that promotion, the family moved to Moscow, where they lived on the second floor of the Agro-Joint building. From Groyer's job description, one gets a sense of the kind of work in which Agro-Joint was engaged. He was in charge of the electrification of collective farms, building the water supply and irrigation system, anything to do with planting orchards and vineyards, and sheep breeding.

Another important aspect of his work was international affairs. He spoke German and English fluently, in addition to his native Russian. He was charged with receiving foreign guests and was a key member of the team engaged in fundraising in the United States.

He also championed a position within JDC that was later used as the basis of an indictment against him. After the Nazi takeover in Germany in 1933 and amid growing antisemitism in Europe, JDC looked for countries that could absorb Jews who needed to flee their countries of origin. The Soviet Union touted itself as the homeland for working people from all countries, and it was therefore a natural refuge for these Jews at risk, at least on paper. Groyer convinced his superiors that JDC should assist Jews from Germany, Poland, Romania, Lithuania, and other environments in which they were persecuted to resettle in the USSR. Groyer was in charge of the program for JDC. Several contingents of Jewish doctors, refugees from Nazi Germany, were the most prominent of the arrivals.

The program for German Jewish physicians was abruptly ended with the onset, in the late 1930s, of the "Great Terror" – Stalin's murderous rampage against internal enemies, real (few in number) and imagined (the vast majority). The NKVD spelled out precisely why the doctors' program had to be aborted: "Apart from preparing bacteriological war by throwing bacterial bombs from planes, air spraying of bacteria from planes, and spreading epidemics with the help of aerial vehicles, the intelligence department of the general staff pays special attention to the planning and executing of acts of bacterial terror including through agents who are deployed especially for this purpose."

All this was nothing more than paranoid hysteria on the part of the Soviets. There was no such menace. Nevertheless, primary suspects included foreign nationals who, it was assumed, took Soviet citizenship in order to destroy the USSR from within. Who could be more suspect than immigrants from the USSR's prime enemy, Nazi Germany? The fact that these were Jews fleeing the Nazis was not considered. Those who had fled Nazi terror several years earlier to refuge in the USSR, where they were welcomed, were all eventually executed by the Soviets.

If the doctors were suspect, the agent who facilitated their arrival in the USSR was similarly guilty. Groyer had even more things working against him: He was a fluent German speaker, he had made numerous trips to Germany, and, of course, he was a Jew.

Most JDC employees at the time were arrested as counterrevolutionaries on orders signed by military tribunals. Groyer and two other JDC senior staffers were arrested on November 28, 1937, based on orders signed by the supreme leader himself.

Groyer was interrogated on January 23, 1938. While most of his erstwhile JDC colleagues were charged with "Zionist activities, agricultural sabotage, and anti-Soviet manifestations," Groyer was tried on far more serious charges: "terrorism, espionage, and sabotage on behalf of German intelligence." He was tried on March 14, 1938. At his "trial" he signed a confession that had clearly been coerced by torture.

At this point the narrative is taken up by Irina, Yehezkel's daughter:

> Shortly after my father was taken away, a representative of the security services burst into our flat and made an inventory of everything that we owned. He refused to give a reason. Several months later, in late 1938, we were told that father was sentenced to ten years of imprisonment without the right of correspondence. At about the same time, Joseph Rosen, the JDC director in the USSR, arranged for a meeting with the Soviet foreign minister, [Vyacheslav] Molotov, to plead for his employees who had been arrested. Molotov told him that my father had, in fact, been spying for Germany since 1922, before his JDC employment, and that the government had nothing against JDC as an organization! [This was shortly before JDC was formally expelled, and clearly after a decision to do so had been taken.] Rosen arranged for a generous JDC severance package for all the families of employees who had been arrested and sentenced to imprisonment, but there was nothing he could do to facilitate my father's release from incarceration.
>
> We never heard from our father again. In the initial period we convinced ourselves that the sentence was being carried out according to its conditions – namely, internal exile. Father was to serve ten years and could not correspond with us during that period. At the end of that period, there was no change. Gradually, our hope faded, and we came to understand that father was probably no longer alive.
>
> In 1957, we received a letter from the Military College of the Supreme Court of the Soviet Union posthumously rehabilitating father. They included a letter stating that records indicated he died in prison on April 10, 1943, quoting a death certificate issued in

Moscow at that time. I was summoned to the military tribunal, where they officially informed me that my father was not guilty. I burst out crying. The members of the tribunal were surprised and even acted as if they were concerned for me: "Why are you crying? Everything is going to be good for you now. Your father's history will no longer be a liability for you."

How could I respond? A miserable life in which my father is murdered, and I am persecuted for his alleged treachery – and they expect it all to be erased in a moment? Basically, they are telling me that all will be good in my life except for the memories. That is not life.

In the end, we learned that they were cynically lying to us. We now know he was executed the day after his trial in 1938. Molotov lied when he met with Rosen later that year and hinted that my father was still alive. Even when he was rehabilitated, the official documents were based on the lie that he had "died" in 1943, at the height of the war, when so many others died, as if to mitigate the severity of the sentence. We were to understand that many citizens died during that period, as if my father was just one among many other casualties of war. But the fact is that he was murdered, plain and simple, and I have lived with that every waking day of my life since then. Only because he wanted to help his fellow Jews.

It is difficult to escape the irony that underlies this story. At a time when the USSR was isolated from the world (the United States had not yet granted diplomatic recognition), in the aftermath of the trauma of the revolution and subsequent civil wars in Ukraine and parts of Russia, Agro-Joint made a major contribution to the well-being of hundreds of thousands of its citizens, Jews and non-Jews alike. Tons of food, seeds, machinery, and livestock were brought into the country, in addition to hundreds of experts and consultants on agriculture and industry. It was virtually the only foreign assistance. But in the end, ideology was more important than assistance. Employees of foreign organizations, and especially of a foreign Jewish organization, became inevitable targets. Any contact with foreigners made one suspect – and for many, this meant death.

A circle is closed – almost. There was one more request that Irina made of our staff, who interviewed her after learning of her history:

> My mother is buried in Donskoy Cemetery. Obviously, we never knew what was done with my father's body. Last year my nephew went to pay respects at his grandmother's grave. In the cemetery's office, he found a list of people who had been executed by Stalin and buried there. To his surprise, he found his grandfather's (my father's) name, and a statement that he was buried in a mass grave for criminals there. Each year on October 29, the official memorial day for victims of the Great Terror, there is a ceremony at that site. An Orthodox priest says prayers at the gravesite. When I inquired, they apologized that no rabbi comes. They know Jews are buried there, but they don't know how to organize a visit from a rabbi. Could Joint arrange that next year?

Jewish Anti-Fascist Committee (May 26, 2006)

I have just come across two documents – letters – of extraordinary historical value that are in the American Jewish Archives, on the Cincinnati campus of the Hebrew Union College. Because of space limitations, I will share the contents of only one of the letters here. The one I will not reproduce is dated November 16, 1942. It is signed by a coalition of six American organizations, three of them Jewish (JDC, American Jewish Congress, and B'nai B'rith). The letter is addressed to Cordell Hull, then the US secretary of state. It describes the plight of minorities in Nazi-occupied Poland and is a plea for permission to circumvent the American embargo on aid to people trapped in enemy-occupied territory. Given the addressee, and the date, the letter is incredibly poignant. It describes the suffering of Jews caught in the Nazi juggernaut and how the sending of food packages could alleviate their plight, at least minimally.

The request was subsequently denied.

The letter that *is* reproduced below is from the same period. Dated October 7, 1943, it is written on JDC letterhead and signed by Paul Baerwald, honorary chairman of JDC at the time. The subject is proposed assistance to the general population in the Soviet Union in regions where there were large concentrations of Jews. Although the Soviet Union was considered an American ally in the war, the US administration wanted to be the exclusive channel for any large-scale material benefits that Soviet citizens might receive. Individual packages were not an issue. Broader support for larger swaths of the general population that an official delegation of Soviet Jews had requested as a way of ingratiating the Jews with Stalin required a waiver of the policy, which the letter was requesting.

There are several noteworthy things about this letter. The first is the sum of money mentioned within it. Baerwald sketches the magnitude of support that JDC had funneled into the USSR in the decades prior to the writing of the letter, in the hopes of helping Soviet Jewry adapt to a post-revolution reality for which most of them, as small shopkeepers, were singularly unsuited. Given that much of this assistance coincided with the Depression throughout the Western world, the amount is staggering.

A second point is the persistence of the JDC leadership in looking for ways to help this segment of Jewry. This is in the midst of the Second World War. The demands on JDC's resources were enormous. It would have been understandable for them to concentrate exclusively on those imprisoned in Nazi-occupied territory, as did the letter mentioned above. But the JDC leadership felt a sense of responsibility to *all* Jews in need and they were undeterred by the organization's limited resources.

It is worth noting the lengths to which JDC would go in order to supply the aid. The letter seems to cry out, "If we can't send packages through our normal channels, we will go as far as necessary to make this happen, even to Tehran if need be." It was, of course, easier to operate from there than in occupied Europe. Therefore, beginning in 1942, JDC moved a major part of its field operations to Tehran.

Baerwald recognized that JDC support of Jews, exclusively, could be a problem. He declared a willingness to make serious concessions in order to ensure that JDC's primary recipients get what they need. If this meant that some of this assistance had to be made available to others, as the Soviets insisted, they were prepared to do it. This approach was repeated during JDC's first food package distribution when we returned to the USSR in 1990.

Baerwald emphasized JDC's insistence on adhering to American law, which is why he wrote to Hull asking for State Department permission to help Jews in the USSR. He reported on the Soviet-sponsored visits of Jews to the JDC to address any suspicion that these meetings were furtive and had an agenda that ran counter to American interests and policy. And finally, he noted that JDC conformed to Soviet laws in its activities in the USSR, presumably as reassurance that should American attitudes toward the Soviet regime change in the future, JDC would not be an impediment to an improved relationship.

This letter was written long after JDC was forbidden by the Soviets to operate in the territory of the USSR. The Joint had officially been expelled five years earlier, its employees severely abused and several murdered by Stalin's regime, but the search for ways to maintain contact with Jews was ongoing.

It is interesting to note that official representatives of the Soviet regime engaged in discussions with JDC, which the same regime had labeled an enemy a short time before. Clearly, the prospect of relieving serious shortages, the existence of which might contribute to civil unrest, superseded ideological incompatibility. It is striking how these themes recur in JDC history in so many different guises.

One final note: Reference is made in the letter to two representatives of Soviet Jewry with whom JDC met, Professor Solomon Mikhoels and Lt. Col. Itzik Feffer. These men were key players in the "Jewish Anti-Fascist Committee," a body of Jews set up by Stalin to garner support for the Soviet war effort in the capitalist West.

Mikhoels and Feffer were dispatched to the US on speaking tours to galvanize American Jewry to press for American government support for the Soviet government and its people in the fight against the Nazi invaders. Both were famous Jewish intellectuals, one a Yiddish actor and one a Yiddish poet. (Mikhoels's portrayal of King Lear in Yiddish is still occasionally written about in theater circles as one of the most memorable of all time, in any language. Snippets of it still exist on the internet.[1]) Within five years, the war was over, and both were murdered, having outlived their usefulness to Stalin.

---

1   "MIKHOELS playing King Lear 1935," Moscow Jewish State Theater production of *King Lear*, YouTube, https://youtu.be/AU838zh5ysw.

Below is the letter:

October 7, 1943
Honorable Cordell Hull, Secretary of State
Washington, DC

Dear Mr. Secretary,

We believe that it may be of interest to you to know of the recent discussions which we have had with Professor S. Mikhoels and Lt. Col. I. Feffer of Russia, as well as with Dr. Lebedenko, representing the Russian Red Cross in this country.

You will, of course, recall that the Joint Distribution Committee and its affiliates were able to conduct a substantial program of relief and constructive assistance in Russia between 1921 and 1938. Our work was conducted on a nonsectarian basis in regions where there were large Jewish populations. JDC expended independently from 1921 to 1938 approximately $12,000,000 for various types of relief and reconstructive activities in Russia. We developed a program for settling over 300,000 Jews on several million acres, training them to become farmers and at the same time helping over 80,000 Russian peasants, neighbors of the Jewish colonists. This agricultural program was conducted through our operating agency, the American Jewish Joint Agricultural Corporation (Agro-Joint).

All these important enterprises were, of course, carried out with the full knowledge of the State Department and with the active and continued cooperation of the Soviet Government. These activities came to an end in 1938. In recent months, in response to many requests from interested relatives and groups, we have sought to find ways of rendering service within Russia through the sending of parcels of foodstuffs, clothing, etc. to needy individuals in that country. The shipments are being made from Tehran with the help of the Intourist Bureau under arrangements made with the Soviet Government. The food packages are sent through the Russian parcel post, and full Russian customs duties have been paid.

Within the last few weeks, we took advantage of the presence here of Professor S. Mikhoels and Lt. Col. Feffer and discussed these matters with these gentlemen. We indicated our interest in being of help on a more substantial basis in other directions through the food parcel program. During our conversations, it developed that greater benefits could be conferred if shipments were made in bulk, rather than individual parcels. These could be shipped into regions where, through the channel of the Russian Red Cross, a distribution could be effected to the needy population without regard to race and creed, but where there was a substantial Jewish population. In our discussions with them, we pointed out that naturally we would want to submit these plans to the State Department.

We can well understand your present burdens and that you have very little time to spare. However, should you desire to have us confer with one of your associates, we hold ourselves in readiness.

Respectfully yours,
Paul Baerwald
Honorary Chairman

In a letter of response from Secretary Hull, the request was denied.

Chairman Kab (October 19, 2007)

The Central State Archive of Lithuania, in its sections on the KGB and Communist Party archives, contains some fascinating material on JDC's activities in that region. Of particular interest is the immediate postwar period, from 1945–48.

JDC sent packages into the western regions of the USSR, including the Baltic states, during this period. In July 1947, for example, JDC headquarters allocated thirty thousand dollars per month for three months to send dry goods and clothing into these remnant communities that had survived the Nazi occupation. These years coincided with the apex of Stalin's power, when his control over the empire was nearly absolute. We can assume, though, that in the rush to rebuild a devastated country in the aftermath of the war,

some of the controls on contacts with the outside world were unintentionally weakened, as the rebuilding efforts took precedence over everything else.
Mikhail Beizer, a JDC historian, relates what he uncovered in the recently
declassified archives:

> Documents in the archives attest to quarrels among the members
> of the Kaunas (Kovno) Jewish community in the post war period.
> For example, ninety-seven members of the Kaunas community
> sent a protest letter to the authorities in 1947 requesting that a new
> election be held to replace those authorized by the community to
> distribute JDC assistance within the community. Apparently, these
> protestors were not confident that the Jewish leaders in charge
> were fulfilling their responsibilities. The debates were internal,
> and sometimes bitter, and they revolved around control. And they
> turned to the government authorities to mediate the internal com-
> munal dispute.

The situation in Lithuania changed dramatically about a year later. Two
months after the 1948 murder of Solomon Mikhoels, the Yiddish actor, as
part of a general purge of Jewish cultural luminaries by Stalin, it became clear
to the Jews remaining in Vilnius (Vilna) that Jews throughout the USSR
were now targeted by the Stalin regime. Sycophancy became a survival tac-
tic. If previously the government would be called on to help resolve internal
disputes, now fear of anything that might attract government attention pre-
dominated. The protocol of a community meeting at that time, written in
Yiddish and carefully edited, was sent to the New York headquarters of JDC:

> The chairman Chaim Kab takes the floor and declares the fol-
> lowing: "Taking into consideration the discontinuance of the
> rationing system [which was originally imposed during wartime]
> by our benevolent [Soviet] government, as well as the brilliant cur-
> rency reform of our leader Stalin, the conditions of all working cit-
> izens have improved a great deal. Inasmuch as each person is able
> to get everything he needs in the open market at very reasonable
> prices, I therefore believe that we do not find it necessary to accept

any further aid from the Joint. I propose that we inform the Joint to discontinue their support, as this American aid is of no benefit to us."

Until now this is what historians of the period knew about this situation. Clearly fearful that connections with the Joint could put their loyalty to the Soviet regime in question, the community leaders asked that the assistance be suspended.

Recently, Beizer uncovered the postscript to this story, an unintended consequence of the cessation of material support to the Jewish community as they rebuilt their lives after the war. We now understand that the food packages were not merely classic welfare assistance to the indigent – those packages also functioned as a magnet that attracted Jews to Jewish communal life. In the course of picking up their packages, the Jews in need, or those who acted on their behalf, were exposed to Jewish community events and activities. Furthermore, KGB sources connect the increased number of circumcisions of Jewish children in the city in those years to JDC's material support. Apparently, the outside support increased the sense of economic security for many younger people and made them more willing to identify as Jews.

These Jews who had just gone through the hell of the Shoah were initially fearful of further suffering because they were Jews. But they remained connected to the community because they needed the material support offered through the Joint. And this support gave them further reassurance that the bad times were behind them.

Once the leadership of the community through Chairman Kab rejected the JDC's material support, being labeled a Jew became an unmitigated liability, with no advantages to it. You could easily be identified for persecution and discrimination. Previously, the benefits of the food supplements outweighed the risk, but now that these were no longer available, Jews lowered their profile and began to desist from making any public affirmation of their identity. A visit to a Jewish communal institution was now a public declaration of being Jewish with no attendant benefit, and that was dangerous. As a result, according to documents of the time, when JDC food packages stopped arriving, the community infrastructure collapsed!

Relief in Transit (September 30, 2005)

I write these lines several days before Rosh Hashanah 5766. We each have our own ways of observing this period on a personal and communal level. At the very least, we are bidden to engage in *cheshbon nefesh* – a kind of soul-searching – to examine who we are and where we are going. The letter that follows provides a possible frame for these questions.

While the time of year at which the letter is written is, at first glance, immaterial and the events described in it have nothing directly to do with the Rosh Hashanah season, I believe that there is a theme here that is very appropriate to this period. The letter is a request, the background of which will be clear in a moment. The nature of the request, and the fact that it is directed to JDC, should give each of us pause.

The letter was written to a JDC official in London who directed part of a JDC program known by its initials, RIT (Relief in Transit). This program has not had widespread exposure. Due to its nature, while in operation it was a secret program, which accounts for its innocuous rubric. It was an effort by JDC, working in partnership with the highest levels of the Israeli government from the early 1950s, to ensure that Jews behind the Iron Curtain would not be hermetically sealed off from the Jewish world, despite the best efforts of their governments to do so.

JDC support, financial and often logistical, played a key role in the program's development and execution. One facet of the operation involved sending in individuals posing as tourists with instructions to meet Jewish activists. These "tourists" smuggled in things like Jewish books, Stars of David, tapes of Jewish music, and posters of contemporary Israel – all to let these Jews know that they were not forgotten, and to give them an opportunity, even if clandestinely, to express their connection to, and identification with, the Jewish people. It was in this context that I made my first trip to the USSR in 1977, well before I began working for JDC. Only years later did I learn of JDC's involvement in this program.

One aspect of the RIT enterprise, which at its peak accounted for millions of dollars of JDC's annual budget, was a program to send packages of clothing to Jews in difficult straits in the USSR and other Eastern European countries. The clothing was primarily for Jews who had been dismissed from their jobs after submitting an official request to emigrate to Israel, although it was also given to Jews who were persecuted for other reasons. The recipients would sell the contents of the packages and use the proceeds to support themselves. Packages were sent from dozens of European addresses so as not to arouse the suspicion of the authorities. To this day, you can meet Jews of Soviet origin in Israel and elsewhere who talk of these packages in terms of salvation. The source was generally anonymous to them.

The process worked as follows: One day, totally unexpectedly, in the midst of a difficult period in which the future looked particularly bleak, the designated recipients in the Soviet Union were summoned to the local post office to receive a registered mail package with new clothes. This was during the time when Communist bloc countries imported very little from outside the bloc. The various regimes gave little consideration to consumer needs or desires, so a thriving black market developed. The contents of this type of package, when sold, could sustain a family for months at a time. A pair of western jeans, otherwise unavailable in Soviet stores, was gold.

The needs of these Jews were not limited to physical sustenance. Read this letter from 1947, translated from the original Yiddish, to the director of the JDC package program in London soon after the program was developed. Notice the pathos with which it is written. Read and put this in the context of the work JDC does today, considering both the impact we can calculate and the impact that we, or those who succeed us, will learn of only at some future time. It is, to my mind, something to contemplate in this season of taking stock and considering our Jewish commitments. Note especially the currency to which the writer refers:

Sir,

Since you are helping everyone who needs help, I am asking you, in the name of all Jews from our little town who survived the war, to help us to complete the work we began of making mass graves a suitable tomb for the remains of the holy martyrs who were killed by the followers of Hitler in our small town.

I will tell you the whole story of our slain brothers, sisters, parents, and friends:

Now I am living in Vilna, but before the war I was living in a town by the name of Utian, which is 140 kilometers [eighty-seven miles] from Vilna. This town had about twelve thousand Jews before the war. When the war broke out, those who could do so escaped eastward to Russia; those unable to flee remained. When the Hitlerites came, they were determined to exterminate all whom they found who had not escaped. The slaughter [took place] three kilometers [two miles] out of town, in a forest. There they killed about eight thousand of our twelve thousand Jewish brothers and sisters.

In 1946, when I came back from the army to Utian, the peasants there told me what happened and showed me the place where our martyrs were killed. At first, I collected money from the surviving Jews, and we built a monument in honor of the victims.

Now terrible things are happening there. There are such evil people who couldn't even leave the dead bodies of the martyrs in peace. What have they done, those shameless hooligans? They are digging out the dead bodies and looking for gold teeth. It seems they are finding what they are looking for. Several peasants I know came to Vilna to tell me that. I immediately left my work and went over to the place. When I came to the graveyard, I nearly passed out. The graves were in many places dug out, and arms, legs, heads, and even the rotten clothes of our martyrs were lying about.

I decided to do something. I returned to Vilna and went to see some people from our town. We collected some money and we decided to put cement on the graves. But we do not have enough money to cement all the graves. And we do not have any possibility of getting it. So please, good sir, could you help us with whatever you can to enable us to cement all five mass graves? The one grave, the largest one, forty-one meters [135 feet] long, we will try to finish, but we still owe the workers for the work they have done till now. This grave should cost us – I have figured out – from five to six parcels of clothing, the ones you are sending to help us. And the other graves (four of them) should cost around eight to twelve parcels, as well as some good material for suits or coats. This will enable us to pay the workers for cementing the other four graves, so that our holy martyrs may rest in peace.

Sir, I am asking you, please take the necessary steps as soon as possible and send us the required help. I believe that it is a duty for every Jew to assist such a case, and I hope that all Jews in London, led by the Joint, will help in this matter. I am waiting for help and a decision of your welfare committee. In helping us, you will do a great act of faith.

With regards,
Yossl Z.

PS: I am sending you four photos where you will see how I am leading the work in cementing the very large grave, the one which is forty-one meters long. On a recent visit I found the graves, now paved over.

Four Key Decisions (December 17, 2010)

I've just finished a fascinating book by Ian Kershaw, a British historian of World War II, who wrote about ten key decisions made during that period that changed the course of the war, and by extension, the course of history.[2]

The book is part of a genre that looks at how turning points in history are often the unintended consequences of decisions taken by people in positions of authority. The notion that history is often determined by accident rather than design has enormous implications.

With respect to our work, we can identify four key decisions during the first twenty years of our FSU operations that set the stage for the program we now run. Some of these decisions had anticipated consequences that were realized more or less as we expected; many did not. Are these in fact the four most crucial decisions, the decisions that most determined where we are

---

2 Ian Kershaw, *Fateful Choices: Ten Decisions That Changed the World, 1940–1941* (London: Allen Lane, 2007).

today? Perhaps, although others could undoubtedly come up with alternatives. But as an opening gambit, this list is as good as any.

JDC began to work in the USSR in the late 1980s, not knowing very much about the context in which we were to work. We, the original staff, were not neophytes in JDC. Our experience extended from North Africa to Asia to Eastern Europe. But we had scant knowledge or understanding of life in the USSR; few outsiders knew much of anything about it. There were educated estimates of the number of nuclear warheads in the Soviet arsenal, but hardly anything was known about how a family in Gorky managed its monthly budget. Western intelligence agencies knew little about daily life and what people thought and felt, and of course were generally caught off guard by the way things imploded within just a few years.

Decision number one: JDC's focus would be on Jewish community, and we would work through communal structures, where they existed, in order to realize our goals. Where they did not exist, which was almost everywhere, we saw it as our challenge to help cultivate them. This had been part of our organizational DNA for the previous ninety years, in a most pronounced fashion in our reconstruction efforts in postwar Europe. JDC's expertise as an organization was not to be realized in a particular classroom in a Jewish school or in large events attracting myriad Jews. We were there for the long term and would work on creating community infrastructure, building block by building block.

The implications here were manifold, not all of them easy for us. Others could run programs; our focus was on assisting organizations. Others could hang a banner advertising their organization's contribution to a particular event. JDC nudged community leaders and community organizations to the forefront as the sponsors, even if they were only channeling JDC funds into the program. Service to the elderly was not provided by JDC but by the community Hesed.

The programs we establish or sponsor need to be run by local professionals and have a local governance structure. They have to conform to values we impose, because it has been our experience that these are universal values in Jewish communities, even if they are not widely embraced in this region: the importance of encouraging people to volunteer, the expectation that all Jews are welcome to participate in community life, the notion that transparency is a foundation of proper governance, and more.

An insistence on working through community subjected us to attacks from others who felt that we were encouraging illusions and creating unreasonable expectations. Community, they said, could not be created from the ashes of a Soviet society that, contrary to its ideology, fostered a perverse kind of individualism – that is to say, ultimately everyone in the Soviet Union was out for himself or herself, and had no commitment to the collective. No one would volunteer, they predicted. "The organizations and the programs you create will all be yours and yours alone. They will be foreign and transplanted, rather than genuinely indigenous." But the naysayers were proven wrong, and Jewish communal life was reborn. Legitimate and authentic communities began to sprout.

Decision number two was not to become involved in welfare. Contemporaneous with our entry into the USSR we had major welfare programs for the elderly in most of the countries in which we worked. If we extrapolated from a place like Hungary, with one hundred thousand Jews (or so we believed), and a welfare budget that came close to two million dollars, then to assist the needy Jewish population in the USSR in the same fashion would have required a commitment equal to our entire global budget at the time. Also, how could it be done? Jews in most of the countries in which we worked were to be found in one or two major cities and a handful of smaller ones. To provide welfare to Jews spread out across the vast expanse of the USSR was more than daunting. It was logistically inconceivable.

On the other hand, while some of us felt that welfare was too big a task for us to take on, others didn't believe there was much of a need. Poverty is normally correlated with education, they argued, and most Soviet Jews were not merely literate, but educated. Given the many impediments to achievement because of antisemitism, the generally accepted notion was that Jews had to be outstanding in their chosen professions in order to stand a chance at succeeding on an uneven playing field. Excelling in education was one way to do this, and therefore these were presumably not impoverished people. There were at that time few studies documenting Soviet poverty. Even vaunted Western intelligence agencies were not aware of the depth of the problem. The population may not have been wealthy, but there was no reason to believe they were very poor.

Rumors began to reach us on our early visits that there was a netherworld beneath the surface that we saw, which contained cases of real poverty. We started asking questions, and the answers were ominous. We saw few elderly Jews at community events. We saw no one in wheelchairs. We were visiting apartments on the fourth floors of buildings without elevators. We wondered how elderly residents negotiated the stairs. Indeed, *did* they negotiate the stairs, or were they homebound?

We could not escape the welfare issue. Given the scope of the need, however, we had to be careful not to compromise on our commitment to community. There was a risk that the budgets required for welfare, and the nature of the program, would overshadow everything else we did and make community development a meaningless aspiration. Instead, we consciously decided that the welfare program would not become the exception, but instead would serve as the foundation of our community-building efforts. A strategy was formulated in which welfare services were delivered through a community-based organization – the Hesed. Local professional talent was nurtured and boards were created. Community values were the standards by which the programs were evaluated. Delivering a food package became a means for creating community rather than an end in and of itself.

It took several years for the program to develop. By the late 1990s it was established. The physical and human infrastructures were in place to reach and serve every needy Jew. Our ability to operate in this sphere was now primarily dependent on funding, which was inevitably in short supply.

The time came to enter new arenas of activity, to help bring communities to the next level. A community needs to care for its needy, but a community that focuses *only* on its needy will not be able to sustain itself over time. Which led to the third major decision, and our next organizational challenge.

In the late 1990s, we realized that a building is a sine qua non of community. There is no Jewish community anywhere that does not have physical space among its varied assets. If you don't have a place for Jews to congregate, for a community to call home, a physical site in which the community is centered, you will not have a viable community. So, decision number three was to build, purchase, or renovate space for Jewish communities.

Newly minted Jewish organizations rented space commercially in their cities. This situation was unsustainable over time as the costs of rental space skyrocketed as countries adapted to new, post-Soviet economic realities and real estate markets began to emerge. Programs for special-needs children and for Hillel and for adult Jewish education and for so many other programs critical to community development would not be able to afford to compete for commercial space in large cities.

A shared building also serves as a catalyst for interchange among organizations that otherwise have no point of interaction. Boards have to make decisions about communal priorities through the act of allocating space. Buildings foster a pride in Jewish engagement – in Odesa we were told of a taxi driver who corrected a passenger who had asked to be taken to a particular street address: "Why don't you just say to me to take you to that beautiful new Jewish home, Beit Grand." The Odesa Jewish community has an address, which is tangible evidence of its existence in the eyes of local Jews. It is the first time in their history since early Soviet times that this is the case.

From a historical perspective, the decision to acquire space marked a turning point in our work in the FSU. Until this point in 1998, when the decision was formally taken, we generally spoke about the "window of opportunity" with which we were presented in the FSU. The implication was that the window was open, but only temporarily. At any moment it could close. Our presence there was temporary, and tenuous. The USSR had previously undergone periods of liberalization and then the dark forces once again got the upper hand. Was this change that permitted us entry also part of a cycle? Would we work in the FSU for a few years and then be forced to close up shop as the "evil empire" reemerged?

By deciding to invest in property, we were making a statement: Our engagement in the FSU was now long term, and buildings were the concretization of this.

Decision number four is in many ways a product of all the decisions made before it and is a perfect example of the law of unintended consequences. By the middle of the first decade of the millennium, all three of the previous decisions had collectively become a potent force for our meta-mission. We were looking to reclaim Jews for the Jewish people. Community was turning into a valuable tool for doing this; the building blocks of community were in place almost everywhere, and these were the organizations and programs that were attracting Jews. The basic needs of most of the Jews at risk could be addressed by bodies operated by members of the community. And the lion's share of communal activity in most communities of substance around the FSU was taking place in facilities purchased with JDC's help.

But it was also becoming clear that what we had created could not be sustained exclusively by JDC budgets. This, of course, was never the intention. Together with our local partners, we made efforts to engage oligarchs in local life. Some showed interest, but in general their involvement revolved around their business ventures. Where contributions and commitment advanced their business interests, they could be enticed. Where the rewards for involvement lay elsewhere, they displayed little inclination to contribute.

After much thought and study, decision number four was made in 2005: to begin a massive move toward self-sufficiency in community operations with which JDC was connected. Where possible, a fee-for-service regimen would be implemented. Buildings in large cities would be viewed not as liabilities but as potential assets that could generate funding for their operations through commercial rentals of space that the community could relinquish for the short term. The most creative minds among our staff were mobilized and local partners were challenged to be part of the process.

Success would require a change in organizational culture and identity, a move away from traditional philanthropy into new arenas. We needed to operate in a different way. There were legal hurdles that needed to be surmounted. "Partnership" took on a new meaning. If Jews were to pay to participate, programs needed to be more responsive to their needs and desires. Things like business plans and focus groups to determine needs became part of our modus operandi. Evaluation had to be done differently, and a new set of metrics needed to be developed.

The unintended consequence was the involvement of a whole new socioeconomic group in community life. For the first time, the nascent middle class began to turn out for programs. This group, previously absent from Jewish communal life, not only existed but could be engaged by the community. The middle class was assuming the role of the backbone of the community, as it is in many places in the Jewish world.

Another unintended benefit was the ability to survive the global economic downturn without excessive damage to our community development program. As JDC's traditional sources of funding constricted, they were gradually supplemented – and in some instances replaced – by locally generated income. Thus, a severe reduction in JDC support did not automatically mean that programs would close, which had been the case in the previous philanthropic model.

Four decisions were made over the last two decades of operations, each with enormous consequences. They are not the only important decisions that were made and one can certainly take issue with the choice of these four. But these four provide some insight into the way one international Jewish organization has chosen to assist the Jews of the former Soviet Union.

The Meaning of Renewal (February 18, 2011)

Recently uncovered documents in a Moscow archive contain a laconic notation about one Solomon Goldberg Gurevich, born in 1897. A military panel of judges ruled in 1956 that "according to the newly discovered circumstances, and an investigation that followed, the sentence he served was abolished due to 'the absence of *corpus delicti.*'" Therein lies a tale. This piece is dedicated to his memory, to bringing his story to the attention of all of us, professionals and volunteers alike, who strive to realize JDC's mission in the FSU, a mission for which he sacrificed his life.

Our story begins in a more contemporary setting. Rafael Goldberg served as the head of the Tyumen Jewish community when we began our operations there several years ago. Tyumen is a regional capital and an oil-producing area in the heart of Siberia. As in many similar locales in Siberia, here too there is a small Jewish community. Throughout the Communist period, there were financial incentives for people to settle in these regions in order to extract their plentiful natural resources. Many Jews took advantage of these incentives, because the standard of living was much higher and educational opportunities often less restricted for Jews in these places. So the Jewish communities of Siberia are generally of more recent vintage, without the rich history of the communities further to the west and south, within the traditional Pale of Settlement of czarist times.

Rafael spent his professional career as a journalist and the editor in chief of the local newspaper, the *Tyumen Courier*. When the political environment eased somewhat in the late 1980s, he began taking tentative steps toward organizing local Jews into a cultural organization. When JDC first came to the region in 1994, Rafael and his society, called "Aviv," were natural partners. From the outset Rafael proclaimed that one of his goals was to have the local synagogue restituted. The building was in an advanced state of decay but Rafael was undeterred. He felt that the building was rightly the property of the Jewish community and would be critical to the efforts to revive Jewish life. He personally raised significant sums of money and the authorities returned the building. Their condition that it be reconstructed was not a problem and since the early 2000s, the synagogue has been functioning as a house of worship and a community center. This was a major achievement for the Tyumen community, and Goldberg spearheaded the efforts.

At this point we move from Rafael's public life to his private life. He was raised by his mother, and queries about his father were often met with incomplete answers. He was told that his father was an agronomist and had something to do with a Jewish community in Moscow. In any event, it was clear that it was a line of questioning not to be pursued. He suspected that there was far more to the story. He was sure that the Jewish connection made his mother uncomfortable, and even fearful of telling all that she knew. This was not because she was in any way ashamed of her own Jewish identity, but because she wanted above all else to protect her son by shielding him from *his* Jewish identity, as was common among her contemporaries. One way to provide that protection was to downplay the Jewish elements in his past by keeping those elements from him, lest they limit his opportunities in Soviet society, which was an intolerable prospect to her.

As he matured, Rafael's curiosity was piqued. He became more and more interested in the mystery of his father's identity. Rafael was a journalist by profession, but even more important, he had the *soul* of a journalist. He was increasingly driven to find "the story behind the story," to uncover his father's fate. He understood that this information might be painful to learn, but he needed to know.

Through connections he was given limited access to the files of the NKVD, which he suspected might contain his father's secret. In that archive he finally tracked down the file of one Solomon Goldberg Gurevich, whose background matched his father's. Goldberg Gurevich had indeed been an agronomist – he'd worked in the Ministry of Agriculture and collaborated with Joseph Rosen, the director of Agro-Joint.

The file contained documents indicating that, in the eyes of the NKVD, Solomon Goldberg Gurevich was a member of the Central Committee of the "counterrevolutionary Zionist organization, HeHalutz." He was in fact a member of that organization, which was founded in Moscow in 1923. It united leftist Jews of the time under a political banner, but also served a social purpose: it helped Jews establish collective agriculture farms to conform to the regime's wishes. HeHalutz partnered with Agro-Joint and was instrumental in the operations of these collectives. HeHalutz was banned by the Communist regime in 1928 because it was considered a threat to the hegemony of the party (presumably because of its Zionist leanings), but its members almost certainly continued to meet underground. Its leadership reported to JDC's USSR director Joseph Rosen in distant Moscow about how the collectives were faring and what was happening to the Jews of the region. Agro-Joint's support of HeHalutz was clandestine. It did not want to put its general activities or its staff at risk of an NKVD crackdown. Government policy shifted frequently, and what was permitted or even encouraged at one time could, without any forewarning, become a justification for persecution.

Once banned, HeHalutz continued to operate secretly and to enjoy Agro-Joint support. According to its agreement with the Soviet government, Agro-Joint was to deal in specific areas of interest to the government. But its internal budget presented to JDC leadership in New York for annual approval contained a clause called "Cultural Activities." This clause was exploited to the fullest both overtly and covertly. Knowing that Jewish organizations had nowhere else to turn for support, Rosen made sure some Agro-Joint assistance went to synagogues, Maccabee sport clubs, museums, and Jewish and Zionist groups.

Eventually, Goldberg Gurevich was caught in the NKVD web. The file Rafael uncovered contained the arrest warrant and a questionnaire filled out by his father. There was a receipt for the prisoner's seized property, a list of other confiscated documents and money, and the full transcript of the interrogation that had been conducted in the Lefortovo prison, steps away from the Kremlin in downtown Moscow. Finally, there were the minutes of the sole meeting of a panel of military judges of the Supreme Court of the USSR, on April 21, 1938. The "trial" lasted about fifteen minutes, according to the official record. A confession allegedly signed by Solomon was submitted to the court. The confession was quite explicit, referring to his involvement in an "underground counterrevolutionary Zionist organization aiming to overthrow Soviet power through espionage, sabotage, and terrorist acts against the leaders of the Communist Party and the Soviet government." Furthermore, he was an agent of "one of the foreign intelligences [sic]." This was a commonly used pseudonym for JDC in Soviet legal parlance.

The final document was the verdict: "Solomon Goldberg Gurevich is hereby sentenced to the extreme penalty – to be shot and all of his property expropriated by the state. The sentence is final. There are no appeals, and according to the law of December 1, 1934, it is to be carried out immediately." Solomon was executed on that same day, April 21, 1938. His son, Rafael Goldberg, was born on May 2, two weeks after his father's execution.

Rafael's search was over. He now knew his father's fate. His father had been an agronomist and could have supported his family in that field. But his work with HeHalutz allowed him to contribute to the education and spiritual welfare of the Jewish people, which was so important to him. HeHalutz members were harassed from the time it was established. To be involved was a way of realizing a commitment to the Jewish people, a commitment that carried with it substantial risk.

Rafael took comfort in the fact that well before he knew of his father's work and the risks he had taken to help his fellow Jews in the USSR, he, Solomon's son, had chosen a similar path – although admittedly with far less at stake personally. He felt that, in his life's work and through his dedication to the Jewish revival in Tyumen, he had lived his father's dream.

And a further lesson for us in a contemporary setting: The term "Jewish renewal" has an important subtext, namely, to "renew," rather than create de novo. JDC's history in the USSR did not start in 1989 when it officially returned to the USSR. The communities with which we work have roots stretching back generations. In the intervening years, those under Communist rule were profoundly disconnected from those roots. But for many, the move to Jewish life and connections is a return to the family of the Jewish people.

So, too, for JDC as an organization. Our work in the FSU and the professionals who work there on our behalf are part of a chain extending back to people like Solomon Goldberg Gurevich. They are continuing his work and helping realize his dream, a dream for which he paid with his life.

Righteous Gentiles (June 17, 2002)

Odesa was the site of a well-known ghetto during the Second World War. It is this fact, rather than the killing grounds elsewhere, such as the Babyn Yar ravine in Ukraine, where German troops and their collaborators massacred tens of thousands of Jews in September of 1941, that defines the wartime experience for the city's community. Those who helped Jews survive the ghetto experience are often the objects of commemorations, and the number of local citizens who assisted Jews in the ghetto is remarkably high. It has bred a concern for the welfare of righteous gentiles unlike anywhere else I know in the FSU.

As a consequence, the Odesa Hesed, Gemilus Hasadim, runs a "warm home" for elderly righteous gentiles. It is a place for the elderly, generally in one of their apartments, to gather in an informal social setting on a weekly basis, to relieve their loneliness, to share memories, and to give emotional support to one another. The "mission statement" of the warm home clearly and movingly articulates its goals:

> The relationship between the Jewish and Ukrainian peoples has always been complicated and difficult to understand. Ukrainians were the policemen hired by the Fascists to put into practice the idea of killing all the Jews. The attitude of the Ukrainian population was generally quite passive in the face of these efforts. Still, there were many examples in which Ukrainians risked their own lives and those of their families to save Jews.
>
> Today, the people of Ukraine are reconsidering the issues of Jewish-Ukrainian relations from a positive perspective. There is mutual understanding that the two peoples have much in common: the genocide of the Holodomor, contemporary poverty, and life under lawless regimes for many years. Today, Ukraine and Israel are two sovereign states that embody national revivals and

efforts to right historic wrongs. A warm home, sponsored by the local Jewish community with gratitude for the righteous gentile population of Odesa, is aimed at fostering the links between these two peoples."

This mission statement does not whitewash history. A record of difficult relations does not allow one to forget those instances in which thanks are due. And it goes one step further in drawing a parallel that is supposed to inspire empathy among the Ukrainians who learn of this initiative. The local Ukrainian intellectuals (all non-Jews) who drew up the mission statement make reference in it to the Holodomor, the famine enforced by Stalin in order to collectivize Ukrainian peasants in the 1930s. Millions were starved to death, often while nearby granaries were full to capacity.

There are fifteen participants weekly in the warm home, twelve of whom are recognized by Yad Vashem for having risked their lives to save Jews during the Shoah. Each, of course, has his or her own story, but in a room together they appear to be a group of unremarkable elderly gentiles thankful for the assistance of a Jewish community, which knows no bounds of gratitude to them for their courage. The extraordinary thing is the extent to which they feel indebted to the Jewish community for this assistance. They don't have a notion of entitlement or good deeds repaid; as far as they are concerned, this is simply an act of Jewish beneficence.

What Is Political? (June 4, 2003)

I just returned from a brief trip to Moscow, where the buzz is about the president's State of the State Address. The reference is, of course, to Putin, and the issue preoccupying those with whom I met was the president's broadside aimed at NGOs. He issued what is best characterized as a grim warning to nongovernmental agencies, accusing them of "getting financing from influential foreign and domestic foundations, [and] serving dubious groups and foreign interests."

Anyone with even passing familiarity with JDC's history in the USSR can't help but get goosebumps. Jewish artists, doctors, and intelligentsia prematurely met their Maker at Stalin's hand when they were accused of these very same things in the 1940s and 1950s. So, we ask ourselves, what does this mean for the Jews?

First, lest anyone think otherwise, Russian government officials are not alone in these suspicions. Similar doubts about the motives of NGOs are voiced in Ukraine and remain unspoken but not far from the surface in Belarus and the Asian republics. Fears about the role of NGOs have recently been magnified (and in the minds of certain leaders justified) by events in the region. Regime changes in Serbia, and subsequently in Georgia, are attributed (correctly or not) in large measure to the activities of NGOs in those regions that supported the creation of "civil societies." This term is increasingly seen as a code word used to impose alien Western notions of participatory democracy on this part of the world. A country like Ukraine, with bitterly contested elections, is particularly sensitive to "incitement" of this nature.

We can reassure ourselves that JDC is immune to this type of attack, as we are careful to comport ourselves in a strictly apolitical fashion. Assuming that the current regimes are not simply looking for excuses to harass Jews (so far true), we should not be concerned.

Well, not quite.

The first problem is where one draws the line. That is, how exactly does one define "apolitical"? I can assure you that, put in a room together with an "average" citizen of an FSU country, no reader of this briefing would come to an agreement with an FSU counterpart on what is and what is not "political." Creating and training boards of directors for a JCC has a political overtone; empowering representative leadership, as it does, and making it accountable to those it represents are clearly political notions. If one extrapolates from there to governance of society, JDC can be seen as fomenting "threats."

If that seems far-fetched – and I assure you that in a society hypersensitive to such issues it is not – the following presents its own set of problems. We are engaged in an enterprise that, to some, makes the state look negligent. The more we publicize our work on behalf of indigent elderly, the more we bring the state's failings to the consciousness of the world. It is a source of embarrassment that these governments cannot provide for the basic needs of their most vulnerable populations. For some reason, NGO work with children is sanctioned. In fact, the states often give support to local NGOs for orphans and homeless children. At the other end of the spectrum, though, the problems of the elderly are seen as an embarrassment – certainly some-thing that should not be given a high profile. This may explain why there are so few indigenous NGOs working on behalf of the elderly in the FSU successor states.

Finally, JDC could be targeted by extension. A local Jewish community newspaper that enjoys JDC support might carry an article or letter to the editor attacking government welfare policy. The head of a local Jewish com-munity with whom we cooperated may turn into an opposition activist after leaving Jewish communal life. All the scenarios cited above come from our experience; it all depends on how wide the net is cast. Add to all this a tradi-tional Soviet suspicion of foreigners, and we are vulnerable.

So, should we worry? Local analysts and pundits with whom I spoke this week confirmed our sense that we are not currently at risk. NGOs on the radar screen are those primarily engaged in more overtly political activity, things like sponsoring "democracy film festivals" or training political activists in how to organize demonstrations, monitor abuses of civil rights, and so on.

But one never knows. A single bureaucrat can decide to make our lives miserable. A particular position could be misinterpreted, a local employee could run afoul of the authorities, and JDC would sustain collateral damage. The situation, while not presenting an immediate risk, is cause for concern, and we are carefully monitoring it.

Family Camps (June 4, 2003)

Family camps have become a flagship of our efforts in informal Jewish educa-tion around the FSU. For an average of ten days during the summer, parents and children live in a resort setting and simulate Jewish communal life, learn-ing and relaxing together. The experience differs at each site, but until now we have always considered the goal to be the same.

The enterprise enjoys enormous popularity. As they prepare for this year's group, a cadre of young FSU Jewish educators, brimming with enthusiasm, spread out across tables and all over the floor, acting out scenes, drawing murals, and composing songs. A non-Russian-speaker would catch the occa-sional familiar term – "Shabbat," "Yerushalayim," or "Montefiore" – above the din and chatter.

With all of this, we need to ask a fundamental question: What is the purpose of these camps? The answer is not as obvious as one might expect and speaks to broader issues in Jewish communal life in the FSU:

1. Is the education at these family retreats to be rooted in values education? If so, how do we teach Jewish values in a sensitive, effective, and nonproscriptive way? Or:
2. Is the purpose of these camps to give the participants the basic skills of Jewish living? Should they concentrate, for example, on the life cycle and the calendar, and leave more amorphous issues, like Jewish values, for a later date? Or:
3. Is the ultimate goal to empower the participants to engage their Jewish identities directly through the study of primary Jewish texts, as opposed to imbibing texts "off the shelf" from rabbis and teachers who come from elsewhere for brief, or even extended, visits to the FSU?

It would be easy to declare that we need to find the right balance among all three of these options, but in the brief time available we risk being a mile wide and an inch deep, with nothing sustainable at the end. The dilemma is further sharpened as we attempt to build on this summer experience within a JCC context when the families return to the city. We want to channel the enthusiasm to ensure continuity of the camp experience throughout the year, the question for us being what will most likely be sustainable outside of the intense cocoon of the family camp.

When we are asked about our role in education in the FSU, the questioner generally has in mind a response in the context of a school setting. In fact, though, this kind of educational work doubtless has as much impact as any formal setting on the creation of community and its direction and is a unique JDC niche in the FSU.

Klara (April 18, 2008)

This was our last address for the day. From early morning, we had been distributing food packages to needy elderly. We were bringing ten-kilogram packages of critical items to homebound elderly throughout the former

Soviet Union – thousands of elderly Jews whose only income was a state pension that was set far below the poverty line. In apartment after apartment, the picture was the same: larders that were empty, refrigerators that contained a moldy potato and perhaps a few shreds of cabbage.

This last apartment, like many others, was on an upper floor of a building with no elevator. It meant that many of these homebound elderly had not been outside for years. Klara was no exception.

Hers wasn't really an apartment. It was a room in a communal apartment, a common living arrangement from the Soviet period, when there were severe housing shortages. She had a tiny room to herself and shared a toilet and a walk-in kitchen with six other family units. "Tiny rooms" in communal apartments were often the private living quarters of entire families. Divorced couples who separated because of abuse, addiction, and similar issues were frequently forced to share that "tiny room" for years due to the lack of alternatives.

Her plight was like that of many other elderly people in the former Soviet Union. She was dressed in her housecoat, her only real outer clothing. A smile graced her face when she saw what we were bringing. Soon, though, the smile turned to tears.

She received a monthly package of basic food items. This package held something more. It was a week before Passover, and in addition to the fish, canned meat, flour, oil, and other standard items, there was a one-kilogram package of matzah to help these elderly mark the holiday that still held a place in their memories. It was this box she focused on, and it soon became clear why.

She took me by the hand and shuffled with me into the communal kitchen, all the time murmuring in an agitated state, with tears streaming down her face. Each resident of the apartment had a little cubby in which to store his or her food. Klara's cubby was empty, except for a small package, maybe two inches by two inches. Slowly, she took apart the paper wrapping. What was uncovered was another wrapping that looked like it was made of red velvet. It was not clear to me what was inside the wrapping, but whatever it was, it clearly had tremendous value for Klara.

She slowly unwrapped the velvet, and as she peeled it away, she revealed a piece of matzah. The tears became more intense, and so was my puzzlement until Klara explained: "I have not been able to observe Jewish tradition for many years. I have been too ill to go out and have not been able to visit the synagogue.

"But in my parents' home, Passover was always a special time. I remember the cleaning, the preparations for the holiday, and so on. I resolved years ago that if, under the Communist system here, I could do nothing else, I would always eat matzah on Passover, to remember who I am.

"For the last nine years, I have not been able to leave this apartment. I cannot climb the stairs. I no longer know the exact date of Passover, but I know it is in the spring. So, each spring, I take this piece of matzah and put it on my table for a week's time to remind me. Even if I don't have enough to eat, it will be here to remind me that I am a Jew.

"And now, you angels from Joint have come and brought me something I could never have dreamed of. I can be a part of my people once again."

Does Size Matter? (May 15, 2009)

At what point does JDC decide to withdraw from a city or town, and on what basis? Decisions are rarely clear cut; we need to make choices, sometimes very painful ones. When we say that we cannot "afford" to maintain programs in a place, we are not really saying that we don't have the money to do so. We are saying that when we weigh the needs, and the advantages and disadvantages of working in a particular place, we conclude that our resources are more effectively expended elsewhere. We can reallocate them if we choose to do so, to maintain operations in all of the places where we currently work, but for a host of reasons we will not.

When JDC's strategic visioning paper communicates that, in the next few years, we will withdraw all but critical, lifesaving services from "the periphery," the translation of that into practice is by no means obvious. What are the factors we need to consider when determining that a place is in the category of "periphery"? Is it geographic location? The size of its Jewish population? Its viability as a community over time? Its strategic importance, or its traditional role? Why one place and not another, even if the characteristics of both places, on paper, appear to be similar?

Which brings us to a city where this question has become very real for us. It is a place that I am sure no readers of this weekly have ever been to, although many dream of going there while travel is still an option. The place is Nizhny Tagil. It lies on the Tagil River – which is a cross between the Mississippi and your local sewage outlet. "Nizhny" means lower, to distinguish it from Verkhny Tagil, which lies on the upper end of the Tagil River. It is in the Ural Mountains, which demarcate the Europe-Asia boundary in Russia.

The town has an estimated population of 390,000, of whom about 2,500 are Jews, down from some 3,000 at the end of the Soviet era. It is a small Jewish population in a region that is not easily accessible.

During Soviet times, Nizhny Tagil was a closed military area. Visitors were allowed into the city only with special permission. Even locals from the region could not enter the city freely. The Soviet government was concerned that permitting free access would compromise important state secrets in the chemical and metal-working factories that employed most of the city's citizens. These same factories spewed air pollutants with impunity. Cynics might say that the real reason to keep people away was so that the extent of environmental abuse would not become widely known. The area is gray and often overcast due to the pollutants. It is a very unwelcoming place.

On paper, there is not much reason for optimism about the long-term sustainability of the local Jewish community. There is no history of Jewish life in the city before the Second World War, when factories were moved from the west to this region to protect them from the Nazi blitzkrieg. So Jews have no deep roots in the area. There are no old synagogues or other evidence of communal life. Moreover, the city has many qualities that would drive away its mobile inhabitants – and mobility is a characteristic of Jews. There are severe ecological problems, a crumbling infrastructure, and little serious cultural life. In other cities that contained this number of Jews just ten years ago, few Jews remain.

But the Jews remain here. And their community thrives. Why?

One gets a hint of the answer on visiting the address given for the local JCC and Hesed. They are found in a large, deteriorating, multistory building that hosts nine minority groups in the city. Among these nine ethnic groups, the Jews stand out.

Enter the building and turn left into the "Jewish property." You will be stopped by Moise, the guard. He will sternly ask for identification and check your bag. After a cursory glance, and upon establishing that you are a *lantzman*, Moise will engage you in conversation.

He is hardly the intimidating type. He is a ninety-one-year-old volunteer, and one gets the impression that he has assumed this grave responsibility for one reason: to find the right guest who can engage in Yiddish banter with him. The Yiddish jokes pour out of him, his smile is a mile wide, and his hug can suffocate you. The pervasive sense of heaviness and squalor outside give way to the warm embrace of community within the building, and this is only the beginning.

Get past Moise and you begin to hear the chatter and squealing of pre-schoolers, and the choir of the Hesed practicing for an upcoming performance. The walls are covered with posters on Jewish themes. A schedule of activities on the board is totally covered with notes on which groups meet when, when large community events are held, when family camp takes place, when youth clubs meet, and so on.

The question is sharpened: Why is this community flourishing when so many others of similar size are moribund? There are, of course, a host of reasons, but experience teaches us that it all comes down to people. In the case of Nizhny Tagil, the X factor is a thirty-six-year-old dynamo named Ira Gutkina.

Ira started volunteering in the Hesed when it was established, when she was in her early twenties. The child of a father who was evacuated during the siege of Leningrad and a mother who was raised in Ukraine and moved to the city in Soviet times because of government incentives, she elected to stay put and enrich her own life through community activism. She stood out in the Jewish community from the outset of her involvement, and JDC professionals invited her to move from her engineering career into a role as a Jewish communal professional. She set two conditions: that JDC provide her training opportunities to build on her own abilities, and that JDC not abandon the community as long as it reached performance targets. From that point on, she never looked back.

The director of the Hesed eventually entrusted Ira with additional responsibilities when JDC allocated funds to broaden community programming to include other age groups in the JCC. Ira set about engaging volunteers and put special emphasis on what she called "caring projects." The young and middle-aged were challenged to help run programs for the elderly, and the elderly became teachers of Jewish culture for the young. Issues of personal responsibility to the community became a hallmark of programming.

In a recent study JDC carried out in the field, Nizhny Tagil was the only community of its size in which the level of voluntarism had remained stable over the last ten years, a remarkable accomplishment given the population shrinkage. In interviews, the volunteers stated that they feel they are partners in the community, and individually feel responsible for its fate. They "own" the community. They noted that they were regularly consulted on the direction of the organization and the community, and that their voices were heard. Moreover, they felt that their work was meaningful, and that they were making a real contribution.

Always on the lookout for more challenges, Ira used the Hesed as the convener of a council of NGOs in the city. She was elected chairperson and represents this group in dialogue with the local authorities. She is committed to attending at least two JDC-sponsored professional workshops a year on a range of subjects, including a JCC directors' course for management, a seminar on how to plan a community's future, and a course on using public-relations tools to reach out to the unaffiliated.

Now, in the season in which budgets are allocated, we have to take a careful look at our choices. Jewish communities in large cities are clearly underfunded, and the amount of money available for Nizhny Tagil is not great; the $130,000 spent on elderly welfare clients will be used even if we pull back, as these clients will continue to be served. The same holds true for the $34,000 for children at risk in Nizhny and its environs. The "discretionary" sum of about $14,000 for Jewish renewal is up for discussion. And we ask ourselves if that sum of money can be utilized in a more meaningful and purposeful setting than this small but vibrant community.

Proportional Response (January 16, 2009)

I deliberated all week as to whether to send a weekly briefing. The current war in Gaza takes precedence over all our other concerns, as well it should. In the end, I decided to share an impression of how the war looks from there (Russia), and then something that struck me in the media here (Israel).

Several people I spoke with during my recent visit to Russia, among them opinion makers in Moscow, agreed that Russia understands and supports Israeli actions. They all stated that Russia would not publicly break ranks with Europe in its condemnation of both sides and call for an immediate cease-fire, but they said not to pay too much attention to that. Russia's position, as reflected in behind-the-scenes conversations between governments, differs from what it says in its public statements.

The notion of "proportional response" is a case in point. While Westerners express grave concern that Israel's response to Gazan rocket fire be "proportional," among the Russians with whom I spoke, the issue is irrelevant. Those in Moscow say that the pictures of Russia's war with Georgia this summer were evidence of the extent to which this matter is not a factor. Russian media at the time simply did not report on civilian casualties or damage on the Georgian side. As far as they were concerned, there was a goal to be accomplished and military means were called for. Once that happens, any price can be paid to achieve the desired end. If anything, they perceive Israeli efforts to avoid civilian casualties as a weakness.

These are impressions, of course, and cannot be empirically demonstrated. But it is certainly a different view from what one sees in the international media.

From Moscow to Ashkelon: Israeli television last week carried a story about an elderly couple who live in this coastal city just north of the Gaza border. The couple immigrated to Israel from Ukraine several years ago. They are Holocaust survivors, and the reporter was interested in getting their reaction to the shelling of their neighborhood with missiles originating in Gaza.

The report was heartrending, perhaps even more so for those of us who deal with this population regularly in the FSU. How often we sit with these people on home visits and see in them the victimization of Jews in the twentieth century. This couple are simple people who lost their families in the Shoah. In its wake, as they reconstructed their lives, they were further victimized – first by a cruel and unforgiving Communist tyranny and then by the implosion of the Soviet Union, which wiped out any savings they may have had and made them reliant on inadequate pensions paid by impoverished societies.

The wife told the interviewer that they are both too old and too weak to run down the steps from their apartment to the building's shelter when the siren goes off, warning of an incoming missile in their neighborhood. The time allotted to reach safety does not suffice for them. Their apartment has no protective room in which to hide. During the interview, the siren went off in anticipation of a Grad missile heading toward the area. The woman began to cry. You could see displayed on her face a feeling of despair and helplessness.

This sweet elderly couple in their twilight years finally found refuge from the daily misery and indignities they were subject to before moving to Israel. In Israel they found a home where they were welcomed and felt valued. And then that dream was shattered by the sirens and missiles of a conflict they don't understand.

The interviewer didn't ask, so we are left to imagine what talk of "proportional response" means to them.

Of Buildings and Bureaucracy (April 18, 2002)

As part of our efforts to revive Jewish life in the FSU, we have begun to purchase, renovate, or contract for long-term rental properties to serve the needs of Jewish communities. In most cases the building will host the Hesed and a Jewish community center, and other organizations where space allows. It took a number of years for us to realize the importance of property for the creation of community. A building, even a rented one, gives a sense of permanence to communal institutions and organizations, all of which are of recent vintage. It gives the community a place, an *address*, which makes it real, even to those who don't regularly participate in its events. And it eliminates the burden of being subject to the whims of market forces that make planning unpredictable.

Purchasing a building is normally fairly straightforward, with a set of rules that govern how the transaction proceeds. There are the legal aspects: agreement on terms, adherence to any relevant governmental regulations, and so on. What follows is a window into this process in the FSU, based on our current efforts in Odesa to renovate a property we purchased recently. It's a good example of the procedure, because what we are going through in

Odesa is similar to the challenges we face in this realm all over the FSU. And it is a process probably unlike that in any other country.

JDC purchased a building in downtown Odesa to be developed into a combined Hesed/JCC facility. The Odesa Jewish community suffers from a paucity of communal space in the city, which is arresting the development of communal life. Donors to the project expected construction to proceed on a set timetable.

The municipality has an interest in the advancement of this Odesa property, and, indeed, the property was purchased from the city authorities. This was of interest to us, as it often means that the bureaucracy inherent in private property purchases can be bypassed, or exposure to it limited. The municipality's interest is twofold: the building is centrally located, next to the main square of the city. Thus, they want to be sure that the building's development is in line with the plan for downtown growth and will be an attractive addition. A reasonable expectation, but for the fact that the chief architect's position mimics the game of musical chairs in which each new occupant has his or her notion of what that development plan should be and does not hesitate to share it with our professional staff in the form of revised regulations. In addition, the city administration wants to curry favor with its Jewish residents, perhaps to procure campaign donations or win votes, and having a relationship with an international Jewish organization like JDC puts them in the good graces of the Jewish community. One would expect that to work to our advantage.

So why the delays? The building was bought with the assurance and written opinion of lawyers that there are no third-party claims on it, and it was listed thus in all municipal documents. However, it turns out this wasn't entirely true, which apparently is a Ukrainian euphemism for a bald-faced lie. There are phone cables on the roof, which the phone company agreed to move for a reasonable fee…until the date of the move arrived! It then became apparent that these were not ordinary phone cables, but civil defense wires for emergency mobilizations. Needless to say, moving them is a serious infraction of the law that requires the approval of bureaucrats too numerous to mention.

After many months of running from office to office, we succeeded in procuring the documents for putting in the new phone wiring. There are 157 "permissions" to be secured, each one with between eleven and fifty-three signatures on it. This applies only to installing phone wires.

The second surprise came with the heating element found in the basement. It was checked before purchase and found to be faulty and needed to be replaced. What was not discovered at the time was that this massive unit does not serve our building, but rather the building contiguous to ours, as our heat comes from yet another place, with a boiler less than one-third the size. In other words, building number 27, a residential building with probably fifty housing units, has its boiler in the basement of our building, number 25. A boiler as a squatter! We have been told that disconnecting the boiler and letting the residents of number 27 fend for themselves is out of the question, as most are elderly pensioners, and the Hesed's values and reputation wouldn't tolerate a move like that. Paying to transfer the boiler to their basement would ordinarily be a solution, but their basement space is owned by a nonresident of the building who adamantly refuses to concede any space for this purpose and is within his legal rights to do so.

Issue number three: The city has decided not to let us hook up to the electricity grid at the entry point nearest our building, despite a previous commitment to do so. As they put it, "Sorry, we are not bound by commitments, even written ones, of the previous mayor. He was a thief." They want to move the local power station from prime downtown land to a spot closer to the port, quite a distance from our building. The hookup will cost us about six times what was originally estimated. Here we have legal recourse, but the wheels of justice in Ukraine move at such a slow pace that progress is often imperceptible.

And so it continues. The architectural plans are in place and, barring any unforeseen difficulties, we expect to start construction within the next several months. In any event, this is the bad news. We have to confront issues like this with all of the buildings we purchase. The good news is that in Kharkiv and Minsk, JDC-owned buildings officially open next week – so the obstacles are eventually overcome. We just need to ensure that our donors and partners understand that construction here is unique – which perhaps gives insight into why the reconstruction of the FSU states has taken so long.

A Jewish Lobby (April 18, 2002)

The Russian Jewish Congress, a local body we partner with and which purports to represent Russian Jews, recently made a decision to set up what they call "an AIPAC-type organization" in Russia. Of course, the analogy is incomplete for a host of reasons, but it is interesting on several levels. First, imagine: a Jewish lobby to influence the Kremlin! More significantly, it is being organized publicly, without fear on the part of those involved that it will feed into a "dual loyalty" canard. It attests to a growing sense of confidence on the part of certain elements in the Jewish community, although not all by any means. It also reflects a level of comfort that changes in Russian society are irreversible. It needs to be stressed here that we are dealing with Russia and not the entire FSU.

A second recent development is on the street. Anti-Israel partisans have demonstrated in Moscow, Kyiv, and Baku, and more demonstrations are to be held this week in Kharkiv, Rostov, and Krasnodar. However, the Jewish community is beginning to respond publicly. Yesterday, approximately seven thousand people participated in a pro-Israel demonstration in Kyiv, a larger turnout than the antis earlier in the week, and a major demonstration outside the main synagogue in Moscow is scheduled for next Thursday. These public displays on behalf of Israel are very serious statements in that context – outward expressions of Jewish identity, typical of the refusenik era, are very atypical of the period of "community development" of the last ten years. Some of the elites have been unabashedly Jewish, but this has generally not been true for the common man and woman. It is another milestone in the maturation of these Jewish communities in their move toward normalization.

A Culture of Corruption (May 27, 2005)

Shortly after I began working for JDC in 1986, in my capacity as the JDC country director for Yugoslavia – at the time still a confederation of six republics that swore allegiance to a single government in Belgrade – I learned an important lesson about the work JDC does that is relevant to our contemporary experience.

In the Croatian capital of Zagreb, for the first time in the Eastern Bloc, there was to be an exhibition of Jewish art at the most prestigious art museum in the region. This exhibition was breaking all sorts of taboos about culture, nationality, and related issues. On my first visit, I was taken to meet the chief curator of the museum, who had agreed to hold the exhibition at some personal risk and was therefore a hero to the members of the Jewish community, for whom this was "the breakthrough of our lifetime." I, though, had come in the middle of a full-blown crisis that threatened the exhibit.

The exhibit was to begin in Zagreb and after a period of three months was to be transferred to Belgrade, the capital of the Serbian Federation. There was much the Serbs and Croats hated about each other (a hatred that would have severe consequences several years later, when Yugoslavia unraveled), but they also shared a great deal. One of the things they shared – well, almost shared – was a language. The language in question is called Serbo-Croatian, a Slavic tongue. Much of the language is the same, although for historical reasons it is written in different script in the two countries – Cyrillic in Serbia and Latin in Croatia. The Serbs were Slavs; Croatia had been part of the Austro-Hungarian Empire for generations.

All of this is relevant because of a major difference in the shared language in the two republics, which was the root of the fiery debate raging when I arrived. The exhibition was accompanied by a catalogue. There was only enough money to print one edition. The issue of which script was to be used was resolved in favor of Serbian Cyrillic, which all Yugoslav citizens could follow. The debate now centered on a very sensitive issue. The word for Jew was not standard across the republics. In the Serbian regions, Jews were colloquially referred to as *Ivrei* (Hebrews), while in Croatia, a Jew was referred to as a *Zhido*. The key problem was not this difference, because in any event the terms were understood as referring to Jews in either region. The problem was that where *Ivrei* was used, the term *Zhido* was an offensive way of referring to Jews. In Croatia, however, the opposite was the case; there *Ivrei* was considered the insulting term. In other words, each republic's reference to a Jew was understood by the other as a "kike." In the Balkans, where ancient battles were justifications for contemporary atrocities, language was of similar importance.

The ultimate resolution of the crisis is unimportant. Far more important was the lesson. In an organization working in over sixty countries, with as many cultures and sets of norms, sensitivity to local environment is critical for success. Often, though, the line between sensitivity to different ways of doing things and the need to impose standards that may be universal is not clear.

Which brings us to the subject for consideration this week: corruption. It is an issue that every one of the post-Soviet successor states faces and, for many, the ability to overcome it will determine to what extent these states can begin to function normally.

Corruption is not new to the region. The old saw about the culture of employment in Soviet times speaks directly to the issue: "We pretend to work, and they pretend to pay us." An entire subterranean economy is in place, fueled by corruption, with its own pricing structure, language, and rules. It is pervasive; bribes go to teachers, doctors, butchers, police – basically to everyone.

In her story "The Bottle," Charlotte Hobson writes of a present-day mayor in a Russian town who is on the verge of signing an agreement to privatize the local vodka factory, the largest employer in town. The mayor and his cronies (apparatchiks) are slated to be personally enriched by the factory's new owner. On the morning the deal is concluded, the mayor wakes up profoundly hung over and discovers that he has metamorphosed into a drained vodka bottle. In this one-factory town, where vodka is a currency alongside rubles, the empty bottle is quickly returned to the factory to be refilled. The "vodka-bottle mayor" then begins his odyssey through the gray economy, handed from one citizen to another in exchange for favors and wages and more. As the town's second currency, the mayor tours the town's formal and informal economies, learning harsh truths that turn even his seasoned stomach.

It is a timeless phenomenon in the FSU. One major financier with connections to the area labeled the entire region one big kleptocracy. Two investigative reporters for a European newspaper recently uncovered the details of a deal made in Ukraine between a government official and prominent local underworld figures to purchase two nuclear weapons for six hundred thousand dollars, with only two thousand dollars down. In a meeting we had with the new prime minister of Georgia, he noted that the biggest challenge the new government faces in a country that barely functions is corruption.

When we first began working in Russia, our staff had difficulty delivering food packages in one neighborhood because the police had gone on strike and closed down a major artery connecting the city center to a neighbor-hood with a large number of elderly Jews. The issue? Large numbers of traffic police had been promoted and as a consequence had been taken off speed patrols. While the promotion was welcome, the end result was a reduction in take-home pay because of the "supplements" that came with stopping motor-ists for traffic violations. And this is the police!

How does all of this affect our work and the Jewish communities with which we work? A Hesed director in Russia makes $750 per month – a good salary for the region, but a paltry amount compared to the fantastic sums for which he or she is responsible. That person oversees a major operation, often running into six-figure sums on a monthly basis. The temptation for kickbacks, skimming, etc., is enormous. We have an audit committee. We spot-check. We monitor pricing. We do the due diligence that must be done. But that will not change the environment, the temptations, and the norms and values that in many contexts in the FSU do not discourage corruption.

Moreover, in an environment that encourages looking out for yourself, you are expected to help friends and relatives. Corruption is not simply tol-erated; it is often expected. It is even occasionally characterized as an entitle-ment, an anticipated offset to low wages; the term *entitlement* carries with it certain understandings that are vestiges of the Soviet period.

Like the nascent governments faced with this in their societies, we too see corruption as an enemy of the community development for which we strive. Where the greater good is pushed aside in the quest for personal gain at any price, the community will be dysfunctional and unattractive.

I would propose that the focus, given the above, should not be on the negative. Rather, we should turn our attention to how extraordinary it is that so much functions well. Many outsiders in the know – from local American ambassadors, to managers of international auditors like Ernst and Young, to managers of other NGOs not connected to the Jewish community – have commented on the manner in which FSU Jewish communities function. We often hear from them how impressed they are that these fledgling commu-nities exist as islands of sanity – and yes, probity – in an otherwise difficult environment that actually encourages dysfunction. We trust, but we also ver-ify. Our auditing system is comprehensive and vigilant, and it finds the occa-sional errant worker or uncovers the scheme designed to cheat. But in light of the general context, if these knowledgeable outsiders are to be believed, the situation is one to be proud of.

By investing in the people who work in the system, we try to give them a sense of mission, to ascribe to the work they do the value it deserves, to elevate it from simple employment to the status of a holy mission, and to constantly remind all involved that people's lives literally depend on the integrity and sense of responsibility of those who work for us on their behalf. Corruption hurts needy, elderly beneficiaries of Hesed services more than anyone else.

We have been blessed with a staff in the FSU that generally understands and identifies with this sense of mission. Most left careers as engineers, teachers, lawyers, and the like to begin to work for institutions in the Jewish community. We must remember the risk that this entails for them. They relinquished employment that often had some assurance of continuity for something new and untested – a job in a Jewish community that was dependent on a foreign organization for financial stability, with no job security and with no evidence that the employing institution was sustainable. They generally made the leap of faith because of their own desires to identify as Jews, and to contribute in some way to this new enterprise now that such an opportunity existed. These are generally people driven by their own idealism to play a role in recreating Jewish life. After seventy years of intensive efforts by their government to erase any connection to Jewish life, this phenomenon is nothing short of wondrous.

Setting Priorities (May 8, 2009)

It is a given that the work we do does not have a road map we can follow. It is more of an art than a science and is filled with dead ends, surprising turns of events, unanticipated successes, and failures that occur after we have done the same thing ten times successfully.

What follows are questions with which we struggle in our FSU work on a regular basis. In a sense, the answers to these questions are less important than the questions themselves. Every day brings new dilemmas, some of which put us in a position of having to do the correct thing at the expense of our long-term goals. Here are two, culled from a much larger pool.

The first problem: Needy Shoah victims are entitled to support from restitution funds that we receive from the Claims Conference and other sources.

Once the eligible individual dies, the surviving spouse, if he or she is not a Nazi victim, continues to get support from our "nonrestitution" sources. It is generally a given that if the couple was eligible while married, the need persists when the Nazi victim passes on.

But what happens if the surviving spouse is needy...and not Jewish? Of course, we would want to continue supporting the spouse. It would be cruel on a human level to stop support, especially since this person is now even more vulnerable than before because of the death of his or her mate. Moreover, by marrying a Jew the surviving spouse had tied his or her fate for years to a pariah class, and undoubtedly paid a price for it.

What happens, though, if, because of this system, the percentage of non-Jewish clients climbs to levels that exhaust budgets in local Heseds, so that local elderly Jews with no connection to the Shoah can no longer get the support they need? In a situation in which there is not enough money to go around, what needs to be done to ensure that our core constituency is ensured the support for which this program was created? Or should no distinction be made?

The second dilemma: *Empowerment* is a word often used in the setting of goals for our work. Ultimately, we want locals to take over tasks that JDC has assumed. We've learned through the years that this is never black-and-white. Empowerment is measured on a spectrum, and we need to be sure that we are moving in the right direction in everything we do. But what happens when the cost of empowerment is borne by the constituency we need to serve, and those recipients are not a party to the decision?

The conundrum: A Hesed director who is a capable and admired professional has asked for a larger say in the way budgets are allocated. She is included with her colleagues in all decisions JDC makes concerning budgets, but she now wants to determine programmatic priorities for her Hesed without being bound by external dictates.

She has very strong feelings about the current needs of the elderly. She believes that their primary need is medication, and she is prepared to move funding from home care in order to bolster the budgets for medicine.

The decision to set home care as the priority for JDC funding came from much study and work with a selection of Hesed directors around the FSU. It was an exhaustive process, and the decision was taken to set this as the priority because the home care recipients are considered our neediest clients. These people are generally aging and homebound, and under other circumstances would be in residential facilities. But because such facilities don't exist in the FSU, they need to be helped at home.

This particular director does not care for this program. While she does not deny the need, she contends (correctly) that it is costly per client: it utilizes a high percentage of the budget and it is labor intensive, requiring people to be hired for undesirable work, and subsequently supervised.

Here, then, is one of the dilemmas her request poses to us: We respect her judgment, although we respectfully disagree with her opinion. If she were given the power to enact the change she desires, a situation would be created in which a needy, bed-bound client living in an area served by another Hesed gets the home care services he requires, while a client in exactly the same situation serviced by the Hesed of this director will be knowingly underserved so that other programs can be better funded.

Insisting on some sort of conformity within a particular range of options is characterized as the antithesis of empowering by some people with whom we work. We have our own view, based on research and data, that the home care direction is the most effective use of limited resources and has the greatest impact. This is a reasonable disagreement, the consequences of which extend far beyond the beneficiaries of the welfare program. We insist on what we believe benefits the maximum number of the needy. In doing so, we have limited the scope of independent priority setting of the local professionals whom we seek to empower.

Diana's Story (May 21, 2010)

We spend a lot of time thinking about impact. What is the impact of our efforts in the FSU? On whom? How can we measure it? Scan the literature produced by and about the nonprofit world and you will find reams of paper and theories galore addressing these issues. The subject is an important one and it deserves to be addressed and supported by data. But before doing that, some thoughts about impact from an anecdotal perspective.

In what follows, I want to use one person as the paradigm, and through her personal history enable each of us to draw conclusions about JDC's impact on Jews in this part of the world. I found her story extraordinarily compelling and, from what I know of JDC's history in the USSR and later in the FSU, it represents a not-insignificant number of Jews from that region.

I will let Diana speak for herself:

I was born in 1969 in the "City of Lights" of the USSR, Khust, in the Carpathian Mountains. Residents of Khust today are citizens of Ukraine, but at different times in the last century the same residents of that city were citizens of Romania, then Hungary, followed by the USSR, and, as of 1991, an independent Ukraine. All four of my grandparents were survivors of the Shoah. All four were survivors of Auschwitz-Birkenau. My maternal grandmother encountered Mengele there, as he believed (erroneously) that she and her younger sister were twins.

After liberation, all four grandparents settled in Khust. It was a city with a relatively large and warm Jewish community, and it had a functioning synagogue. The city was newly incorporated into the USSR, and little had changed from its Hungarian, pre-Communist milieu.

I was raised for several years as a young child by my paternal grandparents, as my parents were living in a different city during the time they were in their medical training. In my grandparents' home, I was exposed to Jewish life. My grandfather put on tefillin every day, and Jewish holidays and Shabbat were observed to the extent possible. My grandparents spoke warmly and admiringly of Israel in the privacy of their own home, out of earshot of their neighbors; in the 1970s, the Cold War was at its peak and Zionism was a dirty word in the Soviet lexicon. I learned to recite the phrase "next year in Jerusalem" long before I had any idea that this might have practical implications. At home, I was raised in Yiddish, although once outside we all spoke a mixture of Ukrainian, Hungarian, Russian, and Khustit, a local dialect.

I still remember the taste of the challot my grandmother baked every Friday. We used to bring chickens to the local ritual slaughterer, who prepared them for us according to Jewish law. Once a month, a traveling *mohel* would come to perform *britot* on all of the boys born the previous month. We knew it wasn't strictly according to the law that dictated that it had to be done on the eighth day, but it was an accommodation we were forced to make because of the Soviet environment in which we lived. The *britot* were done furtively, in my grandparents' house. As a child, I always referred to that day each month as the "day of the screams." I also knew it was not to be discussed with anyone outside of my immediate family, due to the risk that the authorities might find out about it and punish those involved.

Each Shabbat on the way to synagogue, our non-Jewish neighbors would call out to us, "Gut Shabbes." Khust was at one time a predominantly Jewish town. Many of the locals even knew some Yiddish from that period. We got along with them quite well. Remember, all of this happened in what at the time was the USSR, but the antisemitism promulgated by the regime in the Kremlin was not uniform throughout the empire.

In the early 1970s, we began to periodically receive packages from America. The packages contained very warm, fur-lined coats – protection against the bitter winters – and children's clothes. To this day, I remember one pair of shoes I received in one of the packages – the most beautiful pair of shoes I had ever seen, far more exquisite than those of any of my friends. Later I learned that these packages were from the Joint and were designed to help Jews who were at risk because of their Jewish activities. The Joint wanted to provide these Jews with a way to support themselves, as these items could be sold on the black market. Most of the package contents were sold and we lived off the proceeds, as my grandfather's employment situation was always tenuous due to his Jewish activities. But I was allowed to keep those shoes. They made me feel special, and privileged, as a Jew.

I have a vivid memory of coming home from first grade one day in tears. My grandmother hugged me and asked what had happened.

"They made fun of Grandpa," I told her.

She was a wise woman and surmised immediately what had happened: "Did they call him a Jew?"

"No," I responded. "Worse."

"What could be worse than that?" She was genuinely perplexed.

"They called him a millionaire!"

My grandmother smiled and reassured me. "That is no curse. To be a millionaire is not a bad thing at all." And so, I was introduced to the dissonance of our existence. The Soviet system that taught us good and bad was often quite the opposite of what I learned at home. It was a situation that could not have been easy for a first grader to understand, but it marked our existence as Soviet Jews and informed our lives as long as we lived in the USSR.

In 1977, my grandparents were allowed to leave for Israel. My parents and I were refused permission to leave for another two years.

Finally, on our way to Israel, we again had contact with the Joint. This time, we met representatives of JDC in Vienna. We were technically not in their care, as they assisted refugees going to Western countries outside of Israel, but I remember that they were very kind and gentle people who treated us wonderfully. It was also an opportunity for my parents to tell their two young children about how that organization of American Jews stayed with the Jews of the USSR during the most difficult times.

When I was drafted into the Israeli army in the late eighties, I did my service with Lishkat Hakesher, a nonmilitary government office that dealt with issues involving Eastern European Jewry. My unit was involved in producing material about Israel in the Russian language, in a cultural context that would be familiar and appealing to the Jews of the USSR who were contemplating living in Israel. The JDC's involvement in this enterprise has not been fully documented, but we were very aware of the role JDC played in these specific efforts. So, here again, I met this organization, although this time I was not a recipient of its assistance but was able to serve it in some small way.

In 1992 I completed my BA and applied for marketing positions in multinational firms. I was turned down, told that the positions involved a good deal of travel and would not be appropriate for a young and "delicate" woman.

Then an advertisement caught my eye, and I applied for a position with the newly established JDC department for activities in the former Soviet Union. I was actually quite intimidated at first. How could I work for an organization that was a legend in my family? I was hired, though, and during the next six years I traveled back and forth to the FSU. I, the "young and delicate woman," traveled to places that more seasoned travelers avoid like the plague, on planes in which I stood for the entire flight, or in cargo bays with goats and calves. The planes were often no larger than the kitchen in my apartment, held together with little more than glue and tape. Apparently, JDC thought more of me than these multinationals and I was the richer for it.

You need to understand what this meant to me. When I looked back on my life in the USSR, I saw the critical role that JDC played for us on so many levels. It was JDC that ensured sustenance for my grandparents. It was JDC that sent materials into the USSR that ensured we could fulfill our spiritual longings. It was JDC that gave my parents the assurance that, even in the most difficult times in that most difficult place, we were not alone. And now I would be representing that very organization.

When JDC speaks of its mission in the FSU, "reclaiming Jews for the Jewish people," it is a mission that very much resonates for me.

Impact is measured in many different ways. Few, to my mind, can be as compelling or as illustrative as Diana's story.

CHAPTER 3

People

Natasha (September 27, 2002)

Natasha Chernets remembered hearing, as a little girl, her grandmother's story of how she fled from Kherson to Kharkiv in Ukraine to avoid falling into the clutches of the advancing German army in 1941. Her grandmother traced her fear of being identified as a Jew to that formative experience. Natasha later learned that, on arrival, her grandmother had changed her name to fit into Soviet society and to erase any Jewish associations that could cause her trouble again. Her father also kept his Jewish background secret. He was a lawyer and feared the consequences of being identified as a Jew.

Natasha had very little Jewish knowledge. Her grandmother remained a link to her Jewish identity. Although her grandmother's name was no longer recognizably Jewish, in the confines of her apartment her Jewish character could find expression, and Natasha understood that. But the identity was never a public one, and it faded with her grandmother's death.

While studying professional lighting and design, Natasha played basketball in her spare time. Her coach knew her family and her family background. He had recently taken on a part-time position as the coach of the Beit Dan (Kharkiv JCC) basketball team. He invited her to play on the team. She agreed, mostly because of the convenience of the schedule. That the team was housed in the JCC was not germane to her decision.

Natasha's involvement with the team exposed her to its sponsor. Professionals in the JCC saw the leadership potential in this woman, and the rest, as they say, is history.

We speak often of the need to provide multiple entry points to Jewish life in each community. Natasha recently graduated from the JDC Young

113

Leadership Program and now directs the Jewish drama club at the JCC. A return to Jewish life via basketball. Stranger things have happened.

Polina (December 27, 2002)

We have just over 263,400 names in our management information system for welfare clients throughout the FSU. I often worry that the numbers obfuscate rather than enlighten. They force us to focus on the bigger picture, and we lose sight of what, and who, those numbers represent. Here is an example of one of those numbers.

Polina was a physicist in Moscow until her retirement. She grew up in Belarus and came to Moscow in 1942 to contribute to the war effort and subsequently stayed. She traveled extensively and loved to cook. She retired in 1990, just prior to the collapse of the Soviet Union. Her husband of thirty-two years died three years before that. They had no children. She is an impressive, intelligent woman with a certain dignity that her life circumstances could not suppress.

Because of her work, Polina was entitled to a pension that would have kept her comfortable in retirement. She had meager savings, as those did not matter much in the Soviet era. With the collapse of the state and the economy in the early nineties, whatever savings she had squirreled away were wiped out.

She lives in a room in a communal apartment in central Moscow. She owns a small refrigerator, a rickety table, a television set, and a bed that doubles as a couch. The apartment is immaculate, although after an initial glance one sees how old and worn everything is.

Polina receives a pension equivalent to $53 per month. The official subsistence wage is $60 per month. The average pension is $43 per month in Moscow. So, theoretically, she is better off than many, but earns below what would afford her the basics. She spends $11 per month on housing and utilities, $2.80 a month for a small garden plot outside of Moscow. Her bill for medicines comes to $4 per month. She supplements her income when she can by doing chores for neighbors, often related to caring for their children, which she is finding increasingly difficult. She has about $1.20 per day to spend for food and sundry necessities.

She husbands every kopeck. She carefully plots out her monthly spending in order to be able to have enough to eat at the end of the month. Unexpected expenditures, like repairing a leaky window, buying a lightbulb, or making an unanticipated trip to the doctor for a checkup often cause budgetary crises for her. Her shoes are worn through; she goes barefoot at home, lest she wear them down more.

She eats no meat and practically no fish. As food is such a major expense for her, she travels to the cheapest market she knows, a one-way excursion of just under two hours, to buy staples like eggs and vegetables. She stops on the way to buy black bread because it is three cents cheaper in one market than in her usual haunt. Her diet consists mostly of inexpensive vegetables like cabbage, potatoes, carrots, and radishes. Often these have been discarded in the market because they are rotten. She cannot afford fruit, although she does have an apple tree on her plot of land, from which she harvests apples and makes jam for the wintertime.

Polina finds the humiliation of her circumstances more difficult than the physical hardships – she was a physicist. As noted earlier, the FSU is the only place in the world where poverty does not generally correlate with education. She showed me a piece written by a friend of hers: "Politicians don't look at our generation as the people who created the material and cultural base that they are now dividing up and privatizing. Together with our generation, they are rejecting everything we've done. I'm an educated person. They are inculcating in the minds of young people that we are the people who organized life the wrong way. What was wrong? Everything we built with our own hands. I have been honored by the Council of Ministers and done much to help this country. And now?"

Polina recently began receiving fresh food packages from the Jewish community. A volunteer fixed her television, which had been broken for six years. She started attending the Hesed day-center programs, which provide the social support she so desperately needs to alleviate the oppressive boredom. When I encountered her this week in Moscow and heard her story, however, I understood the significance of a program I had not fully appreciated. Two weeks ago, she signed up as a volunteer in the Hesed to be responsible for contacting ten elderly Jews in her neighborhood every day to provide them with human contact and a caring ear, and to enquire if they have any immediate needs to report to the Hesed operation that can respond.

Why write all of this? These stories are known by now, and in any event, there are far worse cases that make for much more heartrending tales. I felt compelled to write about this because of a conversation I had with a woman in a position of importance in a major Jewish federation in a large American city, who recently returned from a visit to Moscow. She had gone on some home visits and commented that while she had not had extensive conversations with the clients, she was not impressed that their situations were so bad. After all, one of the women she met was formerly a professor of languages at a local institute and lived in modest but clean quarters. She was well spoken. She, and others, certainly did not appear to be needy.

That could have been Polina. On the face of it, all true. But scratch just a bit beneath the surface and you find a needy Jew, a woman not literally starving, but often hungry when confronted by unanticipated costs for basic commodities or medical services. A woman whose self-respect and dignity are at risk due to a situation entirely beyond her control.

Moisie (April 11, 2003)

A reflection from a recent trip that I'll carry with me to the Seder next week: a ceremony commemorating the 1903 Kishinev pogrom was held at the site of a memorial plaque in the middle of a park in downtown Chişinău, as Kishinev is now known.

That pogrom marked a major turning point in the history of Eastern European Jewry. The poet H. N. Bialik came to the city from Odesa, his home at the time, in the immediate aftermath of the pogrom and wrote his seminal work "In the City of Slaughter." Evidence that the czarist authorities collaborated in the murders and did nothing to protect its Jewish citizens spurred large-scale emigration of Jews throughout the Russian empire, with Ellis Island and the coastal city of Jaffa in Ottoman-ruled Eretz Yisrael as the primary ports of disembarkation.

Due to Bialik's poem and the waves of Jewish refugees in the wake of the pogrom, the Kishinev events were seared into the national consciousness of the Jewish people. They were later considered to have foretold the blood-soaked century that was just beginning for European Jewry.

The recent commemoration was well attended despite the bitter cold. As I stood on the podium looking out at the assembled faces, I was drawn in particular to the elderly, who were there in large numbers. Afterward, while the ceremony droned on, I walked into the crowd and spoke to some of them to try to understand what meaning this had for them.

One encounter in particular stands out. Actually, it wasn't even the conversation; it was the man's age. His name is Moisie, and he is ninety-one years old, a truly prodigious age in the FSU.

I was so struck by his longevity that I don't even remember much of what we talked about. He was born in 1912, into a czarist Russia that had created the environment for the pogrom several years earlier. He lived through the revolution and then the counterrevolution, which was bloody and difficult for Jews, who were targeted by antisemitic bands during the chaos of the period. He lived through the ravages of Stalinism, the horrors of the Shoah, the indignities of the post-Stalinist Soviet period, and then saw what little he had left disappear in 1991 when the state collapsed. After all that, he lives out the final years of his life with a monthly pension of the equivalent of $9 (yes, *nine dollars*)!

I asked him how he had the strength to survive all of this. From where does one draw the inner resources to continue? He looked at me and shrugged his shoulders as if the answer were self-evident. "A Yid." As if to say, "This is just what Jews do."

Vera (March 12, 2004)

During the last generation, the study of history in universities has undergone a major shift. Until recently, historians were often concerned with the "big picture," the sweep of history, concentrating on trends, on causes and effects, on the direction of history. Leaders, in all spheres, were often the focus of historical studies.

More recently, though, there has been a growing focus on the individual, the "average man or woman," how they led their lives in a given era, and how history affected them. History from the bottom up, if you will, as opposed to from the top down.

What follows is Soviet and post-Soviet Jewish history as represented in the life of a single Jew, Vera Yakovlevna Bukhbinder. She was, by no stretch of the imagination, a heroine. But there is a lesson in the life she led. In the description of her life, you can understand Soviet Jewish history in a way that history books will miss. The major events are here: the two World Wars, Stalinism, Nazism, Communism, the aftermath of the collapse of the USSR and what arose in its ashes, the Jewish revival, and more. Instead of looking at the broad sweep of these events, you will see it from the other side, the impact of the events on the life of a single Jewess – one of 240,000 elderly Jews who are currently receiving welfare assistance from the Joint.

I am writing now about Vera because she died this week. Her death was not marked in any significant way. She died alone, having long outlived all her family and most of her friends. But I would like to mark her death in some small way by retelling her story, for it is a story that serves as a background for much of what we do today in the FSU. This story came to us from her caseworker at one of the welfare organizations we support in Moscow, who provided her succor in her last years and wrote during this period:

Vera was born March 22, 1909, in Vitebsk, Belarus, where she lived until the outbreak of the Great Patriotic War. Her mother was a painter whose works were exhibited in Minsk. During her childhood, she lived in France with her father, who worked there as a photographer for a few years.

While in school, Vera was an active member of the Communist Pioneer Movement and a member of the All-Union Leninist Young Communist League, known as the Komsomol. The whole town knew her and her family because she was one of the promising next generation of Communist Party leaders, and she was the driving force of many events that took place in her school and in the town.

Vera's husband fought in World War I before they were married. They had been together for a year when her husband was repressed for five years. "Repressed" is a euphemism used in various ways in reference to Stalin's victims, often convicted on trumped-up charges, who served as a warning to conform to "the leader's" wishes or suffer the consequences. He was sentenced to internal exile for that period, presumably to Siberia or its environs. Vera gave birth to a baby girl a few months after her husband's repression began. She graduated from a medical college and entered the Minsk Medical Institute but couldn't complete her higher education because of World War II.

When the war began, the remaining family (Vera, her mother, and her daughter) fled to a small village near Tambov, in eastern Russia, away from the front. On their way to evacuation, the train was constantly bombed, and most passengers were killed, but Vera and her family managed to survive. In Tambov, she started to work as an accountant. When Nazi troops approached the village, its residents were evacuated or fled to Central Asia for refuge. By that time, her husband had been released from captivity, but before he could be reunited with his family he was drafted and shipped to the front.

In Asia, Vera worked harvesting vegetables in fields, where she eventually fell ill. She had pneumonia and had to spend six months at a hospital where she caught typhoid. She left the hospital with severe physical disabilities, but due to her medical training, she was able to work in a hospital as a nurse. Her mother died from typhoid, leaving her alone with her child.

Vera's brother served in the NKVD and, using his contacts, bribes, and false papers, he managed to help her to move to Moscow toward the end of the war, where she again found employment in a hospital.

When the war against the Fascists ended, she tried to find her husband, whom the Red Army considered lost. After months of following numerous fruitless leads and ultimately despairing, she managed to find him only by chance, and he met his daughter (who was ten years old by then) for the first time. Three days later he was drafted yet again for the USSR's short war with Japan in 1945. Her husband later returned from the fighting having lost a leg. For many years Vera took care of her husband, who was bed-bound. He couldn't work, so she was the sole breadwinner. In 1979, her husband died.

Vera's daughter died in 1993 as a result of a hospital stay after she was injected with the wrong medication. Vera was left totally alone, her brother having also died several years earlier. She was in despair and even admitted to contemplating suicide, but she managed her grief and plodded on.

Vera worked for forty-five years as a nurse and was highly regarded in the hospital in which she worked. Three years ago, she was diagnosed with cancer. For a long time, she lived with the thought of the impending end of her life. Every month, her doctors told her that she did not have long to live. But she is still here.

Today, she spends all her time in bed. She is still a very social woman; she likes to talk, to tell about her life, which was full of suffering and disasters. She is a humble person, so she doesn't like to boast that she knew Marc Chagall in Vitebsk. As she recalls they played chess often, and Marc was fond of her.

In spite of her age (she is ninety-five years old) and illnesses, when Vera smiles, her face changes and begins to radiate happiness and fulfillment, despite her personal travails. To smile, after all that she has been through! Remarkable.

As I noted at the outset, Vera died this week. May her soul be bound up in the bond of everlasting life.

The *Baal Agalah* (October 29, 2004)

Twice a year, all our staff joins together for five days of discussion and study away from our respective home bases. A theme is chosen and becomes the lens through which we assess our work.

This year's retreat focused on a new kind of theme. Cognizant of the multicultural composition of our staff, a decision was taken to use an entirely different lens through which our work can be understood and evaluated. The goal this time was to visit places where we work that are rich in the Jewish history of the first part of the last century. The grand theme would be looking at our roots, not as an organization or even as a department, but as individuals who help shape the direction of JDC's involvement in the FSU. What would an examination of our personal roots contribute to our understanding of our work, and could an encounter with our own personal histories be of functional value in our work? At the same time, each of the regions represented a broader theme in Jewish history, which also served as a subject of study.

Groups traveled to Odesa (the Enlightenment and the rise of political Zionism), Vinnytsia, Ukraine (the shtetl), Warsaw and Kraków (the Shoah and interwar Jewish intellectual and political activity), Bulgaria (the Sephardic diaspora), Lviv and Ivano-Frankivsk (Chasidut).

The experiences in Lviv that follow will give you a taste of what we wanted to achieve in these meetings and provide a context for the discussions we had as a staff about how the lessons of these trips could be incorporated into our work.

Finally, and perhaps most important, these vignettes reveal a great deal about the milieu of the Jews with whom we work today. Each story is individual, and in essence *sui generis*, but together they are representative of Eastern Europe's twentieth-century Jewish population, toward which much of the JDC's resources have been directed during the last ninety years.

Dr. Zvi Feine, a veteran JDC professional, joined our group in Lviv. Zvi's family has its roots in the Volyn region, near Lviv. This particular region was Galicia, which was part of Poland for an extended period, and at other times (and currently) part of Ukraine, with a period under the rule of the Austro-Hungarian Empire as well. The entire family, except for one small branch, left for the US between 1904 and 1907. That remaining branch, consisting of an aunt, an uncle, and three children, stayed behind in Volyn. Eventually contact was lost, and the family was murdered in the Shoah. The details of their last years were unknown and were the purpose of Zvi's visit.

Our group traveled three hours from Lviv to the outskirts of the town, Borovichi. Then, according to plan, we disembarked from the vehicle in which we had come and climbed aboard a wagon pulled by horses for a trip around the village. It did not take much to secure the driver and the wagon — to this day, villages in that region are heavily trafficked by horses and wagons. Life, at least to the Western observer, does not appear to have changed much in generations. Judging by what we saw, wood is the primary heating fuel, and there are still numerous wells rather than running water. In short, modernity has not yet arrived.

Shortly into the ride the driver, who was a non-Jew (there are no Jews left in the town), engaged his passengers in conversation. He was curious to know what had brought them to this town – the last tourists were registered there nineteen years ago, and then they had wandered in by mistake. Zvi told him about his roots search, and the driver, who was in his seventies, asked for the family name. When Zvi told him the names of the uncle and aunt, the man filled in the names of the other three children; he had clearly known the family.

It gets better. The driver – henceforth referred to by the proper Yiddish term for a wagon driver, *baal agalah* – invited the group to his home. There the neighbors gathered around an old woman, who brought with her a picture that had been taken at the elementary school graduation of Raizel, the daughter of Zvi's family. In response to Zvi's anxious inquiries about the fate of the family, he was told the following: Shortly after the Germans began their occupation in the fall of 1941, all of the Jews of the town were herded into a ghetto in a neighboring village. Four times, Raizel, the fourteen-year-old daughter, escaped the ghetto and snuck back into Borovichi. There, the mother of the *baal agalah* gave her some provisions to take back to her family in the ghetto. On one of her returns to the town, Raizel brought with her a small token of appreciation from her family to the family of this *baal agalah*. Zvi's relatives, of course, had very little with them in the ghetto, but clearly their sense of indebtedness was such that they wanted to make a gesture.

At this point in telling the story to us, the *baal agalah* breaks off, goes into the kitchen, and emerges with something wrapped in a cloth. He carefully unwraps a small knife. This was the gift his mother had received from Raizel, and he hands it to Zvi. This, then, was all that was left from Zvi's family – the only tangible link to five close relatives with whom connection was lost more than seventy years ago.

Feige (October 29, 2004)

Peremyshlyany is one of many villages within a three-hour radius of Lviv and is typical of what one finds throughout the region. Today, it has about fifteen hundred residents. On the eve of the war, it had two thousand citizens, of whom 60 percent were Jews. This was not at all uncommon for the region. Most nearby villages were between 40 and 60 percent Jewish. Jews generally were traders, skilled craftsmen (e.g., shoemakers), or involved in the logging industry, for which the region was well known.

As we walked through several of the towns, the older residents pointed out where the Jews lived and worked. The size of the Jewish presence was remarkable. Most of these towns are now bereft of Jews, although many have names that have been preserved among groups of Jews. They were the birthplaces of founders of Chasidic dynasties, and the followers of these rabbis retain the names: Belz, Sadigura, and myriad other Chasidic sects are named for towns that we visited or passed by.

During our visit, we had some extraordinary encounters. A grainy, sepia-toned picture seemed innocuous until our guide explained the context. It showed soldiers facing two young girls holding a tray. A careful examination of the photograph revealed that the soldiers were German officers. And then our guide told us that the girls greeting them were Jews. When German troops occupied the city in 1941, they were welcomed with the traditional gift of bread and salt by the local population, and these delegations often included the Jews who lived among them! The reason is incredible, especially in retrospect, and speaks to the kinds of evil both the Germans and the Soviets represented.

After the partition of Poland into Nazi and Soviet spheres shortly after the outbreak of the war in September 1939, this region was ruled by Moscow. During the two-year period of Soviet rule, local populations (including the Jews) were viciously persecuted and quickly alienated by the Bolsheviks. They yearned for the relatively enlightened rule of the Austro-Hungarian Empire. The assumption, shared by many Jews, was that the conquering Germans in 1941 shared a culture with the Austro-Hungarian rulers and therefore would be more benign than the benighted Soviets. German rule was therefore welcomed, and they were greeted as saviors from the hated Soviets! Jews actually welcomed Nazi officers into the city as liberators – liberators who were shortly to become their murderers.

Back to Peremyshlyany. Our guide for the day entreated us to stop in the town on the way back to Lviv. We had to meet the last Jew in Peremyshlyany – Feige Lechter. Feige was ninety-two years old and bedridden due to a recent fall. Our visit with her was more than we had bargained for. She spoke several languages, among them a heavily accented Galicianer Yiddish. She was born in the town and had had a middle-class upbringing as the daughter of a Jewish lawyer. She remembered holiday celebrations from her childhood: the questions the children asked at the Seder, and her father's "long" answer, going to shul on Rosh Hashanah and hearing the shofar.

We visited her in the room she occupied on the top floor of a spartan and immaculate building that seemed to be a dormitory of some sort. With tears in her eyes, she hummed "Hatikvah," the national anthem of Israel, and the Yiddish children's song "Oyfn Pripetschik." She was my grandmother – the same round Eastern European face, the soft blue eyes, the deeply Jewish personality. It was a very special moment, but a painful one for reasons to be spelled out. At one point, she asked us to close the door so that what she had to say would not be heard by those in the corridor, and she proceeded to tell us the following:

At the outset of the German occupation, she got papers as an Aryan, but it soon became clear that they would not help her. She sought and received refuge in the home of a school friend whose father was an Orthodox priest. He built a false wall in their attic and Feige and three others hid there for the duration of the war. She alone survived from her family. She stayed in Peremyshlyany and was its only Jewish resident for many years. She insisted to us that she retained her great sense of pride as a Jew throughout her life. In the Soviet period, the fifth line of the internal passport, which every citizen had to carry at all times, was reserved for the declaration of one's national identity. Despite opportunities to change it, Feige kept hers as "Evreika" – Jew. She told us several times during our discussion that she saw her life's purpose as praying for the welfare of the Jewish nation. She did so every day and was proud of it.

Lying in her bed and speaking in a broken Yiddish, Feige Lechter was like so many of the Hesed clients we serve regularly throughout the FSU – with one major difference. After the war, in gratitude for having been saved by the local priest, Feige Lechter converted to Russian Orthodoxy. Today, she is known [for reasons unclear to me. AO] by her German title, Schwester Maria, and is the Mother Superior at the convent in which we visited her.

During those three days in the region, we were immersed in the Shoah, in seeing a world that had been destroyed. A catalogue of the pictures taken by the members of our group would have a disproportionate number of images related to death – cemeteries, tombstones, mass graves. This particular visit with Feige was a reminder that the damage suffered by the Jewish people was not limited to physical destruction.

Later in the day, we were in Ivano-Frankivsk, called Stanislavov before the war, and today a city of about twelve thousand, of whom fewer than a thousand are Jews. The main synagogue of the city had been restored to the Jewish community in the last few years. It is enormous, a tremendous draw on local resources just to heat in the harsh winters. At one time, though, it was clearly a center of learning and prayer for a vibrant Jewish community.

On the synagogue's outer wall that faces the main street of the city, there is a wreath opposite a moving sculpture. It is a beautiful memorial which one initially assumes is connected to the synagogue, for a community that is no longer there. But the explanation does not jibe with the expectation. We are told that the memorial is to thirty-one Ukrainian "martyrs," killed by the Nazis on such and such a date in 1943 on this site. None of us can begrudge a memorial to those murdered Ukrainians, but there is a message in the fact that a moving memorial to these thirty-one victims is put on the wall of the only extant synagogue in the town, and there is not one public reference – not one – to the nine thousand Jews of the town who were slaughtered at the same time.

Zaira (May 4, 2012)

Zaira Jacobashvili grew up in Tbilisi, the capital of Soviet Georgia. For all sorts of reasons, not the least the physical distance from Moscow, communal life among Georgian Jews was not decimated during the Soviet period. In Zaira's home, Jewish traditions were not strictly observed. Her father attended synagogue on the High Holidays and on the anniversaries of his parents' deaths. Whatever Zaira knew about Jewish customs she had learned from her maternal grandmother, who came to Tbilisi from a small provincial community in Georgia called Poti, where she was born. Her grandmother lit candles on Friday evenings, and she dressed as Jewish women dressed in that region a hundred years earlier. She often spoke to Zaira about life in her own home when she was a young girl. She even tried to teach her granddaughter some prayers, "especially the one when one lights the Shabbat candles." Zaira remembers her grandmother lighting wicks in oil dishes on the anniversaries of the deaths of her own parents and that of her husband.

As a young girl, Zaira attended the Tbilisi synagogue on the High Holidays, but she spent most of her time in the courtyard outside. She could not read Hebrew prayers, nor could her mother. Like other girls her age, she attended camps for Communist "Pioneers" and knew about the history of the great Communist leaders. She was a sincere and devoted follower of Communist Party teachings.

Her father worked in a factory but managed to supplement his small salary with unofficial business activities. Georgian Jews were known to be skilled operators on the free market. In an environment in which almost everything was forever in short supply, there was always something an entrepreneur could buy and resell. Occasionally, a Jew was caught dealing unofficially in selling commodities and was taken into police custody. The Jewish community then mobilized to collect money to buy his freedom or reduce his prison sentence. It was rare for a Georgian Jew to be sent to the Gulag for economic crimes, as happened routinely in other parts of the USSR. Solidarity among the members of the Jewish community was generally effective in preventing that.

Zaira knew nothing of the "adult" business life her father and other Georgian Jews led. Her family was not short of food nor of other basic needs, as was the case with many of her "Pioneer" friends, but she never questioned the reasons for that.

When the "Great Patriotic War" (World War II) broke out, young people volunteered for army service. Those who did not volunteer were impressed directly off the streets. Zaira excelled in her army duties and soon became an officer. She willingly took on difficult tasks and often volunteered for dangerous assignments. Her patriotism was sincere. She was deeply convinced of the cause for which she was fighting.

She was wounded twice on the front, the second time quite seriously, and spent half a year in an army hospital. When she recovered, she insisted on rejoining her unit on the front. Promoted in rank and bedecked with medals, she contributed whatever she could to the final victory or, as she was wont to say, to "the crushing of the fascist enemy."

In the army she met a Russian officer, a non-Jew, whom she married before they were both demobilized. When her parents learned about it, they were proud of their daughter, who already had a reputation as a distinguished officer and was now married to one. They missed their only child and pressed her and her husband to settle in Tbilisi.

That was not to be. Her husband was assigned to a distant town in Siberia. Zaira, too, was given a job in the military in what was a "closed military town." Access to these towns was forbidden to ordinary citizens, with no exceptions made. These places did not appear on maps up to the end of the Soviet era (and often even beyond).

When Zaira's son was born, her parents applied for permission to visit their daughter's family. Permission was repeatedly denied because they did not have the necessary security clearance, presumably because they were Jews. And Zaira was rarely given more than a few days off at a time, as was the practice for officers in her unit. Therefore, they had to be satisfied with letters and an occasional telephone call.

Zaira integrated well into her new Russian community in Siberia. She made friends and felt very comfortable in the community she was part of. Her Jewish identity was unknown, even to her closest friends. In fact, even her husband did not know that his wife was Jewish. It was not a factor in her new life.

Years went by. Her parents no longer worked. They lived modest lives dictated by their small pensions. When her mother took ill, Zaira was finally given permission to undertake the long trek to Tbilisi with her son. After an exhausting journey by train, Zaira and her adolescent son arrived home, and her elderly parents met their grandson for the first time. He was not a Georgian but was nevertheless "a fine young man." During the visit, Zaira's mother passed away. Zaira witnessed how the community took care of all the funeral arrangements, the burial ritual, and the prayers during the burial. Her father, who had never been a strictly traditional Jew, insisted that everything be done as custom demanded. He himself wore a black jacket, the collar of which was cut as a mourning ritual. During the entire week of mourning, many people came to pay their respects and joined the prayers in the house. Zaira was quite taken by this communal solidarity, and by the help offered to her bereaved father during those difficult days. The customs were alien to her, but she was impressed by the consolation the rituals provided to her father. Her son asked few questions and associated all of the rituals with those of ethnic Georgians. He had no context in which to see them as Jewish.

Back in her assigned city of duty, Zaira immersed herself in her work and her social life. She lived as a non-Jew among non-Jews. She did not know if there were any Jews in her environment, but that did not trouble her.

Her son, Ilya, qualified as an engineer. He married and moved to Kazakhstan, where the central planning bureau in Moscow had assigned him. It was quite far from his parents, but he had no say in the assignment. Visits to his family were infrequent because of the distance and cost. Zaira's husband retired, and soon after, she did as well, and they lived comfortably on their military pensions. She learned of her father's death but did not return to Tbilisi. When her husband died, she began thinking of the Tbilisi Jewish community of her youth. Some of her distant relatives were still alive. She had an unexplained yearning to return to her birthplace, to live among the people she had known in her youth. With no family around her, she now felt lonely in Siberia. She thought that among her own people she would not be so lonely, so she returned to Tbilisi in 1988.

Her pension remained adequate for her needs. Her military service and the work she had done gave her some privileges. Her relatives, though not close, were a source of comfort.

In 1991, quite unexpectedly for many citizens living far from Moscow and the political center, the Soviet Union disintegrated. Zaira's life fell to pieces. Georgia quickly claimed independence. New currency, a new economy, and a new government changed everything. Pension responsibility passed to each newly independent country, with little advance planning and despite these countries' nonviable economies. Her new Georgian pension was not sufficient for her to live on, so she sold some clothes, jewelry, and furniture to keep herself alive.

Eventually there was nothing more to sell. In her old age, she did not have enough for her minimal needs. Her relatives had emigrated, most to Israel, some to Austria, and others to the United States. She was again all alone in her town of origin, but without any means. She had occasional contact with her son, but he could not help her. Even when his salary sufficed, he was paid in a nonconvertible currency. Travel now involved crossing huge swaths of territory and borders and became prohibitively expensive.

Her Jewish neighbors were kind to her. They would not let her starve, although they, too, had little to spare. Eventually the Hesed learned of her situation and sent a social worker, who saw to it that each day she received a warm meal, clothing for winter, and gas for heat and cooking. She lived modestly, but her needs were simple. She felt that her decision to return to Tbilisi, to be again among her own people, was the right one. Jews did not abandon Jews.

I visited Zaira, and she told me the story of her life. She spoke with pride about her army service. She had a good life with her husband. She showed me photographs of her youth, her husband, and her son. She lived in the past. She was grateful for all the help she received, and deeply thankful to the good people who took care of her.

She had only one request: Would we see to it that she was buried in the Jewish cemetery where her mother and father and other ancestors were buried? She lived most of her life as a non-Jew among non-Jews, but she wanted to be buried among Jews. And she wanted a religious burial service, like her mother and her grandmother had had. With a wan smile she made this last request. "I know that Jews will not abandon me, even when my end comes. Jews always look out for other Jews."

Vitaly (January 20, 2006)

Remember the dark days of the Cold War? Remember the talk of intercontinental ballistic missiles (ICBMs), bomb shelters, and the like? Did you ever think about the "other side," or about who was attending to these missiles? What was his or her life like? Was he or she totally committed to the ideology that so threatened the West? I present for your consideration the story of Vitaly Kanov.

Vitaly was discharged from the Red Army in 1991, after thirty-six years of distinguished service. He was a colonel at the time and had spent most of his career as a missile specialist in the Army. During the latter part of his service, he was a commander of an ICBM base in Ukraine. "His" missiles were aimed at the east coast of the United States.

First, a bit about Vitaly, and then how we know him today.

Vitaly was born in 1944, to a Jewish mother and non-Jewish Russian father, while his family was in Uzbekistan, to which they had been evacuated in the wake of the Nazi blitzkrieg. After the war, he relocated to Ukraine with his mother, as his father had been killed at the front. After he graduated high school, he entered the Sumy Artillery School, majoring in nuclear rockets and destined for a career in the military. He graduated with honors and continued his education at the Leningrad Artillery Academy. He was nominated for further training, but his file revealed that, unbeknown to either of them, his wife was also Jewish (his documents listed him as a Russian, after his father), and he was therefore not allowed to advance. Instead, he was placed in Ukraine, overseeing a base with an arsenal of rocket launchers carrying nuclear warheads aimed at the US.

From 1982 to 1988 he served in Hungary, in a missile base that was to be a forward position in the Warsaw Pact defenses, with missiles targeted at American bases in West Germany. He fell into disfavor during the final year of his service there and was charged with "anti-party" activities. He was never told what he did wrong. He believes that a fellow officer, who viewed Vitaly as potential competition for career advancement, was the source of the rumor that was his downfall. As someone with Jewish relatives he was particularly vulnerable and could be punished on the basis of rumor and innuendo alone. His punishment was reassignment to a military base near Sumgait, Azerbaijan, which was essentially tantamount to internal exile. He was quickly promoted to base commander. This was at the height of the war between Azerbaijan and Armenia that erupted in the twilight years of the USSR, when Moscow basically lost control over the populations of its far-flung republics. Ancient ethnic hatreds resurfaced; this war was over the disputed territory of Nagorno Karabakh. Both sides hated the Russians, who were trying to keep both armies at bay. And a special antipathy was reserved for Russians of Jewish descent, who were disdained by all sides.

One day in late 1991, during the height of the hostilities (while the political entity known as the USSR was still extant), Vitaly and his driver were dragged out of his car and beaten senseless by a group of inebriated Azeris. Coming to the realization that this was no longer a position for a "Jewish boy," he resigned his commission and returned with his wife to Ukraine.

They settled in Kirovograd (later, Kropyvnytskyi), a city with a Jewish population of about three thousand. Vitaly had trouble finding employment and did some acting in his spare time. His wife, who was volunteering at the newly formed Hesed in the town, convinced him to put on several performances for the clients. When a position opened up as director of the Hesed food programs in 1999, Vitaly applied and was accepted. His next opportunity came when the director emigrated in 2002. Vitaly was chosen from among the eight candidates who applied. Since that time, he has trimmed expenses and staff size and has won kudos from the clients for the caring nature of the operation.

When asked about the secret of his success as Hesed director, Vitaly smiles and attributes it to the time he spent commanding ICBM bases but does not elaborate.

His is not a unique case. Boris Kapustin is a retired naval captain from the Crimea. He sports a large scar on his abdomen, the result of an emergency operation performed on him on a Soviet submarine returning from service in Vietnam supporting Vietcong troops. His son, Misha, is now the Reform rabbi in Kharkiv. Vladimir Yankelevitch also commanded a submarine, reached the rank of commodore, and now walks around Vladivostok, a Russian city on the Pacific Ocean, wearing a *kippah*. He is the president of the Jewish community in Vladivostok.

We are indeed a peculiar people.

Avraham (March 3, 2006)

Avraham Yagudayev's body was found this past week on the side of a road in Tashkent, the capital of Uzbekistan. He had been murdered.

Avraham was not famous. There were no extraordinary feats that could be attributed to him. He was a simple Jew, a rabbi. A Bukharian Jew who was proud of the heritage of his community.

The origins of Bukharian Jewry are shrouded in mystery. They get their sobriquet from the town of Bukhara in Uzbekistan, an important post on the legendary Silk Road, although not all hail from there. Their religious rites accord with Sephardic tradition. During the most difficult periods of Soviet rule, they managed to maintain a strong communal life that revolved around the synagogue. They had rabbis and religious slaughterers. Their children received a Jewish education. They married within the community because of people like Avraham and the father he venerated (also a rabbi), for whom Jewish community and continuity were paramount values.

It is a very conservative, patriarchal society. They speak a Judeo-Persian language among themselves. While the Soviets generally succeeded in destroying the family as an organic unit throughout its empire, Bukharian Jews resisted that trend, and families often remained intact.

Avraham's father was a rabbi in this community during its heyday in the postwar years. The physical distance from Moscow gave them a degree of freedom to practice as Jews that was uncommon elsewhere in the Soviet empire. He died several years ago. Since the collapse of the USSR, there has been an accelerated exodus of Jews from the Central Asian Republics. What is left of Jewish life there is a shadow of what once was.

Avraham saw himself as one of the last. He refused to emigrate, preferring to remain where he was so that he could serve the Jews who remained, tending to their communal and religious needs. He was extremely modest and lived in dire poverty. His home was a hovel, and he dressed in tattered clothing. He always resisted efforts to compensate him for his work. Several years ago, JDC initiated a bar/bat mitzvah program for the community, which we also saw as a way to supplement his income. He took an active role but refused to be compensated. "It's a mitzvah," he said. "I can't take money for that." Other efforts to redress the situation were likewise rebuffed. He was modest, hardworking, and totally dedicated to the Jewish community, as his father had been.

When we speak of leadership development, we generally look for people who have characteristics that equip them to succeed in societies as we know them: charisma, vision, ability to make connections, ability to plan, etc. I'm not sure how many, if any, of the things we look for could be found in Avraham. He was a simple, pious Jew whose only goal in life, even at the expense of personal comfort, was to help the Jewish community.

His murderers will probably never be brought to justice. The country and its judicial system are too corrupt, and even if the murderers are found, they will find a way to get off. It's not even clear what the motive was for the killing. What is clear, though, is what a tremendous loss it was for the Jewish people.

Avraham left a wife and four children. He was thirty-four years old. He was undoubtedly one of the thirty-six righteous souls of this generation.

Misha (August 20, 2004)

What follows is the description of an artifact, one that is not particularly impressive or notable, but one that has determined the course of the life of a Jew in Belarus. The man's name is Misha Alterman. He lives in a town called Volozhin. And the item is a key. Misha, and the key, are a window into Jewish heritage in that part of the world, and to what it means to so many Jews who live there.

Volozhin is about forty-three miles west of Minsk. It holds a place of honor in Jewish history. During the eighteenth century, there was a titanic struggle in the region over the nature of Judaism. The nascent revolutionary movement, Chasidut, challenged the entrenched rabbinic authority. The latter fought back in a battle led by the Gaon of Vilna and his followers. It was not a trivial matter. The victor would determine the nature of normative Ashkenazic Judaism, and the lives of millions would be affected for generations.

The issues over which the battles were fought are not germane to this discussion. Suffice it to say that a handful of very influential yeshivot were set up in the ensuing years to nurture the leadership that would lead the battle going forward, and the one in Volozhin was one of three jewels in the crown. From that time on, the name of this town was revered in Orthodox circles.

Today, Volozhin is a small Belarusian town that modernity has bypassed. The section in which the long-abandoned yeshivah building still stands is straight from *Fiddler on the Roof*, what we know as a shtetl. The roads are not paved. They are lined with one-story dwellings made of wood, with outhouses and no running water. Prominent in each yard is a well – yes, a real functioning well – that provides drinking water for the inhabitants. Stray dogs and an occasional chicken wander loose. The patches of earth in front and in back of each house contain carefully tended vegetable gardens.

Misha lives in one of these houses. He is eighty-five years old. When asked how he made a living during his younger years, he says he was a "schlepper." Pressed to elaborate, he explains that he delivered packages for elderly people from the state-sponsored grocery store. You can see that at one time he was an ox of a man.

He was one of nine children. All were murdered in the Shoah except for him and a sister, who died several years ago. He was widowed around the same time and now lives alone.

We talked about his Jewish memories. He remembers Seders in his parents' home. During Soviet times, it was considered dangerous to buy matzah in the small towns. (Several of the cities had matzah bakeries but these were primarily for show. There were no efforts to reach the Jews in the periphery, out of sight of foreign visitors and observers.) So his mother baked matzah at home. After the war, he would still hold a Seder for his wife and two daughters, but gradually he forgot the content. Each year the ritual was less complete. In the last thirty years, he says, "We sit around a table at a meal with no bread and try to remember what we can."

His days are still full. There are six elderly Jewish widows in town. He and they constitute what is left of a Jewish population of several thousand on the eve of the war. He tries to attend to their needs. Most important, every three weeks, his home is the drop-off point for the Hesed mobile food packages, medicines, and whatever else is needed. He has no companionship except for these ladies. The neighbors, according to him, are antisemites.

Naturally, we asked him, "Why do you stay?"

Here I should explain that this question can have multiple motivations, often depending on the intonation used when it is asked. It can be rhetorical, an expression of perplexity over why anyone with an alternative (like Israel, for example) would choose to remain in this godforsaken place. Or the question can be asked in a nonjudgmental way, which was the intention here. It was a sincere effort to understand something that was not at all self-evident.

He didn't miss a beat in his response. He pulled out of his pocket a piece of leather that served as a wrapping for a metal object. On closer examination, it held a key. This was his answer to us. With that, he motioned us to follow him. After walking for ten minutes, we came to a field about half an acre in size, surrounded by a low brick fence. It was the Jewish cemetery of Volozhin.

There did not appear to be much left of the cemetery. There was a fairly large monument that clearly received special care, dedicated to the memory of Chaim Volozhiner, the legendary founder of the yeshivah. Most of the surrounding stones were overturned or overgrown with grass and weeds. The vandals had clearly stopped coming. There was nothing left to deface or loot. Six goats grazed on foliage that covered the graves. We followed Misha to what was clearly a relatively new gate that (only symbolically) kept trespassers out. He took out his key, carefully unwrapped it, unlocked the gate, and motioned for us to come inside, through the front door, as it were.

There's much more to tell about Misha and Volozhin, but one thought struck me at that moment: Misha stays behind because, as possessor of that key, he sees himself as the custodian of a glorious past. He will not confront the inevitable passage of that key into non-Jewish hands once he is no longer around. This is the burial ground of *his* people. Those buried here are *his* ancestors. In his mind, the responsibility for this holy place falls on his shoulders, and his shoulders alone. He is the end, and as such won't give up. If you ask him what he lives for, it is this key. If you ask him what gives his life meaning and helps him transcend the aches and pains of an aging body and the loneliness of his life now, it is this key. At the end of the day, a metal item with a net worth of perhaps several dollars.

I was struck at that moment by the value of so many of the small things in the systems we have set up in the FSU, and what those small things have done for the people we serve. We tend to think in terms of JCC programs and concerts, food packages, and home care hours. We often lose sight of the value of the connection to the outside world that the home care worker brings, how a smile from a volunteer delivering some medicine can mean the difference between darkness and light for the homebound, how the insertion of a Jewish calendar in a package of food will reconnect a "lost Jew" to the Jewish people.

The impact of our work is not easily measured, and certainly cannot be predicted. If a simple key and what it represents can have such a profound impact on the life of one Jew, who knows what broader effect our work may have?

Sveta (March 10, 2006)

Recently, I was asked a question and was myself surprised by the answer I gave. At the board meetings last week, a board member asked, "Of all the home visits you have made in the FSU to the impoverished elderly, which was the most memorable?" At first, I was a bit taken aback. To answer that question would mean scrolling through a lot of material, having made literally hundreds of those visits. I have seen human beings in wretched states that often defy description.

But my mind kept returning to one visit, which did not fit at all into that category. It was an hour I spent last year in Chişinău, in the home of Sveta, a ninety-two-year-old survivor of the Shoah. What was most memorable about that visit was not the condition of the apartment, nor was it Sveta's physical or economic predicament, either of which would have made her eligible for Hesed support. What I remember about the visit was that, from the moment we walked into the apartment until we closed the door behind us on exiting, Sveta had us in stitches. We had expected to visit an indigent, suffering woman whom the Hesed was helping live out her last years in dignity, and instead we found a vibrant woman, full of energy, telling stories and jokes and reveling in the laughter she elicited from us.

Sveta fit the profile of so many of our clients: she was physically frail and surviving on a pension equivalent to twenty-three dollars per month. She regularly had to decide how to apportion her meager pension between medicines and food. If anyone ever earned the right to be downtrodden and depressed after a lifetime of carrying the burdens of the world on her shoulders, it was she. Yet through it all she was able to laugh.

More than that, we sat in the presence of a woman born in Czarist times who had lived through the enforced famines in Ukraine during the Stalinist period, and the Nazi occupation a few years after that. She had been a victim of the discrimination against the Jews during the Soviet regime, and her son and husband had predeceased her. And she could still laugh.

On further reflection, I realized that Sveta was representative of a phenomenon that we have encountered repeatedly through the years in the FSU. We often speak of the creativity and commitment of this Jewry only recently released from Soviet shackles. We admire their inner grit, a resilience that helped them not merely to survive the vicissitudes of their history but to outlast those who tried so hard to destroy them.

We can point to many characteristics that helped these Jews survive: the role of the family and community, the importance they always placed on education and achievement, and much more. Another aspect of the collective Soviet-Jewish personality that enabled Jews to survive those difficult years, an attribute for which they are well known in the FSU, is their very Jewish sense of humor. The ability to laugh, to mock, and to poke fun at life's obstacles served Soviet Jewry well. If we want to understand many of the people with whom we work, we need to appreciate their sense of humor as a critical survival tool.

In that spirit, what follows are selections from a wonderful collection by David Harris and Izrail Rabinovich, which records "Soviet-Jewish" jokes and stories.[1] They are taken from different periods. They include as protagonists representatives of Soviet evil, either lofty leaders or petty bureaucrats, at the hands of whom every Soviet Jew was victimized at one time or another. They serve as examples of how Soviet Jews were able to laugh in circumstances that otherwise had no redeeming features. Perhaps this humor, more than it is a window into the Soviet Jewish experience, was actually a factor contributing to the resilience of Jewish life in the face of monumental efforts to obliterate it.

During the Yalta Conference in 1945, Stalin, Roosevelt, and Churchill decided to take a break from the work of discussing the projected post-War situation. Out of curiosity, Roosevelt and Stalin asked to see Churchill's watch.

On the back they found the following inscription: "To Winston Churchill, with fond remembrance, King George VI."

Churchill and Stalin then asked to see Roosevelt's watch. They found the following inscription: "To Franklin Roosevelt, from his friends and admirers in Congress."

Churchill and Roosevelt then asked to see Stalin's. On the back, they found the following inscription: "To Rabbi Moishe, from the Jews of the city of Warsaw."

---

1   David Harris and Izrail Rabinovich, *The Jokes of Oppression: The Humor of Soviet Jews* (Lanham, MD: Jason Aronson, 1995).

Abramovitch telephoned the KGB: "Hello. Is this the KGB Headquarters? I was just wondering whether by chance a parrot has come to your office."

"No," came the reply.

"Well, if he should come, I just want to let you know that I don't share his political views."

It's a cold day in the middle of winter in Moscow and a long line has formed in front of a butcher's shop on the rumor that sausages will soon be available.

After the eager citizens have stood in line for an hour, slapping themselves and stamping their feet to keep warm, the butcher sticks his head out the door and says, "Comrades, I regret to say that the lorry has been delayed, and there will not be enough sausages for everyone. All Jewish citizens are required to leave the queue." Muttering and grumbling, the Jews leave the line.

The temperature drops and the wind starts blowing. After a couple more hours the butcher sticks his head out again and says, "The lorry has been further delayed, and there will be a distinct shortage of sausages. Comrades from the Moldavian S.S.R. are required to leave the line!" So, the Moldavians leave, and the remaining citizens continue their vigil as the wind blows harder and snow starts to fall.

A while later the butcher reappears and says, "The lorry is still not here. Comrades from the Estonian S.S.R., please leave the queue!"

So it continues the rest of the afternoon. One by one, the various ethnic groups of the Soviet Socialist Republics – the Ukrainians, the Lithuanians, the Latvians, the Byelorussians, the Kazakhs, the Uzbeks, the Tajiks, the Turkmen, the Kyrgyz, the Armenians, and the Georgians – are all required to leave the line and go home. No one is left but the comrades of the Russian Federated Socialist Republic.

Finally, as night falls, with the snow almost a foot deep, the butcher emerges one more time. "Comrades! Counterrevolutionaries have sabotaged the fuel depot. The lorry cannot refuel, so there will be no sausages today. Everyone must go home!"

Muttering and grumbling, the Russians turn away and start the long walk home through the snow. One old fellow turns to the man next to him and says, "Those damned Jews! Why do they always get all the breaks?"

Moishe is being interrogated by a Russian bureaucrat:

Government Official: "If you had a yacht, what would you do with it?"

Moishe: "Give it to Mother Russia."

Government Official: "And if you had a palace, what would you do with it?"

Moishe: "Give it to Mother Russia."

Government Official: "And if you had a sweater, what would you do with it?"

Moishe: (No reply.)

Government Official: "What would you do with it?"

Moishe: (No reply.)

Government Official: "Moishe, why don't you reply?"

Moishe: "Because I have a sweater."

A longtime Moscow resident was recounting to an American tourist the horrors of Stalin's Great Terror during the 1930s. "You wouldn't believe it," the Russian tearfully explained. "People simply disappeared from their homes and offices. Countless people were killed."

"But it's unbelievable that something like that could happen," the American exclaimed. "Didn't anyone call the police?"

No sooner did the newspaper kiosk open every morning than Shapiro bought the paper, scanned the first page, and threw the paper away in the nearest litter basket. The newspaper vendor couldn't quite figure out the reason for this strange behavior and decided to ask Shapiro about it. "Citizen, what is it that interests you in the paper?" asked the vendor.

"Obituaries," replied Shapiro.

"But obituaries are listed on the back page, not the first," said the vendor.

"Believe me," said Shapiro, "the obituary that I'm waiting for will be printed on the first page."

In the 1970s, a Russian school inspector is questioning the children. He points to one of the boys and says, "Who is your father?"

The boy replies, "The Soviet Union."

He then asks, "Who is your mother?"

"The Communist Party," came the reply.

"And what do you want to be when you grow up?"

"I want to be a super-human worker for the glory of the state and the party."

The inspector then points to one of the girls and asks, "Who is your father?"

The girl answers, "The Soviet Union."

"Who is your mother?"

"The Communist Party."

"And what do you want to be when you grow up?"

"A heroine of the Soviet Union, raising lots of children for the state and party."

The inspector looks round and sees a Jewish boy tucked away at the back, trying to look inconspicuous. He points and says, "What's your name?"

The boy replies, "Haim Abramovitch."

"Who is your father?"

"The Soviet Union."

"Who is your mother?"

"The Communist Party."

"And what do you want to be when you grow up?"

Haim replies, "An orphan."

Piotr (February 1, 2008)

The small Jewish community of Shymkent, Kazakhstan, with an estimated Jewish population of 350, traces its origin to the post-Stalin years. At that time there was a campaign in the Soviet Union for volunteers to move east to the steppes of Kazakhstan and to develop the vast uncultivated land there for farming. The aim was to make the Soviet Union independent of Western countries (and, in particular, of the United States) for its grain. There were terrible shortages of wheat and corn in the Soviet Union in the late 1950s. Nikita Khrushchev was determined to increase the growth of basic foods for the population. As with many of his plans for radical changes in the economy, this idea too turned out to be a disaster.

Jews were among the first to volunteer to settle in the region and cultivate the land. The Jewish presence in Shymkent is generally traced to that period.

This coincided with the Soviet efforts to dismantle the system of prison camps, generally situated in particularly harsh environments in the farthest reaches of the USSR, known as the Gulag. Most of these camps were established by Stalin and his henchmen. They were meant to serve a dual function during his reign: making dissidents and troublemakers inaccessible to potential followers, and supplying free (slave) labor for projects in sparsely settled regions. When the prison gates were opened after Stalin's death, many newly freed Jewish prisoners, previously exiled for activities deemed antithetical to the state, remained in Kazakhstan, adding to the local Jewish population. It was widely believed that once they were freed, the distance from the major Russian cities in the west would enable them to stay off the radar of the security services, who were convinced that they posed a real threat to the state.

Piotr Galperin's father, Grigory, came east in the mid-fifties of the last century. He was a truck mechanic who had been born and raised in Vitebsk, in Belarus, the birthplace of Chagall. He lived there in a tiny one-room apartment. Because he was able to service farm equipment – a sought-after skill – he was promised more spacious living accommodation if he were to move to Kazakhstan. He came to Shymkent, found good living quarters, and stayed. Piotr was born in Shymkent, went to school and college there, and qualified as a teacher of Russian literature. Though his father was mechanically minded, Piotr loved poetry and classic literature. His father warned him incessantly that one could not earn a living from poetry. The son insisted on following his own inclinations. He wrote poems which were praised by his professors at college. He proudly related to all who would listen that the greatest day in his life was when one of his poems was included in a collection of modern Russian poetry published by the Academy of Russian Literature.

Piotr became a lecturer of Russian literature in the local college. He struggled to earn a decent living, and eventually had to concede that his father was correct; it was difficult to make ends meet with his meager salary as a professor. Piotr's wife taught Russian in the local high school. They lived modestly but happily. Their happiness increased when Tanya, or Tanutchka, as they called her, was born.

Piotr knew that he was Jewish; his wife was not, but nationality meant very little in Kazakhstan. He loved books and filled his modest apartment with books of Russian literature and poetry. Over the years, he accumulated almost ten thousand books, often given to him by relatives of people he knew who had died.

Tanya married a local Kazakh and moved in with her parents. Even the young couple's single room had shelves stocked with books.

The situation in Kazakhstan changed dramatically when the Soviet Union disintegrated in December of 1991. As was the case in many of the new successor states, an independent Kazakhstan moved from being a society run in the Russian language to one administered in the local Kazakh language, which was foreign to most native Russian speakers in the country. Laws were passed to attempt to instill pride in and connection to Kazakhstan, which had never previously existed as an independent political entity. History was now taught through a Kazakh lens. The dominant culture switched from Russian to Kazakh. The legal system was adjusted, and school curricula were revised. It was a process that was repeated throughout the former Soviet Union, as newly independent countries made tremendous efforts to sever themselves from years of Soviet (read: Russian) dominance.

The result was the disenfranchisement of the native Russian population in Kazakhstan, many of whose family trees extended back generations in the region. They did not speak the local language, nor were they familiar with, or attracted to, the local culture. They suddenly took on the status of resented aliens in the only home they had ever known.

Piotr's particular skills and knowledge became devalued overnight. His own position as a lecturer of Russian literature became irrelevant. In his mid-fifties, he was forced into early retirement, with no adequate income source. He had to find private pupils to supplement his meager pension.

It was in this setting that the 350 or so Jews of Shymkent set up a Jewish community. The political changes following Kazakhstan's independence left an enormous vacuum in their lives – one that they hoped could be filled for them through this new community. They identified fellow Jews by word of mouth.

Few of them knew anything about Jewish life. There was no synagogue in Shymkent, nor was there anyone who could call up memories of the Jewish communal life of a previous era. Undaunted, they acquired several books. A small group among them decided to arrange a celebration on Purim. Piotr read from a book he had about Purim. Almost half of the Jews of the city came to their celebration, which was held in a café. Two older men told them the story of Purim and spoke about the traditions they remembered from their childhood.

From these small, tentative beginnings, the Jewish community of Shymkent began to grow. Piotr organized a Sunday school. He found books that helped him prepare his lessons for the children. Teachers were found for Jewish music, Jewish songs, Jewish-themed painting, and other activities. By the late 1990s, the Hebrew school had almost fifty children. Piotr was the director and main teacher. The community had a permanent rented facility where they met frequently. Those who attended were highly educated individuals, but their knowledge of Jewish subjects was poor. A Jewish community was born in Shymkent; Jews met, talked about Israel, sang Jewish songs, and were glad to be with each other.

Piotr insisted that we come to his home. He gave us a tour of his library, the old records of classical music, and the small room where his daughter, her husband, and their baby lived. His wife served tea and jam. Piotr spoke to us about Israel and his great desire to go there. He was eligible for immigration, and he was convinced that he could be helpful to the many Russian immigrants in Israel.

But he had a big problem: his library. What would happen to his books? He could not leave his books behind. This represented a lifetime of effort. He had spent a fortune on his books. He had spent many hours acquiring them and reading them. He loved his books. No, under no circumstances could he leave without his library. He was prepared to donate his library to a university in Israel, or to any institution willing to accept it, house it, and make it available to him whenever he wanted one of his books. Unfortunately, no such institution could be found, and today Piotr is still in Shymkent with his library, living in his small apartment, attached to his books.

To the question, "Now that you can emigrate why don't you?" there are many answers that are given by Jews who live in circumstances that seem to justify resettlement. For some there are family reasons. Others are intimidated by the prospects of learning a new language at an advanced age, adjusting to a new culture, etc. In this case it is a whole life's meaning contained in a personal library.

We have no right to pass judgment.

Nadezhda (August 24, 2007)

There is much talk of the plight of so-called non-Nazi victims in the FSU. The term refers to those who are ineligible to receive support from the German government (via the Claims Conference), because they were not directly impacted by the Shoah, generally because they were born in areas not invaded by the Nazis.

I have always felt uncomfortable with "non-victims," the shorthand term often used to distinguish these elderly people from those who are beneficiaries. They are not "non-victims" by any stretch of the imagination. They may not have had the exact same experiences in life as those who fall under the category of Nazi victims, but anyone who had the misfortune to live under the Soviet regime can certainly be considered a victim. The regime was cruel, callous, and uncaring. The vast majority of its citizens were fearful, persecuted, oppressed, and in general mistreated in a way no human being should ever be.

What did it mean to be a victim of the Soviet system? Myriad interviews and testimonies of people whose lives were ruined speak of that experience. Perhaps ironically, one of the most painful parts of this story is the "afterward"; that is, after the Soviet Union fell apart, those who held out hope that what rose on its ashes could be more just and more compassionate were inevitably disappointed. The dreams of 1991 did not materialize for so many. They were victims then, and perhaps in different ways, they still are.

Nadezhda Vlasendo was born in 1924 in Siberia. Both of her parents had been exiled at the beginning of the Soviet regime. Today, Nadezhda lives in Kharkiv, Ukraine, in a tiny, shabby, lopsided, one-room house. The walls are covered with worn rags in various places where the wallpaper has peeled off. An unshaded lamp casts a dim light over a sparsely-furnished room. The house has no running water, and the nearest well is three houses away. Homebound due to poor health, Nadezhda must ask someone else to fetch the water she needs for washing and cooking. She heats her house through an antiquated radiator, for which she also needs water. Sometimes a neighbor will help her. At other times, she has to wait for the Hesed home care worker who visits her once a week. The municipality has no budget for home care, and Nadezhda did not work long enough to earn a pension that even comes close to the poverty line.

All of Nadezhda's household conveniences are outside, including the washing stand and a small wooden outhouse with a round hole in the floor. She says she is afraid to go outside in the dark and in the bitter cold. At night, and especially in the winter, she prefers to stay inside and use an empty bucket as a toilet.

She is a sick and lonely woman who suffers from depression. She often cries when she remembers her husbands. They both died tragic deaths – the first during World War II, the second from a head wound in a workplace accident that left him in a coma for the last few years of his life. Her two sons also passed away within a year of each other. After their deaths, she leads what she calls a miserable life.

Other than the Hesed home care worker, a very old, black-and-white television set and a miniature radio are Nadezhda's only connection to the outside world. She cannot read due to cataracts. She also suffers from what her doctor describes as myocardial ischemic gastrointestinal tract diseases, hypertension, nephrological diseases, and arrhythmia.

She subsists on a meager monthly pension of seventy-four dollars. Without the Hesed's help she would go hungry and would have to do without the medications she desperately needs. The Hesed provides her with subsidies for the purchase of medications, weekly home care services, and diapers.

"Even in my most dreadful nightmares, I could not imagine that I would have such a horrible and lonely old age," says Nadezhda. The caregiver and the volunteers sent by the Hesed are her only hope and help in this world.

Nadezhda spent the years of World War II far from any of the fronts. As such, she is not entitled to funding from restitution sources. In the shorthand used by some she is a "non-victim," but her reality belies this term.

Fima (April 18, 2008)

Marusya Margolin had long ago given up any hope of influencing her only son, Efim, whom she called Fima. Ever since her husband abandoned her and their only child, Marusya had gradually pulled back from disciplining her son, and finally gave up altogether. She worked long hours as an orderly in a hospital. This meant starting in the predawn hours to serve breakfast to the patients and staying late until all the supper dishes had been collected, washed, and stacked away ready for the next day. From the time he was very young, Marusya had to leave the house long before Fima left for school. By the time Marusya came home, Fima was already out with his friends. No one knew how he was getting on at school, or if he had even *been* to school. Marusya did not bother to inquire. She saw no recourse, even if his truancy could be established.

In fact, at the onset of his teen years Fima had, without his mother's knowledge, left school altogether. He met with a group of school friends every day in a café. They played billiards, smoked stolen cigarettes, and walked the streets. By the age of fifteen he had begun to come home late, well after his mother was already asleep. Marusya sometimes asked her son where he was and why he came home so late. Either he did not answer, or he made up an explanation, which his mother knew was untrue. After a full day's work at the hospital, she had neither the strength nor the will to argue with her son. She knew it was futile to talk to him. There was no way she could control him, and she had nowhere to turn for help. The local social services were not sympathetic; the education system had no trained professionals and lacked the wherewithal to assist her.

Fima was intelligent, shrewd, and far too worldly for his years. He had charisma and was a natural leader. The group that coalesced around him became known as "Fima's gang." There were other gangs in their city – Pavlodar, in

Kazakhstan – but Fima steered clear of them. Each one operated within a well-delineated territory. No one was allowed to trespass into a neighboring area.

Fima knew how to defend his territory. He never gave way to others. The gangs knew that it was dangerous to invade Fima's territory. He had a reputation as a ruthless opponent, and he ruled his group with an iron fist. Any infringement of discipline was severely punished. Any show of weakness meant exclusion from the gang. The boys listened to Fima; they feared him and worshipped him.

Gangs need money. The café had to be paid regularly. It began with small pilfering and escalated to organized theft from shops until finally the gang developed into a group of highly skilled and fearless burglars. A target was chosen during the day and staked out. A plan was drawn up, and the gang went to work at nightfall. It could be a men's clothing shop that was emptied during the night, a carload of shoes, a television store, or a computer supplier. Fima was an expert in the value of stolen goods and knew where to dispose of them, and he had acquired a reputation on the street as a tough bargainer. The money was divided according to the degree of risk taken. Fima naturally received the biggest share. His followers considered him violent but fair.

The police did not bother his gang, or for that matter the other gangs. There were more serious crimes to be solved than theft. If one of his gang got into trouble with the police, Fima dealt with the situation with a lawyer, with bribes, and in any other way that would be effective. He was loyal to his "soldiers."

Fima brought food home to Marusya. He filled the refrigerator with all the household necessities. His mother understood that her son must be involved in crime. When he brought a silk blouse as a birthday gift for his mother, she told him that she would not accept it if it was stolen. He assured her that he had bought it for her, and she did not challenge him. Perhaps she needed to believe that her son was not a criminal. She accepted the gift, kissed her son, and thanked him.

Soon Fima's gifts to his mother increased in value. He regularly brought home food and clothing, and even suggested that she reduce her working hours and rely on him for more. Marusya refused. She was not prepared to be wholly dependent on the suspect money of her young son.

After a while Fima's gang began to traffic in drugs. The danger was considerably greater, but the reward was greater too. At first Fima was reluctant for the gang to move in that direction. He recognized that the police were not the only source of danger for him. There were organized crime groups in Pavlodar, and they tolerated no competition. He was too young to protect himself and his followers from professional gangsters. But, ultimately, the temptation was too great.

By chance, one day during that period he passed the Jewish community center in Pavlodar, which had been founded by JDC. Fima was told once, as a child, that he was Jewish. In fact, most of the members of his gang were Jewish. They knew that from their family names, and from local lore. But this part of their identity meant nothing to him or to his friends. It had no distinguishing elements, nor was it significant in any way. It was purely a happenstance of birth. For reasons that he cannot explain to this day, when he passed the sign on this building, his curiosity was piqued, and he had some time to kill before his next meeting, so he went inside.

He was surprised to find a good billiard table, two Ping-Pong tables, and a whole array of equipment for muscle development: bicycles to strengthen leg muscles, weights, and three treadmills.

He saw a young man of about seventeen lifting a barbell and boasted that he could do much better. The young man challenged him to prove it and, to Fima's great disappointment, he could not lift the bar. Weights were removed until Fima finally lifted the now-much-lighter bar with great strain. He was embarrassed and upset. Fima, the leader of a gang, could not do as well as the skinny young man who had challenged him. Fima thought that there must be a trick to lifting weights. He was told that the trick lay in the time devoted to training.

The following day Fima came to the Jewish community center and started training. He could not abide being less able than other young men. He devoted hours to strengthening his body. The sports guide at the center warned him not to overdo his training. There was a method to the system. He was taught how to start, how to progress slowly, and how to combine weightlifting with other exercises.

Attendance at the JCC occupied much of Fima's time, and he gradually lost interest in his gang. He'd put enough money aside so that his lifestyle was not affected; he was now more interested in building his body than in running the gang. He became a regular at the JCC sports hall.

One unusually hot day in early spring he left the exercise room after a difficult workout and gravitated toward an air-conditioned room down the hall. It was a class on Jewish history. Fima, the junior-high-school dropout, was intrigued by the discussion. The class ended with an announcement that there would be a Passover celebration that evening. He insisted that his mother join him. She was delighted with her son's new interests. She herself did not know about the center, but she remembered what a Passover Seder was from stories she had heard from her grandmother. Wearing the blouse Fima had given her, she attended the Seder.

The evening impressed them both. The class aroused Fima's curiosity about Jewish culture and tradition, and he began to attend other courses at the center. The notion of having a Jewish identity was both baffling and challenging to him. That he had a connection to a country far away that was considered to be the homeland of the Jewish people – now *his* people – instilled in him a pride that surprised even him.

Unfortunately, during this time, the money he had saved ran out. His mother never mentioned that the refrigerator was again poorly stocked. She gladly worked additional hours from early morning to late at night. Marusya reclaimed her son and, in the process, she found her own identity as a Jew. She is now part of a community that provides her with the support for which she was so desperate as a single mother. She speaks of how close she now is with her son.

Even though they now live thousands of miles apart, she speaks regularly and candidly with Fima, who recently settled in Tel Aviv with his wife and newborn child.

Arkady (December 4, 2009)

Murray and Arkady are two people I know. Murray was born in 1927 in New York, and Arkady was born in 1928 in Kazan, Russia. Today, Murray lives in New Jersey, while Arkady still lives in the apartment in the central Russian city in which he spent all of his adult life. Both are war veterans: Murray served in the American army in Europe and was in tank intelligence. Arkady was in the Red Army, first in the Far East and then in Stalingrad after the decisive battle there. Both Murray and Arkady were professionals in the field of education. They both have families, and their children are grown and have children of their own. Both are still married, in each case for over fifty years. And both are in advanced stages of dementia.

Murray now lives in a nursing home in New Jersey in a special ward for dementia patients. The ward has a staff equal in size to the number of patients. The staff feed Murray and bathe him; in fact, they take care of all his basic needs. He has no single primary caregiver.

His wife is in another wing of the same institution. She has become physically frail, but she is basically self-sufficient. They lived together in the same house until about a year ago. An aide came in every day to help with Murray, but eventually the challenge became overwhelming. It was no longer safe to keep him at home, and so Murray's family searched for an appropriate facility in which both he and his wife could live, with their respective needs addressed. In the end, they had a number of facilities from which to choose.

Arkady is not so fortunate. There is no institutional option in Russia for him. His family is not faced with the painful decision of when to move him out of his familiar surroundings and into an appropriate facility. They simply have no choice. Arkady is a Hesed client, but he falls into the category of non-Nazi victims, and is therefore entitled only to a minimum level of care. One of the Hesed's home care workers visits him six hours a week. Sometimes that means an hour a day. At other times – for example, when he has to be taken to a doctor – half of the week's budgeted time can be used for one trip and is deducted from the total allotted to him. The door of the apartment in which he lives is always bolted so that he cannot leave unescorted. If his wife needs to go out to the doctor or go shopping, it requires major planning so that Arkady is not endangered by being left alone. His wife – age seventy-nine, and with daunting physical challenges herself – is his primary caregiver. Such as it is.

Murray is regularly taken for walks outdoors. Sometimes he sits outside for hours, alone with his thoughts. He is exposed to sights and sounds and movement. He spends most of his waking hours in a dayroom with others. There are exercises he can do from his wheelchair. There is movement. Stimulation. Music in the background. All of this is supposed to be good for him. Who knows?

Arkady spends all of his time indoors, except for occasional doctors' visits. He looks always at the same four walls. The peeling paint, the musty smell. Day in and day out. No variation, day after day. No stimulation. No socialization. For budgetary reasons, most day centers have been eliminated or cut back in the Hesed centers, but even where they still exist, the demand far outstrips availability, and Arkady would not be a candidate. The reason is alien to Jewish tradition but dictated by current circumstances: Arkady is too far gone.

The nursing home's staff makes sure that Murray takes his medicines at the appointed time. If they notice anything untoward, they summon a doctor who is on call. Adult diapers are taken from a pantry in the facility as needed.

Arkady is eligible for a medicine allowance from the Hesed because the couple's combined income from their pensions is under $160 per month. His children pick up eight adult diapers a week from the Hesed for their father's use. That is all that he gets. Eight. One day a week he gets to use two.

Recently Murray's children met with a social worker and accountant, who outlined with them a plan for the next few years, should there be a need, to ensure that government entitlements can be supplemented by Murray's savings, insurance, and pension. They considered several scenarios based on a model of continuing care, the kinds of institutions Murray needs, and their costs. The course of the disease and the expected concomitant increase in Murray's needs were spelled out, and the necessary financial plans were discussed.

That kind of meeting would seem to Arkady's family like an event taking place on another planet. Government entitlements in Russia are almost non-existent; there are no institutional options, and there is no health insurance.

Murray's family is grieving for his situation. The family patriarch has been reduced to a shell of a human being. But they are consoled by the fact that he is getting good care and is as comfortable as his situation allows. He is surrounded by professionals and gets the attention someone in his situation needs. If there are complaints that seem significant – the diet is not right, his clothing is stained, or he is not changed soon enough after soiling himself – they are put in perspective when one learns of Arkady's situation.

Given my role in JDC, it is hard for me to write about Arkady. The Hesed can do more. Much more. The difference between an adequate level of home care and what he currently gets is budget. The difference between eight diapers a week and what he needs is budget. The Hesed in Kazan can determine needs, deliver what is required, and ensure that it is used properly. Its professional staff can provide all the necessary medicines and good nutrition, and they can address the other needs of the elderly as well. They can do all that is needed, and so can the other Hesed operations in the system. The only thing they lack is resources. And because they are short on resources, they are providing a woefully inadequate response to a devastating situation.

It is also hard for me to write about Murray. He is my father. The efforts to help him, to provide him with the care he deserves and needs, are also woefully inadequate, but for very different reasons. Resources are not an issue. The pain stems from our inability to penetrate the world he inhabits; it is simply beyond our reach. Or at least, so it seems to his son.

Luisa (October 15, 2010)

Every one of the Hesed clients has a story worth telling. A visit with one of these people can last hours and provide insight into the history of the Jews of that region over the last hundred years.

I just came across a report from Zina, a Hesed home care worker in Zaporizhzhia, in eastern Ukraine. In it, she tells of a visit to a woman whose circumstances set her apart from most of the other clients with whom Zina works.

We need to be reminded periodically that even now, in the twenty-first century, people in Europe still live like this. Following the report below, you will see a series of questions that I asked in order to understand the client's plight a bit better. I left the questions as asked and the answers as received directly from the field. Here is Zina's report:

> Luisa Nemirovskaya lives twenty minutes outside the Zaporizhzhia (Ukraine) city center. The road leading to Luisa's home was unlike any I had traveled before. We had to take a special van that could safely travel over the water-filled potholes that led to her street. Luisa lives year-round in an isolated summer home, what is referred to in Russian as a dacha. In truth, it is more of a hut, without gas or running water. We met Luisa in her yard, where she was digging up some plants, preparing for the winter. Outside her door are buckets of factory water left over from the summer, when it is

provided to the weekend visitors who use it to water their small plots of land. Incredibly, Luisa uses this water to drink and bathe, as she has no access to any other running water. Inside, the home was freezing and dark. Despite her surroundings, Luisa seemed happy…until she started crying to us, "I just want a little corner of my own. I cannot keep on living like this."

Born in 1937 in Khabarovsk in the Russian Far East, Luisa lost her immediate family to typhoid and was taken in by her aunt in Zaporizhzhia in 1941. When the war began a few months later and Zaporizhzhia was bombed, Luisa and her aunt Hanna were evacuated back to Khabarovsk, where they lived until 1945. Repeated displacements and moves into temporary housing were a leitmotif in her young life. Luisa later found out that her father was killed at the front in 1943.

After the war, Luisa returned to Zaporizhzhia and worked as a nurse at the hospital, where she met her husband, a doctor. Ten years after they married, Luisa's husband abandoned her and their young son, Vladimir. The remaining family of two lived together in their home in the city until circumstances forced them to move into their one-room summer house. Two years later, Vladimir died unexpectedly of pneumonia.

Today, Luisa – still inconsolable after the death of her son decades ago – lives alone. She takes in stray cats and shares with them what little she has (mostly for the company they provide), leaving only once a month to take the bus to Zaporizhzhia to receive her pension and to visit her son's grave. Luisa's state pension is the equivalent of eighty dollars per month, and she suffers from hypertension and vascular disease. The Zaporizhzhia Hesed provides her with food packages, medications as needed, and winter relief (two tons of coal). Her home is in such disrepair that the wall above Luisa's bed seems ready to topple on her. Unfortunately, the structure is such that it cannot be fixed.

What follows are some questions posed to the Hesed staff member who works with Luisa.

How does Luisa occupy herself each day?

Luisa's main source of food, aside from what she receives from the Hesed, is her garden. She spends most of her day during the spring and summer months taking care of her vegetables and fruits – watering, digging, or picking, depending on the season. The rest of the day she spends resting or playing with the five stray cats she has adopted. According to her, they are "the only family she has."

Choose a day as an example. I would like to know what Luisa ate on any given day. I want to better understand what daily life is like for her.

Luisa's main food concern is to have enough bread at home. As there are no food shops within walking distance of Luisa's house, she makes sure she buys a lot of bread when she goes to the city once a month to pick up her pension and visit her son's grave. Then she brings all those loaves home and keeps them in her fridge (or in the winter on the roof of her hut) until her next journey.

Another "must" on Luisa's menu is a very cheap canned fish, which she shares with her cats. There are always a few cans that can be found in her hut. The rest of her menu is what she grows herself: some beets and potatoes in winter; cucumbers, cherries, and apples in summer. Luxury items from the Hesed food package are stretched throughout the month: sugar, oil, pasta, chicken or fish, milk, and cheese products. Recently, the Hesed mobile has started to bring her bowls of fresh drinking water, as there is no clean source of it available nearby.

How big is her living space?

Twelve square meters [approximately 129 square feet].

Is there any furniture in the house, and if so, what?

Luisa's hut is basically one room. It is so small that it hardly accommodates an old bed, a refrigerator, and an old wooden box used as a table. The rest of the space is taken by the ancient coal furnace. There are no chairs or sofas; Luisa's bed doubles as a chair.

Does she have a TV and/or radio, and if so, does she use either?
There is a forty-year-old TV set and an even older radio in her hut, which have one or two channels each, and poor reception. Luisa says it's enough for her, as the electricity doesn't work well anyway, and so she does not watch TV or listen to the radio often. When she does, she prefers musical concerts.

Does she ever interact with neighbors?
Luisa lives in an area of summer houses, most of which are unoccupied during the winter. Luisa is completely isolated, and the only social contact she has is with the Hesed workers who come to deliver food and water, or to help her with the furnace. Although in the summer more people are in the area, they are usually not interested in her company. I assume they find her quite eccentric and are busy with their own gardens, as is the custom in the region. There is one family that has a dacha nearby, and from time to time in summer, when she asks, they bring her an extra loaf of fresh bread from the city.

One Jew. Eccentric. Alone. Out of sight. But not forgotten by the Jewish world.

Yankl (September 15, 2002)

Recently we hired someone with a mandate unique (or nearly so) in the Jewish sphere. He was told to go to the far reaches of the world (actually, to the far ends of the former Soviet Union, and that is *far*) to find "new Jews."

This term has multiple meanings, depending on the context. For us, it refers to Jews who live so far from the loci of Jewish life in the FSU that they are completely disconnected to the renaissance happening throughout that land. Following are some excerpts from the report our new colleague submitted on his first field trip:

We traveled to the Komi Republic and visited the cities Syktyvkar, Ukhta, and Vorkuta. The Komi Republic is a territory of 416,000 square kilometers [approximately 160,000 square miles]. Vorkuta, the northernmost town of the republic, is 160 kilometers [100 miles] north of the Arctic Circle, where winter temperatures reach minus 50 degrees Celsius. Many of the Jews in these places were prisoners in the Gulag and never left.

We arrived in Vorkuta on August 19, late at night. It is not particularly comfortable to stay in hotel rooms that lack hot water, but this is what they had arranged for us. We knew that the mayor of the town, Igor Shpektor, was a Jew, as I had spoken to him several weeks earlier. Unfortunately, the day we arrived he was called to Moscow unexpectedly, so we were received by Mikhail Voloshkin, a deputy mayor – who also turned out to be a Jew.

From his office, Voloshkin called all the departments of the city administration to ask who knew of Jews. I can hardly believe this happened, even in the retelling. Please imagine the situation in this northern Russian town, where people were loath to talk about Jews for generations: suddenly the telephone rings and a voice of officialdom asks, "Are there any Jews in your department?" It was a question that would have instilled great fear in this place not all that long ago.

At first, the question was met with silence. Several people asked for time to think about it and called back. One answer puzzled the deputy mayor: He was told that the director of the Youth Palace is a Jew. He said this could not be so, because he had known her for over fifteen years, and never "suspected her of being a Jew." He could not remember any indication that she and he shared a heritage.

You should have seen their meeting. They kissed each other and he asked how it could be that he never knew that she was a Jew. She responded that he had never asked!

We decided to convene a meeting of all these newly identified Jews in her living room that evening. People who lived in the same town and had known one another for years were finding out for the first time that these friends were Jewish. A Jewish organization was formed, and a Hesed operation will shortly be in place. The mayor estimates that there are one thousand Jews in the town, although I am a bit more cautious in my estimates. Now they will be organized, and who knows what will come of it?

Indeed. But that was not all.

At the end of the evening an elderly man approached me and asked me to come to his home the next day. It was a strange request in that environment, but he almost begged me to do so, so I agreed.

When I arrived the next morning, he took me to his very small backyard, carrying a shovel. After a few minutes of digging, I heard the shovel hit something hard. He maneuvered around it and brought out of the ground a metal case, about half a meter high. He opened it and then took out wads of wool that were clearly protecting something. When he finally pulled out the contents of the box I was stunned. He told me the following about his own background:

"I am a Jew from Vilna. I grew up in a very Jewish home, in what was a very Jewish city. You know what they called Vilna – 'The Jerusalem of Lithuania.' We had a wonderful life…until the war.

"When the Nazis occupied the city, it was almost impossible to leave. We thought we were too late. But my mother insisted that my sister and I go. 'Go anywhere,' she said. 'But don't stay here.' I was sixteen and my sister was fourteen. We left just hours after my mother urged us to go. When we said goodbye, my father gave me this miniature Torah. It fit into my coat pocket.

"We went east and just kept going. For almost a month we did not stop. My sister fell ill, and within two days I had to bury her. I kept running. I knew one thing: the further I ran from that place – the Vilna in which I had grown up, and which I loved – the safer I would be.

"I won't tell you the whole story of my flight. I settled here in Vorkuta. I never married. After the war, I tried to contact my family but heard nothing back. I lived my life quietly. I bothered no one and no one bothered me. I knew that there were some Jews who had survived the war in the USSR, but to be honest I did not search them out. I was proud to be a Jew in my heart, but I could not live again with the threats. And so, my identity stayed in my heart. I made no efforts to contact other Jews, or to identify as one.

"Several years after the war, I decided to bury this Torah scroll that my father gave to me the night we were separated. To be honest, during Stalin's time it could have gotten me a jail term, or worse. I gave it a real funeral. I remembered some Hebrew from my childhood and recited those prayers.

"Each year in the fall, I would pick a day – I considered it my Yom Kippur – to sit down as long as I could next to this burial site and remember everything that was lost to me.

"You must understand; I thought I was the end – that I was one of the few surviving Jews, and certainly the only Jew here. I have had no contact with Jews or Jewish life. But what I did through the years was a way of preserving what I thought was to be erased from the world upon my death.

"You can imagine how I felt when I was told last week that there would be a meeting of the Jews of this city. To be honest, I was not sure I would come into the hall. I know things have changed, but I am tired, and still a bit afraid. With my personal history, and at my age, it is not easy to change something like that. My head said to stay outside the hall. My legs brought me in.

"I have no use for this Torah. You take it. Give it to Jews who will know how to use it and tell them it is from Yankl of Vilna. That's all I ask."

Aldis (April 17, 2009)

There are few survivors from the wartime ghettos in Belarus. On rare occasions, someone managed to leave the ghetto and save himself. Even those who somehow did leave the ghetto knew that they had escaped into a hostile world, where at any moment they could be caught again by the Germans or handed over to the Germans by antisemitic Belarusians. The only chance of survival was to be hidden by a friendly peasant who was fully aware that if he were caught, he would be shot, together with the Jew he was hiding.

Sometimes one reached a partisan group in the forests that was willing to accept a Jew, but most such groups were unwilling to include Jews in their ranks.

Eric Galperin lived with his family in a shtetl called Koidonova, now Derzinsk. Soon after the German occupation began in the fall of 1941, the Jews were collected in a ghetto and later marched to their place of execution. Eric's mother pushed him out of the marching column and told him to run into the nearby woods. Eric, who was seven years old at the time, did as he was told. He spent his days hiding in the woods and searched for food at night. He was afraid to visit a village during daylight.

After several months of successfully evading capture, he was caught by a Latvian police officer, who handed him over to a Latvian battalion in the service of the Germans, with orders to shoot him. It was never made clear to them that Eric was a Jew.

Eric was incarcerated for several days. One night, he heard his Latvian jailers talking among themselves and understood that they would shoot him the next morning as a suspected "undesirable." When the group broke up, one of the Latvians struck up a conversation with the young prisoner, and Eric asked him if he was indeed to be executed. The man told him that he would not be shot for reasons that he chose not to share. He advised Eric not to mention his former name and never to shower in the presence of other Latvians from this battalion. He gave him the name Aldis and took him under his wing. The man protected him and was able to shield him from his fellow guards.

Because of the efforts of this protector, Eric was eventually adopted by the Latvian battalion as their mascot. The Latvians did police work for the Germans, and when necessary, operated the machine guns when Jews from the ghettos were brought to the killing fields. Eric knew this. In fact, he knew personally some of the Jews who had been killed by those he now "represented."

Eric, now Aldis, was given an army uniform and traveled with the Latvian battalion. At the end of the war, the Latvians returned to Riga, and Aldis went with them. One of the families of the Latvian group adopted this young Latvian orphan. He lived with them and went to school with other young Latvian boys. Throughout this period, he mentioned nothing about his past and took care not to reveal his Jewish roots. Meanwhile, the men of the battalion were afraid that one day the Soviets, who now occupied Latvia, would find out about their collaboration with the Nazi occupiers during the war. The Soviets knew of widespread Latvian collaboration, and regularly made efforts to identify and punish those who had cooperated with the Germans. The group that had sponsored Eric decided to emigrate to Australia before they were caught, and in the postwar turbulence and confusion, the families escaped, taking Aldis with them as the son of the family that had adopted him. By that time, he no longer remembered his own name or his original family name, although he did remember the village where his family had once lived.

In Australia, he became a skilled electrician, married one of the Latvian girls of the group, and settled with other Latvians in a small town near Melbourne. The group helped him build a house. Aldis felt settled. His community never raised questions about his past. He explained his circumcision to his wife as a medical procedure done in childhood. He had a profession, earned a good living, and lived with his family and friends.

But he did not have peace of mind. Frequently, things reminded him of his past. He knew that he was Jewish. He vaguely remembered his family. He remembered the name of the village in Belarus where his original family once lived. He did not remember his family name, nor even his own name or those of his siblings. He did, however, remember that his father had been the only dealer in furs in their small town because furs were always hanging on stretched strings in their courtyard. He assumed that his family had met the same fate as the other Jews of their town during the Shoah. Even though he was now living as a Christian Latvian among Latvians, in his heart he knew he was a Jew.

On a trip to Melbourne, he visited a Holocaust memorial. He told the person in charge what he remembered of his life history and asked her to send a letter to the Holocaust Museum's office in Minsk. Maybe they could find out something about his family, or piece together a personal history from the scraps of information he recalled. A letter from the Melbourne Holocaust memorial was sent to Frieda Reisman, who by now had assumed responsibility for the Holocaust Museum's office in the Jewish campus of Minsk, capital of today's independent Belarus. Frieda herself was a ghetto survivor who had published a book about her survival and that of a friend who had escaped from the ghetto with her.

Frieda began searching for connections. So many years later, with so few surviving documents or memories, it was not a simple task. The shtetl had developed into a small city. Records had been destroyed in the war.

One day Frieda's publisher visited her, and at the end of their meeting, she read the Melbourne letter to him. To her surprise and shock, the publisher burst into tears when he heard the contents of the letter. The publisher was named Eric Galperin, and his father had come from the small town of Koidonova…and had been the only fur dealer in that town.

The Eric Galperin of Belarus took up the story for me from that point. His mother and the other children in the family had indeed been killed. The father, the furrier, was sent to a slave labor camp, where he worked until he was transferred to Auschwitz. He survived Auschwitz, and after the war he married a woman who had also survived Auschwitz. He had a daughter who died at a young age and a son whom he named Eric – the publisher now telling the story in Frieda's office – after his other son whom, he assumed, had been killed. The man in Australia was therefore his half-brother. The father, who was no longer alive, had left two sons, both named Eric.

It did not take long for a connection to be made through the two relevant offices in Minsk and Melbourne. The Latvian wife of Aldis (Eric) was shocked when she heard the story and was not at all happy to find out that she had married a Jew. Hatred of Jews ran deep in this community of former Nazi collaborators. They had no interest in rewriting history. While they did not advertise their wartime behavior, most did not regret it in any way. The community demanded that Aldis – now Eric Galperin – leave their town and repay them every penny they had given him to build his house.

Aldis/Eric sold his house and repaid all he owed the Latvian group. He moved to a new area near Melbourne, where he could settle down without everyday reminders of his erstwhile neighbors and former friends. His wife remained behind with the Latvians, and they were divorced.

Frieda Reisman wrote to Aldis and asked him for a photo, which she subsequently showed to Eric Galperin. Eric saw in that photo the image of his late father. They were very much alike. There could be no doubt that the two Erics were brothers. Aldis and Eric soon talked on the phone, although they barely had a language in common. The first few phone calls were filled with tears.

Aldis came to Minsk to meet his brother. After returning to Australia, he remarried, and he now knows who he is and proudly lives as a Jew. He has not forgotten that the Latvian group in Australia saved his life. He acknowledges a great debt to them and is torn over his relationship with them. But he could no longer live among the people who may have shot his own family, and who most probably shot thousands of others because they were Jews. Aldis visited Minsk four times last year.

Lena (June 6, 2008)

Lena Kossovskaya is from Uzgen, a small town in Kyrgyzstan. She has no living relatives, and most of the small group of her contemporaries in the town died years ago. But she would not characterize herself as lonely. She has family and friends with her at all times. They are just not physically present. Every morning, after putting her room in order and after she has had her tea and bread, soaking the bread in the tea to soften it, she sits down to her daily preoccupation.

She has a shoebox full of family photos. She does not know exactly how many; she has never counted them. She recognizes everyone in these photos – all of them are members of her family.

Lena removes the photos from the box one by one, careful not to sully or damage them. Her eyesight has become poorer over the years, but she can still make out the people in the photographs. The pile of photos is divided according to the branches of her family tree – cousins, uncles, aunts – and acquaintances. She insists that she remembers all of them clearly, even though over sixty years have passed since she left her native Baranovichi in Belarus to escape the German armies.

Lena talks to each photo separately, conversing with the person who appears in the photo. She loves to talk to her brothers and sisters, who are no longer alive. She can talk to them for hours, reminding them of various incidents that happened in the family when they were young. She reminds her sister, Feiga, about a new dress their mother bought for her, but not for Lena. She tells Feiga that the dress was beautiful – the rose ribbon around the waist was a lovely contrast to the white material, and the lace collar was delicate and dainty – and that she remembers clearly wearing it for the first time on Shabbat. These chats with Feiga can last over an hour. Lena discusses everything with her, even events that occurred after Feiga was no longer alive. She argues with her sister, tells her a funny story, and laughs heartily, convinced that Feiga shares her merriment.

After she has had a long conversation with Feiga, she pulls out another photo. It's of her cousin from a village near Baranovichi. Lena's uncle was the tailor in the village, and their family lived reasonably well. There was no synagogue in the village, so her uncle, the aunt, and their four children would come to Baranovichi for Jewish holidays and stay with Lena's family. Sitting at the table with her cousin's photo in hand, Lena has much to say. She remembers that her aunt made delicious cookies and apple cake. She remembers that she once had a real fight with her cousin, Sura, and scratched her. She remembers that her cousin was very clever in math and Russian literature and helped her do her homework. So there was much to talk about.

The morning until lunchtime was not long enough to glance at more than four or five photos. By midday, a warm lunch was brought for Lena from the Hesed. After lunch, she had to rest. She slept poorly at night and needed a break after her meal, but she went back to her photos afterward. Lena lived with all her family around her; she was never alone. So much had vanished in the ensuing years, yet her world remained intact…at least in her own mind.

When the war broke out, Lena was already a girl of fourteen. Her father was immediately mobilized and sent to the front. The family never knew what happened to him. There was no information about where he had been killed or where he was buried. He simply disappeared along with millions of others. The army and the government owed no one an explanation, and none was forthcoming.

When her father was mobilized, Lena's mother took the children – Lena, her older sister Rosalia, and her younger brother Sasha, who was just a child – and left Baranovichi to escape from the German armies. They walked eastward with thousands of other refugees for days on end. The mother took with her some jewelry, whatever money she had in the house, and a bundle of clothing for the children. The many items she wanted to take with them included the box of photos. Most of their belongings were lost or stolen on the way. They walked, and they traveled by cart and by train. They had no particular destination in mind. Their only plan was to move eastward ahead of the advancing German army. Ultimately, they wound up in a Siberian town and found a room.

Lena's mother was sent to work in a factory, and the children attended school. The cold that first winter was almost unbearable. Everything was frozen, and no trains came during the winter. They suffered terribly. Food was scarce, and they were isolated and alone, with no word from their relatives. Lena's mother finally obtained permission to travel to the south, ostensibly to reunite with family, although they had no specific destination in mind. The real reason for the trek was to find weather conditions they could tolerate – anywhere. The prospect of another winter in Siberia was unbearable.

They had to wait until the ice melted on the main river and get a place on a boat sailing in the direction of the train connection to Tashkent, with several stops along the way. There was an epidemic on the boat, and Rosalia became very ill. Without doctors and without medication, the girl succumbed to her illness. She was to be buried at the next port of call. When they arrived, her mother was afraid to leave the boat with her remaining children, lest the boat depart without them, and there was no guarantee that they could continue their journey on some other boat if they were stranded. So mother could not bury her daughter.

Lena pauses and does not finish that part of her story. She continues on about their journey:

The family finally reached Tashkent. Thousands of Russians and many Jewish families were camped around the train station. Lena's mother, desperate to escape from the stench, the crowding, and the diseases, left with the children for the small town of Uzgen in Kyrgyzstan. Traveling from Tashkent to Uzgen today involves a border crossing, but at that time both cities were part of the USSR.

Their mother worked, and Lena and her brother studied. Years went by; Lena became a nurse, and Sasha qualified as an engineer, married a Russian woman, and left for Russia.

Lena's mother passed away in the late fifties, and Lena was left alone. She never married. Her small apartment – one room and a kitchen – was adequate for her. When the Kyrgyz currency was severely devalued, however, the money she had hidden away lost its value. With the cost of living increasing each year, Lena found it very difficult to manage.

Lena had no complaints. Her basic needs were taken care of by her small pension and the help she received from the Jewish people via the Joint and Hesed, although she had no idea who provided this help. Some of her neighbors whispered suspiciously that American Jews took care of her. She was glad to receive the assistance and did not question the woman who visited her with the meals that sustained her. To her, the identity of "the kind angel" was immaterial.

Lena contends that she does not live in Uzgen any longer; now she is back in Baranovichi. She regularly visits her family and speaks with them, connecting through her photos. Most of all she loves to talk to her mother. She tells her everything. She reminds her how they traveled from Siberia. She describes the Jewish holidays they had in Baranovichi when they were all together. She complains about being blamed for misbehavior when in fact her sister was guilty. She thinks that too much fuss was made of Sasha when he was small. She complains to her mother that Sasha never writes to her. She does not even know where he lives. Maybe her mother can tell her. The day is too short for everything she wants to tell her mother, her sister, and her cousins. It takes a long time to go through all the photos in the shoebox. Sometimes weeks or months.

Lena is never lonely, never without her family. She lives in her past but to her, it is very much the present. She is surrounded by all her loved ones. That helps her forget the hardships. She has her photos, a life that was…and to Lena, still is today, in her little apartment, in her shoebox. And she has the international Jewish organization that makes it all possible.

CHAPTER 4

Places

Siberia (November 14, 2003)

Let's start with some very unsystematic ruminations on Siberia and its Jews: This can't begin without some reference to Siberia's size – six thousand miles east to west; five million square miles in total. If it were detached from Russia, it would still be far and away the largest country on earth. When the sun rises on its eastern boundary, it is setting on its western border. It contains three of the world's great rivers, each one with a basin larger than Western Europe. Kolyma, site of one of the many camps of the Gulag, registered a temperature in the last century of minus 97 degrees Fahrenheit.

JDC reaches twenty-one communities of significant size in Siberia. Every one of them qualifies as a "periphery" in terms of size and distance from a major concentration of Jews.

How did Jews wind up there? Sofia's family history gives us an idea about the sundry origins of today's Siberian Jewry. Her maternal great-grandfather was a "cantonist." Young boys, generally around the age of twelve, were pressed into service in the czar's army in the second quarter of the nineteenth century for a period of twenty-five years. The notion was that through this conscription they would become candidates for conversion, or at least shed their problematic (for the authorities) Jewish identities. It's a fascinating chapter in Russian-Jewish history and was the original driver of the growth of Jewish communities in Siberian towns. The cantonists also laid the foundations for the Jewish community of Finland, almost all of whose indigenous Jews are descendants of demobilized cantonists. When demobilized, many of the soldiers remained in their Siberian cities of service, Sofia's cantonist maternal great-grandfather among them.

Her father came to Siberia from Ukraine ahead of the Nazi blitzkrieg in 1941. Most Jews of his kind spent the war years outside the areas conquered by the Germans. At war's end, or soon after, many returned to their original home regions. Sofia's father stayed in Siberia.

Her maternal grandmother, Alina, was born and lived in pre-revolution St. Petersburg. A knock on her door in the late thirties, during the time of Stalin's repression, began an odyssey capped by a show trial for "betraying the motherland." Although she was a devoted party member, her Communist affiliation was meaningless at the trial. A fourteen-year prison sentence in the Gulag ensued.

The Gulag generally meant Siberia. It was an inaccessible, forbidding place, which made it ideally suited as a place of exile. It was a netherworld that conjured up visions of misery and cruelty in the minds of anyone who lived through the Stalinist era. Dostoyevsky referred to Siberia as "a prison without a roof," which turned out to be prescient given the expansion of the Gulag system during Stalin's time. Most who were sent there did not return, and any who did return were generally scarred for life from the experience. Even if one survived the incredibly harsh winters, there was little to look forward to with the change of seasons. The summer climate could be tolerated, but gnats, mosquitoes, and ticks came together to make the summer months as brutal as the winters in their own way. On release during a Khrushchev amnesty, Alina was "too tired to go west," and stayed put in Siberia.

Finally, there was Sofia's husband, Andrei: Born in Belarus, he was lured to Siberia to work at a secret nuclear research plant. And herein lies another dimension of Jewish Siberia. This vast territory contains incredible amounts of valuable natural resources: wood, diamonds, expensive ores, and metals, and of course some of the world's richest oil fields – all of this in some of the harshest physical conditions on the planet. Engineers were needed to turn these resources into marketable commodities. To overcome the obstacle of the forbidding conditions, generous salaries and subsidized food and consumer goods were offered to entice an educated populace to settle there. Many Jews accepted these offers, Andrei among them. The standard of living was quite high.

With the collapse of the Soviet Union, the subsidies gradually evaporated. Inefficient factories and processing plants were shuttered. Salaries shrank to make businesses more competitive, and unemployment rose. Without assets to sell, many Siberians – among them a disproportionately high number of educated Jews – were stranded, without the resources required to resettle elsewhere.

The post-Soviet reality has not been kind to Siberians, and especially to the Jews among them who desire Jewish connections. Jewish roots in the region do not run deep. Many in the community come from families that were alienated from things Jewish for several generations due to their unique histories. To inspire Jewish revival in these contexts is particularly difficult – and poignant when it does occur.

We face unique challenges to provide the support that Siberian Jewry desperately needs. Some Siberian Jews live in areas that are inaccessible for months at a time. But they require assistance, and they receive it. We are regularly asked to approve expenditures from that area for the renting of dogs and sleds to make deliveries of food and medicine. Allocations balloon in September and May, before and after the unforgiving winter, when vast amounts of aid need to be transported before roads close or immediately after they are opened.

From many, the feedback that we get concerns the importance of "connections" – reminders that, although they are far away, they have not been abandoned by the Jewish world. Distance, climate, and environment are not the forbidding impediments they once were. Volunteers in cities like Novosibirsk and Tomsk and Archangelsk stay in touch with the hard to reach. University-age Jewish students travel the region to arrange Passover Seders and Chanukah gatherings. Through determination and passion, supportive communities are established. Jewish life is being nurtured in this most unlikely place.

* * *

A personal postscript: In the early nineties, I traveled to the Siberian city of Khabarovsk during the last week of December, for the dedication of a training program that JDC established to give local Jewish communal leaders some of the skills they needed to properly run their communities. I went in full attire – bearskin hat, *gotkes* (long underwear), and thermal gloves. The centerpiece of my outfit was a new coat, a gift of my parents (see encyclopedia entry for

"Jewish mother"), which would offer the full protection needed against the elements. The coat had a label inside that noted that it was good for temperatures down to minus 45 degrees (Fahrenheit, or minus 43 degrees Celsius). When I saw that before I left the enveloping warmth of my Jerusalem home, I burst into laughter. The prospect that the temperature would ever be so low was preposterous. The note, which read like a warning, seemed like a joke. I showed the label to my wife, Ruth, and asked her rhetorically, "What does this mean? If the temperature dips to minus 50 degrees, the coat won't work?"

At the end of the eleven-hour flight from Moscow to Khabarovsk, we got off the plane into minus-52-degree-Fahrenheit temperatures on the tarmac.

The coat indeed proved to stand up only to temperatures as low as minus 45.

Turkmenistan (December 13, 2002)

A couple of weeks ago, an attempt was made to assassinate the president of Turkmenistan, Saparmurat Niyazov. I won't go into detail about the court intrigues surrounding his regime, but it is an opportunity to discuss aspects of our work in two little-known Soviet successor states, Turkmenistan and Tajikistan. The former is an enormous country in the middle of Asia that is largely desert. Most of the population is concentrated in the capital, Ashkhabad, known for its hand-woven rugs, indigenous ponies, and prodigious reserves of natural gas.

Niyazov is one of the region's last surviving dictators, ruling with an iron fist and not brooking any dissent. He is president for life and has fostered a Stalin-like cult of personality. There are about three hundred Jews whom we know of, mostly in and around the capital. They are descendants of Persian Jewish families. The border with Iran is visible from the country's capital. There is no Jewish community in Turkmenistan to speak of, although most of the country's Jews do know of each other. There does not appear to be any discrimination against Jews, and Turkmenistan maintains diplomatic relations with Jerusalem. Standards of living are quite low, despite the vast quantities of natural gas. Wealth is concentrated in the hands of the few who are close to the presidential administration.

JDC sends in food packages, primarily from neighboring Uzbekistan. While travel is technically not forbidden, it is difficult for citizens of neighboring countries to procure visas to Turkmenistan, and virtually impossible for people from the West. Local Uzbek Jews arrange to bring in the packages on an as-needed basis. There are no efforts to introduce Jewish cultural activities. Local Jews are fearful of anything that would draw potentially unwelcome attention to them. In many ways this place is in a time warp hearkening back to the most difficult years of the Soviet era, in which fear permeated society at every level. This fear keeps Jews apart from one another and, of course, also keeps them from developing any foreign connections.

I was in Ashkhabad during a brief thaw in the country's political situation, when visas were granted to Westerners for the first time since the nation gained its independence in 1991. That thaw lasted only about six months, after which the country reverted to its previous isolationism. Our efforts to contact local Jews while there were unsuccessful; they were presumably frightened that contact with foreigners would put them at risk. Telephone calls ended abruptly when our callers identified themselves.

Ashkhabad was unlike anywhere else I have ever been. Pictures of the "president for life" are ubiquitous. In the center of town is a towering statue of Niyazov made of pure gold, set on an enormous plinth and visible for miles around. He is standing erect, with arms outstretched. The statue revolves to always face the sun as it moves through the sky: the sun, welcomed to Turkmenistan by its leader for life.

To give a sense of how bizarre it all is, for a foreigner to set an appointment with a local is difficult, requiring procedures unlike those followed anywhere else in the world. The names of the months and the days of the week have all been renamed after family members of the "benevolent leader." Thus, if you don't know his late mother's name, you can't set an appointment to meet someone on Monday. Locals are forbidden from responding to efforts to refer to days of the week as they are known elsewhere around the world. It is a cult of personality perhaps rivaled only by the "benevolent leader" of the hermit kingdom of North Korea.

Tajikistan (December 13, 2002)

An even more difficult situation than that of Turkmenistan, albeit without the cult of personality of Niyazov, is to be found in Tajikistan, also a Soviet successor republic located in Asia. Niyazov keeps things in Turkmenistan under control (with an occasional lapse for assassination attempts), but Tajikistan is the Wild West (or East, if you will). Even before the collapse of the Soviet Union in December 1991, civil war raged in Tajikistan among rival ethnic groups. For all intents and purposes, the central government in the capital, Dushanbe, does not function. Visas can be had without too much trouble, but to phrase it delicately, there is not much demand for them. Several times since the establishment of the country's independence, the "last Jew" was rescued from Tajikistan…until more subsequently surfaced. Here, too, we send in food packages, primarily from Georgia or from one of the communities in the North Caucasus region of Russia. We provide help to about seventy-two people on an ongoing basis. Occasionally we are called upon to assist a person who has a serious medical condition, and when that person emerges from Tajikistan, we refer him or her to a Hesed in the nearest Jewish community.

The Jews here are primarily "Tatim," or Mountain Jews. While their history is hard to ascertain, they are akin to Sephardim and more traditional than their Ashkenazic brethren in other regions in the FSU. While Jewish communal life was decimated during the last decade of strife, some still understand the concept of mutual assistance. Also, from time to time we are asked to provide religious articles.

I was recently reminded of our efforts to fulfill the request of what was a community of several thousand Jews there in the early 1990s. That winter, the only matzah-baking factory in the country was either destroyed or simply collapsed due to its age (and presumably a lack of maintenance). We were asked to ship in matzot, not an easy task in a country with such a difficult security situation.

We explored several options and ultimately settled on the only viable way of bringing in matzot: we had to rent a train. The price of this rental was actually quite reasonable, until we were about to sign the contract. Then we were told that we needed to post a bond of over one hundred thousand dollars. The concern? That the train would be stolen after it delivered its load in Dushanbe!

Khmelnytskyi (February 17, 2002)

In Khmelnytskyi, a city in western Ukraine, there is a lovely Hesed, with a charismatic and dynamic director, that serves twenty-two hundred clients.

The city is in the heart of what was once the Pale of Settlement. Some of the towns and villages were more than 50 percent Jewish in the post-revolutionary period.

The Hesed is virtually the only Jewish act in town and serves as the flagship of the Jewish community. In its building there is a small room that serves as a Jewish museum. One of the items in this museum is an official document with a Soviet stamp on it.

It is a birth certificate issued by the local government in the 1930s, and it is printed in Russian and Yiddish! Holding that document in hand was a humbling experience – testimony to a milieu in the early Soviet period that was so Jewish that official, government-produced documents for the entire

An official Soviet birth certificate, in Yiddish and Russian. Birth certificates such as this were issued by local authorities in the Ukraine during the 1920s and 1930s. (Photo credit: The Central Archives for the History of the Jewish People, Jerusalem, RU-2187. The author wishes to thank Benyamin Lukin, who located this image in the Archive).

population were issued not just in Russian, but also in Yiddish. And it is sobering to recall while holding this bilingual document that within a very short time after it was printed, the Jewish presence it represents was virtually obliterated – a job begun with the purges of the Stalinist period and finished a short time later with the Nazi occupation. And here we are, seventy years later, trying to help the local Jews reclaim at least a part of that very rich world.

Minsk (May 13, 2011)

In 1986, I moved with my wife, Ruth, and our six-month-old son, Avishai, to Vienna, to begin a stint as the director of the JDC office there. Coming from a midsized city in Pennsylvania to a central European capital was quite disorienting. I want to focus here on one aspect of that disorientation and relate it to our contemporary work in the FSU.

Vienna had a small Jewish community that at the time numbered about six thousand souls. On the surface, Jews played a very small role in public life there in 1986. There was a Jewish bakery and a kosher butcher to supply the needs of the Jews there. There were a handful of synagogues, a home for seniors, and community offices. But aside from that, unless you knew where to look, one did not come in contact with the Jews of Vienna. They were a tiny minority who kept a low profile in a large, cosmopolitan city.

On Friday morning, several days after moving in and setting up our apartment, I made my way to the JDC office, which was located near the downtown area. At one point on my journey, I noticed something out of the corner of my eye that made me stop and get off my bicycle (my preferred mode of transportation in that traffic-choked city) for a better look. In the bakery window were challot, the traditional breads for Shabbat and holiday meals.

I passed that bakery every day of that week, and I was sure that I had never seen the braided bread. Here it was – Friday. Challot. In Vienna.

I went into the shop and asked the woman behind the counter what the bread was called, and was it a new kind of bread, as I had not seen it previously. (Full disclosure: I was only three days into German lessons, so that's what I was *trying* to ask.)

The woman laughed at the suggestion that this was new. This was not a new type of bread at all. "Quite the contrary," she said. "It is a Vienna tradition, the origin of which is unknown. It is baked and sold only on Fridays, and the origin of its name is unclear. It is called *barkhus brot*."

It was certainly not unclear to me. Braided bread. Only on Friday. With a special name: *barkhus* – a name suspiciously close to *berachos*, i.e., Hebrew for "blessings" in the Ashkenazic pronunciation (as in *boruch Attah*...). It was my first exposure to Jewish Vienna – that is, a city once of many Jews, almost bereft of Jews today.

I later learned of a term used in the downtown market to describe a true bargain. Longtime Viennese merchants referred to it as a *metsiah*. A quick survey the first time I heard it yielded no merchant who knew the origin of the term. Each correctly identified it as unique to Wiener Deutsch, the dialect of German spoken in Vienna. But none knew it came from the Yiddish word for "bargain."

Vienna's prewar Jewish population was about two hundred thousand – enough to leave its mark on Viennese culture and language, to create Jewish artifacts, and more – all that is left in that city, which once had a major Jewish presence.

Recently, I was in Belarus. Like many other places in the FSU, Belarus is a counterpoint to Vienna: Belarus has a great number of Jews but few articles of Judaica. We stayed in a hotel with a Jewish manager and ate in a restaurant owned by a Jew. We had a Jewish guide from a local tourist bureau. There are Jews in the media, in business, and in the arts. Lots of Jews, but little in the way of Jewish markers that identify Belarusian Jews as Jews. Their language is not a Jewish language. They are not conversant with Jewish culture. There are few Jewish books. And so on. Many Jews, but not a strong Jewish presence, in contrast to Vienna, where there is a noticeable Jewish presence but few Jews.

This made our visit to the Belarus Jewish Museum all the more significant. It was a peek into the Jewish past of that region, via artifacts and photos, that showed how really Jewish that area once was. And it sets a standard for what it one day might become. At least that is the wish of Anna, the director. And she leaves no room for skepticism.

The museum is on the Minsk Jewish campus, a facility purchased and renovated for community use by JDC a number of years ago. The term "museum" may be a bit of an overstatement: It takes up a room and a half.

But for Anna, who runs it, size means nothing. Here are reflections on some of the items and what they mean today:

There are two wooden doors on exhibition. They are tall – too tall, in fact, to serve as the doors for a private house. They look quite worn and, ultimately, out of place: What is their connection with a museum of Jewish life in Belarus? Anna explained that the doors are not to a house, but to a town. Small towns often had walls for protection, with one set of doors for those coming and going that were generally locked at night. She gave us the name of this town, which was located in what is now northern Belarus, but that belonged at various times in history to other states, among them Poland, Lithuania, Russia, and Ukraine. I couldn't write fast enough, however, so the name of the town was lost.

Anna pointed out that these doors were like many in the region from that period well into the early twentieth century. She instructed us to look carefully at the upper right half of the doorpost: due to the large number of Jews in the town, as in many towns like this, there was an indentation where a mezuzah was to be hung.

"You know why a mezuzah needs to be hung on the upper third of a doorpost?" she asked, and then answered her own question. "People were poor, and many were reduced to begging. Receiving support from others can be humiliating. But every Jew passing the mezuzah in those days kissed it. To do so, they had to lift their eyes. So, the beggars came to ask for support with their heads up, standing upright and radiating pride because of the mezuzah, and not with their heads hanging down in shame that they need a handout."

And then she added three words that connected these doors, the mezuzah, and contemporary Jewish life in the FSU: "Like with Hesed."

There was a laundry "machine" – two boards through which wet laundry was squeezed to dry and press it. Not particularly notable. We've all seen these, either in early frontier-life reconstructions or in movies. But, Anna told us, this was not used for laundry all year round: For a period of about two weeks, the Jews transformed these washing items into something else: handheld instruments to produce matzah. The dough was prepared in accordance with tradition, and then it was rolled through this instrument to make it flat so that it would bake easily and produce matzah according to Passover stringencies. "As a community, we are not wealthy, as they surely were not,"

Anna explained. "But we will depend on our ingenuity and resourcefulness to reconstruct Jewish life here, just as they made do with what they had to create a vibrant and fulfilling Jewish life."

There was a large, circular metal disk in the next exhibition. At its center was a hammer and sickle from the early 1920s, and it had a circumference of about two feet. It clearly had adorned a building, perhaps a newly constructed Communist Party headquarters in one of Belarus's larger cities. At its peak, in Cyrillic letters, were the words "Soviet Socialist Republic of Belarussia." But as the eyes traced the perimeter of the sign, there were other languages. In fact, the same words were written in the languages of the three other largest communities in Belarus at the time – Russian, Polish, and Yiddish. As noted earlier, in Ukraine, the Jewish presence was so large then that Yiddish was an official language. Government letterheads included Yiddish as one of their languages.

Some sections of a Torah scroll were on display, but they clearly had a peculiar history, as they were not in great condition. I immediately assumed that they had been hidden, perhaps underground, to keep them away from Nazis or others wanting to do the Jews harm.

It was disconcerting to hear the history of the scroll, which had been used as insulation in a house near Gomel built during the war. This was not all that surprising; it was not uncommon for antisemites to defile Torahs by using them for degrading, everyday purposes. This was a way to humiliate Jews by mistreating what was holy to them.

But this story had more to it. When the villager whose roof was insulated with the Torah scrolls redid his house six years ago, he uncovered the scroll, which had clearly been used by someone in a previous generation. He showed it around, hoping someone could identify it for him, as the letters were strange. An elder in his community suggested he approach "the Jews," which he did. When he learned what the item was, he took apart his entire roof and burrowed into the walls to retrieve as much of the parchment as he could and then returned the scrolls to the community in western Belarus. He handed over the materials and asked for nothing in return. The local Jewish community, for its part, took up a collection to reimburse the man. Rather than expressing their sorrow and anger at the Torah's fate, they resolved to thank this person in an appropriate manner for returning the scroll to them.

And so they collected the funds to repair the roof and contracted with a construction company to reinsulate and redo the man's house. Many of those Jews who contributed to this effort live on miniscule monthly pensions. "We are not a wealthy community," Anna explained. "But we are a proud one. And one that knows how to thank those who have done something noteworthy on our behalf."

There were many more objects that benefited from Anna's comments. There was a *ketubah*, a marriage contract, from the late 1960s. In established Jewish communities these are often quite elaborate. This one was very simple and handwritten in very small letters. At the time the Soviet authorities had forbidden all religious ceremonies, so the writing of this *ketubah* was done furtively.

There was also a train ticket from czarist times with a Jewish star on it – this time not as a source of pride. It was a round-trip ticket from Minsk to St. Petersburg. The latter was a city closed to Jews before the Bolshevik Revolution, except under extraordinary circumstances. When a Jew was allowed to purchase a ticket for St. Petersburg, it was generally to complete a business deal. A ticket like this had to be purchased, which marked the bearer as a Jew. It was a signal to the conductor that this Jew was permitted to be in St. Petersburg, albeit for a limited time.

The final exhibit was a picture of what looked like an extended family. The faces were quite small because the group was so large, but Anna made it easy for us: "There are seventy-one souls in this picture, sixty-eight of whom are Jews. If you look carefully, in the middle of the picture you will see an older woman. Short, white haired, well dressed. The picture is because of her." Our interest was piqued. The picture was clearly contemporary, not sepia tinted like the others.

As a child during the war, Charlotte, the white-haired woman, was hidden by a Polish family about twenty-two miles west of Minsk. They saved her life. After the war, she was reclaimed by local Jews, as she was the only member of her family who had survived. She eventually made her way to Florida, where she married and raised a family. Sixty-eight of those people in the picture were four generations of that family – Charlotte and her children, grandchildren, and great-grandchildren. The other three people in the picture were the children of the righteous gentiles who had saved her life.

Among Charlotte's descendants were rabbis and teachers, doctors and accountants, a composer, and numerous academics. Three of her grandchildren have started businesses by inventing medical devices that are now in widespread use. Each of them represents a Jew who was saved, through whom humanity was made richer. Additional pictures showed books on Jewish thought and culture written or edited by members of Charlotte's family.

At this point Anna said to two of our JDC staff, "This is what you do too." Anna had heard our introduction to the visit, reminding the members of our group about the meta-goal of JDC in its work in the FSU: to reclaim Jews for the Jewish people. "Not in the same way. Not physically. But in other ways. We Soviet Jews were lost. And now, through the JCC, and Hillel, and Hesed volunteers, and the preschool, and the young leadership programs, and family camps, Jews are being reclaimed for the Jewish people. Perhaps in two generations we'll be able to hang another picture here – of a large family that stems from one Jew in our time who was 'lost' and then reclaimed through our efforts now."

Kovno (October 7, 2011)

Kaunas, Lithuania, USSR. September 1990. JDC had recently begun sending in staff to scout out the situation of Soviet Jewry, to identify possible areas of activity, and to help us think through what we wanted to accomplish in the region.

It was early September, several days before Rosh Hashanah, and I found myself in Kaunas, the second-largest city in what was then the Soviet Socialist Republic of Lithuania. Change was in the air. While the Soviet Union still existed – and few at that time would have predicted its dissolution a year later – the three Baltic states, of which Lithuania was one, were restive. Kaunas was a center of agitation, although our visit there was unrelated to the unrest. We were there to meet with Jews and to understand how they were organizing their nascent communities. Kaunas, known by Jews for generations as Kovno, had a community that was organized the moment that became possible under perestroika in the Soviet Union of the late 1980s. This was our first visit. We were curious to see what constituted leadership, and how these communities galvanized. What would their key institutions be? How would they care for the vulnerable? How would they organize educational institutions? In brief, how would they reconstitute themselves as a Jewish community?

The visit lasted for two very intense days, with meetings from morning until night. We questioned, we probed; sometimes we were harangued. Emotionally exhausted, we looked forward to sleep on the final night and to an early flight home the next day.

Just before our scheduled program ended, we were invited to visit the new museum of Jewish Kovno. The collection of artifacts was gathered in a small, dank, and musty room off the main section of the synagogue.

The museum itself did not contain any great treasures; those had long ago been pillaged or sold off to enterprising collectors. Individuals in the community had been encouraged to contribute any Judaica they had that was more than a generation old. Together in this room, these items constituted a window into Jewish culture and civilization. There were a few books, some ritual items, and a few pieces of Jewish-themed art. Sweet and moving, given the location, but one could only hope that this would not set the bar for what was to come for Soviet Jewry. At the time, none of us knew.

Just before we left, I noticed something that, from a distance, looked out of place. It was a printed document of calligraphy in Yiddish. The fact that it was in Yiddish was not a surprise. That was the lingua franca of the Jews in that region during the time it was printed. It looked almost like an invitation, which is exactly what it turned out to be. A closer look proved it to be one of the most moving Jewish artifacts I have ever seen, given its context, and one that haunts me to this day.

As I made my way slowly through it, it became apparent that it was an invitation to a fundraising ball. The money raised was to go "to help our Jewish brothers and sisters who are going through such a difficult time in Germany." The event would be held that October, and all funds would be supervised by "the Kovno coordinating council to help Jews in need." I don't remember the exact date of the ball, but I do remember the year: 1938.

This Jewish community was organizing to help its brothers and sisters who were in dire straits. Clearly, Kovno Jewry had members capable of providing assistance, at least at that moment in time.

Little more than two years later, Kovno would be occupied by the Soviets as a result of the Molotov-Ribbentrop agreement. And just a year after that, Kovno would be overrun by elite Nazi units. Those who issued the invitation, and all those who received it, had surely suffered one of three possible fates: small numbers would have survived the war in hiding or fighting with the partisans. A slightly larger number would have escaped eastward into the Soviet Union. Most would have been murdered.

I stared at that invitation for a long time, and I can still see it in my mind's eye. Not one of those people trying to help German Jewry could have guessed that in a short time, his or her fate would be so horrific. Even those who intuited war based on German propaganda had no inkling what that war would mean for themselves. You don't run a fundraising ball if you know, or even suspect, that you are soon to be in the same situation of need as those you propose to help.

Was this Jewish community naive? Was it burying its head in the sand to avoid confronting the reality all around it? The indications that war was imminent were there for all to see. Or was this simply a Jewish response? "If I have now, I must help now. My life will be directed by the positive and constructive."

* * *

As I write these lines, I have on my desk three Rosh Hashanah cards, each wishing a good new year to the recipient. They are part of a collection of historical cards I have gathered on my JDC travels and that I take out this time of year as we approach the holiday. The cards are all from the period in and around the Second World War. Each originates in a community of Jews who could legitimately have bemoaned their fate and expected a new year that would be anything but good. Wishing someone a good new year from the depths of misery and sorrow could be a delusional act, or it could be a reflection of optimism and a messianic vision of a better future despite the odds.

One card is from Litzmannstadt, the German name for the Polish city of Lodz. It is from 1940, from within the Lodz Ghetto. The words and the date give one the chills. But the picture provides the message: if the image of Jews in a ghetto symbolizes powerlessness and victimization, this card wishing a good new year provides a note of optimism. It is, perhaps, not by accident that the words and the date are on the margins, while the picture at the center, the focus of the card, is filled with smiling children.

The second card is from Berlin, printed within a few years of the war's end. It comes from a JDC-run displaced-persons (DP) camp. Berlin in the postwar period was a place of physical devastation and shortages. Every single Jew in that DP camp had family members who had been killed a few short years earlier, and these survivors were now in the city from which all the evil had emanated. But the focus of the card? A child. A future. Hope.

The third card is from a shtetl, possibly in one of the regions that JDC assistance reached in the years just before the outbreak of the war. Contrary to the musicals and cinematic idylls common in popular culture, shtetl life was, for the most part, grueling. But here too, a child surrounded by dolls and toys represents not so much the difficult present but a brighter future. From here, one could draw hope for a better year upcoming.

In the FSU, we confront true suffering on a regular basis. But if we are regularly surprised by one thing, it is the stoic resolve of the Jews we help, and their optimism that their futures will be better.

Adjara (May 7, 2004)

The last few years of neglect and corruption have left Georgia, once a relatively prosperous part of the USSR, in extreme poverty and in political chaos. There are a series of autonomous regions that are technically subservient to the central government in Tbilisi but that, for all intents and purposes, have made a go of it on their own. They thrive on smuggling, thievery, and various other mechanisms that have allowed them to adapt to their predicament as Georgia's downward slide has accelerated.

With the recent change in governments, there has been an attempt to pull them all back into the fold. The new Georgian president has tried negotiating, cajoling, and even begging for a grace period during which Georgia can be rebuilt. This week, the autonomous republic of Adjara gave its answer. It blew up bridges and railroad trestles connecting it to the Georgian mainland, and a standoff began. It looks to have been resolved after a few days of hostilities, but there is no guarantee that it will not flare up again at the smallest instigation.

Adjara was once host to a large Jewish population which has been attenuated due to emigration during the last twenty years. There are about four hundred Jews left. To give an idea of their current situation, just under half are Hesed clients. That is, most of those remaining behind are elderly and have no means to move elsewhere.

We are in touch daily with the Hesed in Batumi, the Adjarian capital, and are exploring ways of getting aid to them. The rump government in Adjara has chosen to align the region with Russia, Georgia's declared enemy, so there are still air links to Batumi via Moscow. We will probably use that route to get in emergency assistance. Full-scale hostilities could yet break out, and we are working on ways to maintain contact with these Jews should they find themselves in a conflagration.

This is a reminder to us that while the upheavals of the early nineties subsequent to the breakup of the USSR are largely behind us, there are still vast swaths of territory, including more than a handful of breakaway republics, that have not yet recovered from the initial trauma of the post-Soviet period. While we often speak of renewal and welfare in the context of a stable though occasionally horrific situation, we should not be lulled into thinking that things are indeed secure – far from it in many areas. And while Jews are not targeted as Jews, they are at risk of being "collateral victims" in quite a few of these areas.

Geographic Disaggregation (August 3, 2007)

Recently, I came across an article written about a reality far from the subject I deal with here, but one that is surprisingly relevant to our FSU operations. The article was written by George Packer and appeared in the *New Yorker* in its December 18, 2006 issue. It is entitled "Knowing the Enemy," and it deals with the war in Iraq. The author doesn't take a stand on whether or not the war was justified, but rather deals with how it is being prosecuted. In the case that he makes there is a profound lesson for JDC, one that we ignore at our peril. And while we are not in a war in the FSU and have no "enemy" there, the point he raises is very relevant to our work.

His basic contention is that Iraqi insurgents can be defeated. His position on that question matters much less than how he suggests that can be done.

Packer interviews an Australian military planner with experience in insurgencies in Southeast Asia. He contends that the first rule of thumb for army combatants fighting an insurgency is "[to] know the people, the topography, economy, history, religion and culture. Know every village, road, field, population group, tribal leader, and ancient grievance." He remarks further that "a war on terror suggests an undifferentiated enemy. Instead, speak of the need to disaggregate insurgencies.... Disaggregation could provide a unifying strategic conception for the war.

"Speaking of Saddam Hussein, the Taliban, the Iranian government, Hezbollah and Al Qaeda in terms of one big war is misleading.... Actually, there are sixty different groups in sixty different countries which have sixty different objectives.... Winning minds and hearts is not a matter of making people like you, but of getting them to accept that supporting your side is in their interest."

On disaggregation, we need to acknowledge that while the term "FSU Jewry" appears repeatedly in our written material, there are no two communities that fit together comfortably under that rubric in that they are identical. Yes, there is a common language and a shared history with one central government, and so on. But the individual histories of these communities, and their current predicaments, mean that each has to be approached in a different way.

For example, compare the Jews of Chişinău, Moldova, with those of Nizhny Novgorod, Russia. The former community still has Jews who grew up in a *kehillah*, a formal Jewish community that had clear parameters for membership and governance before the Soviets took over in the 1940s. They remember what community life was like, and what the role of a community is with respect to the individual Jew. To create a governing board in that community is to revive a governance structure that once existed. A Hesed operation assuming responsibility for the elderly is a given, and hearkens back to what once was not all that long ago. A JCC takes the role that synagogues played in the not-too-distant past. The building may be different, as are the programs, but the notion of a facility that belongs to Jews, services the needs of Jews, and brings Jews together is not new, and certainly not alien.

Contrast this with the Jewish community in the third-largest city in Russia, Nizhny Novgorod, named Gorky during Soviet times, after the writer Maxim Gorky. This was outside the Pale of Settlement in czarist times. Jews were not particularly welcome in Nizhny Novgorod, and those few who did settle there under the czarist regime generally gave up their Jewish identities, or certainly watered them down, in order to win the right of residence. Larger-scale Jewish settlement began there only after the revolution. The Jews who came then were not joining an existing Jewish community, and there was no opportunity to create one. The government assumed responsibility (at least de jure) for many of the community's functions vis-à-vis the individual: welfare, culture, etc. To create a Hesed there based on a sense of communal responsibility and civic duty is something entirely unprecedented in that society. The concept of "voluntarism" is not resuscitated; it has to be created ex nihilo. A governance framework in a voluntary institution or organization is an entirely new concept.

Thus, we need to differentiate our approach in our work in these two cities. We cannot create a board of directors for an organization in Chişinău without including in it elders who are familiar with a model of governance their community once had. In Nizhny, the members of the same kind of board need to be educated from the outset on rights and responsibilities; their education starts in a very different place. They have no firsthand experience with Jewish communal life, nor do they have neighbors familiar with relevant precedents from society at large.

Holiday programs in both cities will be dissimilar. In Chişinău, from a certain age, there are memories of Jewish experiences. People often remember a grandparent's Seder or were taken to the synagogue on Yom Kippur, and the choreography of such events is somewhat familiar, not intimidating or fundamentally alien. In Nizhny, this is exposure to an entirely new culture and way of life, much the way one would learn about a different society in an anthropology class. The key here is how to "market" this Jewish culture, not as something foreign and curious, but as something that intrinsically belongs to the people to whom it is being introduced.

We often speak about "FSU initiatives" and communities as if we were talking of a monolith, of some million Jews who will respond the same way to steps we take or programs we offer. In fact, though, just as individuals differ, so too do these communities, often in ways that surprise us even after so many years of exposure to this field.

* * *

In the last few years, we've engaged in a major effort to build Jewish Community Centers – JCCs – in communities around the FSU. For now, the issue is the nature of these JCCs. If what I wrote above is to be applied to our work, it stands to reason that JCCs, as an authentic expression of Jewish communal life, should not fit a particular template. Every JCC should reflect the idiosyncrasies of the culture of the community and society in which it exists. A trained observer should be able to tell a great deal about the community, its values, and its nature from this institution.

To create the program for the JCC in Tbilisi, Georgia, we hired a marketing firm to do a study on the wants and desires of the Georgian Jewish middle class: What would bring them to such an institution, and what Jewish needs of theirs could such an institution fill? Through a series of focus groups and using other quantitative assessments, they produced an evaluation that will serve as the basis for moving forward on planning the JCC in Tbilisi, and, in fact, those of other, similar, communities in the east.

In the spirit of disaggregation, I want to point out some of the findings that will distinguish this JCC from the one in Minsk (as an example of a community in the western reaches of the FSU). How does the reality of Georgian Jewish life influence the design of the Tbilisi JCC in a way that sets it apart from a JCC elsewhere in the FSU?

1. Georgian Jews were always a significant – and generally welcome – part of Georgian society. This inspired in them a fierce pride in their Georgian identity. Thus, the respondents insist that the JCC must welcome Georgian non-Jews. Some programs must exist in the JCC to explain Jewish life, traditions, and history to their non-Jewish neighbors. In a place like Minsk, Belarus, in which the surrounding environment was generally hostile to Jews, the JCC would be more of a refuge, a place where a Jew went to engage his unique identity, as distinct from that of his neighbors. There is no pressure there for the JCC to engage with the non-Jewish surroundings.

2. The Minsk JCC has a library and a museum. This is common in the JCCs in European FSU. The emphasis on education among these Jews is paramount, and therefore a common way to concretize Jewish

identity is through intellectual pursuits. This emphasis on education is not as pronounced in the east, and these two elements did not come up at all as program areas for the Tbilisi JCC.

3. The communities in the east placed a tremendous emphasis on family. Here, families generally remained intact, in contrast to the horrific state of the family unit in the places in which Soviet domination was more pronounced. These focus groups called for multigenerational family programs in the Tbilisi center, saying, "We want a place that we can visit and spend time with our parents and children for an afternoon." This call is not for separate generational programming, as one would find in the western communities, but rather for programs that appeal at the same time to all components of the nuclear family.

4. The findings of the Georgia study call for a restaurant in the JCC. In western FSU communities, where a restaurant is found in the JCC, it is to generate income. In Tbilisi, where the Jewish community remained loyal to Jewish tradition even during the height of Soviet repression, kosher food and cuisine is an integral part of their Jewish expression. Thus, a Jewish communal house must have a place for them to eat their Jewish foods in the same way that it might have Jewish lectures or cultural activities. Any income generated is a by-product, and not central.

5. Tbilisi Jewry exists in a proud community to which individual Jews have strong ties. And they live in a milieu in which business has always flourished in a way that was impossible in the western areas of the USSR. This shaped their approach to charity as well. The respondents were adamant: free (charity) services are synonymous with low quality. They expressed their belief that service personnel "feel less responsible and don't provide proper service to customers when the latter do not pay." Clearly, there is a very strong stigma attached to support that one receives outside of the family setting, and therefore a value is placed on enterprise and self-support. "Fee for service" becomes a sine qua non in the Tbilisi JCC. In the Minsk JCC, the expectation is that the programs will not be fee-based. "It is the only way we can attract participants."

These are only a few of the more overt differences one finds. In any event, the lesson is clear. The need to "disaggregate" – that is, to treat each community as a distinct and discrete unit – is the key to success for our work in community development. The JCC model is but one example.

Komi (September 4, 2009)

The Komi Republic is a quasi-independent region in the outer reaches of the Russian Federation. Its weather is extremely harsh. It is rich in natural resources, but the population is sparse because of the severe living conditions. During Soviet times, people were offered considerable incentives to settle in the area to provide the personnel needed to mine the resources and to provide the miners with services. Salaries were up to 40 percent higher than elsewhere. Shops were kept fully supplied with commodities unavailable in other places, and, in general, the standard of living was quite high.

Nonetheless, there were not many takers because of the difficulties of living there. The standard joke about the weather was that the region had two seasons: winter and July 15. It wasn't just cold; travel was virtually impossible for extended periods. The region was home to the Gulag, as the distance and difficulties of terrain and weather made for perfect conditions in which to hold prisoners with little risk of escape. In addition, the prisoners could be forced to do some of the heavy lifting that was needed to maintain the economies of the Republic.

In December of 1967, the USSR signed an agreement with the People's Republic of Bulgaria to supply timber from the Komi region for the Bulgarian construction industry. Carrying out the agreement was no easy task, as communities had to be constructed on the tundra for the Bulgarian workers. By the mid-1970s, three settlements were ready to receive Bulgarian workers. One of the settlements, Usogorsk, was in the middle of one of the forests in which the men would work, 87 miles away from the nearest civilian settlement in the region. Three Gulag prisons were within an approximately 12-mile radius.

For vacations, the Bulgarian workers often went to regions in the USSR with warmer climates. Uzbekistan was a popular destination. It was exotic while at the same time "politically acceptable," and not many places fell into that category for Eastern Bloc vacationers, whose travel was severely limited and closely monitored by their government minders. Samarkand, the second-largest city in Uzbekistan, was a particular draw. It lay on the Silk Route and had an exotic (to Bulgarians) middle-Asian culture, unlike anywhere else they were permitted to travel to. Arriving there, you were transported to a different world while still within the confines of the ideologically permissible. In addition to its very mild weather, it had a strong Muslim heritage, and architecture to match.

Samarkand's Jewish community is close knit and very insular. Unlike most Jewish communities elsewhere in the USSR that were ravaged by assimilation, this community maintained its traditions. Synagogues were full, and marriage within the Jewish community was the norm. There were Jewish neighborhoods in Samarkand and semiclandestine but officially tolerated frameworks for Jewish education. The indigenous community was made up of Bukharian Jews, who had their own local dialect, an analogue to other Jewish languages, such as Yiddish or Ladino.

Organized tours of the Bulgarian workers in Komi visited Samarkand regularly. On one of these tours in the early eighties, one of the construction workers met a woman from the Jewish community there and fell in love. The young woman, whose name was Gulya, was very taken by her Bulgarian suitor, but her relationship with a foreigner was frowned upon by her family. Gradually their love grew, and on a subsequent visit they were married.

Gulya was rejected by her family, and she joined her husband back in Usogorsk. She lost contact with her family and community, and gradually gave up all vestiges of Jewish observance. She met no Jews in her new community, and she became indistinguishable from her neighbors in practice and lifestyle.

Gulya gave birth to two daughters, Sasha and Elina. Shortly after Elina's birth in 1990, her parents' marriage disintegrated, and they split. The girls were raised in a "typical" Soviet environment, both inside and outside the home. They had no exposure to other Jews, as Gulya was not in contact with her family. Their passports identified them as Russians. To this day, the girls will say that they may have been told at some point that they were Jews, but the comment would not have registered because it had no context. In Usogorsk, the word had no meaning.

In 2001, Sasha, the elder sister, moved to Syktyvkar, the capital of the Komi Republic and a city with a Jewish population of fifteen hundred, to begin her university studies. In one of her classes, she sat next to a young man with whom she struck up a conversation. He was a volunteer in the local Hesed center, and occasionally he would tell her about how he spent his free time there helping the elderly needy. He readily identified himself as a Jew, but this meant little to Sasha.

On a visit home she mentioned in passing to her mother the young man she had met and his Hesed activities. The mother responded in a casual way that she too was Jewish. There was no great, emotional confession; it was all very matter-of-fact.

On her return to Syktyvkar, the local fellow invited Sasha to visit the Hesed center. It was the night of the Passover Seder. Sasha was intrigued and began regularly participating in Jewish events in the town.

When Elina started school in Syktyvkar, her sister brought her to the Hesed. Her first visit was to a Chanukah party. While she enjoyed the socializing, she was particularly intrigued by the story of the holiday, which touched a chord within her. She began to volunteer with the elderly and soon started a program for young children.

As Elina became increasingly active, the small Syktyvkar Jewish community embraced her. She was nominated to participate in a St. Petersburg–based program to teach young Jews skills in community development and leadership.

As part of her personal project, Elina developed two programs for the Syktyvkar Jewish community: one for outreach and the other a Jewish heritage program to explore the personal histories of members of the community, few of whom had been raised in the region. Both programs now serve as models for small Jewish communities around the FSU.

When I heard Elina's story, I regretted that her extended family from Samarkand – most of whom by then had emigrated to points west – could not see her and her sister now. These women are in many ways the story of Soviet and post-Soviet Jewry. Because of her life choices, her mother was written off; no one would have believed that among her descendants there would be any expression of Jewish identity. They saw Gulya's choice of spouse as dooming her and her offspring to assimilation, which was tantamount to disappearing from the Jewish people. But even those who took issue with that assumption would have had to concede that a decision to live in Usogorsk meant the end of the line for Jewish identity in that family. Studying in Syktyvkar hardly raised the odds that a Jewish consciousness would surface.

And yet, numerous factors – a chance meeting, the existence of a Jewish welfare center primarily serving the elderly, and some other unpredictable situations, together with the care and concern of a very distant Jewry for the fate of every individual Jew – all combined to reclaim these two young Jews for the Jewish people.

There's a further message in this for JDC planning purposes. The bifurcation between Jewish-renewal programming and welfare is artificial and misleading. They are symbiotic. In this instance, the Hesed, which we categorize as a welfare program, has reclaimed two young Jews who otherwise would have been lost to the Jewish people.

Kyrgyzstan (April 8, 2010)

Kyrgyzstan is a mountainous country, primarily agrarian, with few natural resources. It has a population of about 5.5 million, with a GDP that is estimated at $4.7 billion per annum. The average monthly wage is the equivalent of $130. About one-third of the population lives under the state-recognized poverty line. Almost a third of the economy is attributed to remittances by Kyrgyz citizens working abroad. The downturn in the world economy and its attendant unemployment has therefore severely hurt Kyrgyzstan.

The country is divided along geographic and clan lines, the latter functioning as tribes with strong intratribe loyalties and often-nasty intertribe rivalries. The majority of the population, over 70 percent, is ethnically Kyrgyz, but there is a significant native Russian-speaking minority, to which most of the local Jews belong. The Jews are doubly "foreign," perceived both as Jews and as Russians. It should be noted, however, that Kyrgyz society is fairly tolerant of its small minorities, including Jews.

Kyrgyzstan is predominantly Sunni Muslim, but that is manifest more in an ethnic than in a religious way. It has a very unstable political environment. There was a revolution in 2005, for which the motivating factors were corruption and nepotism. But not much changed. Supporters of the regime that recently assumed power utilized many of the same slogans that the entrenched regime had used in its efforts to overthrow *its* predecessor some five years ago.

In the midst of this turmoil live an estimated eleven hundred Jews, most of whom are concentrated in the nation's capital, Bishkek. During Soviet times, the city was named Frunze, after the Soviet hero Mikhail Frunze, but with independence in the early nineties the name was changed back to what it had been before the Soviet takeover in 1919. This was common throughout the newly independent states: erasing the names of cities and streets that had been named after Soviet heroes was seen as an act of independence.

From the 1990s onward, the Jewish community was run by a dynamo named Rosa Fish. Like most of the other Jews there, Rosa's roots extended back to the Second World War. Kyrgyzstan was beyond the reach of the Nazi juggernaut, which made it the destination of thousands of Jews fleeing from the western USSR ahead of the Nazi blitzkrieg. After the war, most returned to their regions of origin. Those remaining in Kyrgyzstan were the forbearers of the Jewish population there today. Among those who remained, or, in some cases, resettled there from elsewhere, was a large cadre of Jewish public-health physicians. Many of the key health positions in the country are held by these Jews, a fact that is not lost on the general population.

Rosa was the founding director of the Hesed, and she subsequently oversaw the establishment of a youth club, a Jewish book festival, a Jewish library, a program for family education, and even an educational program for tolerance in the general school system based on a curriculum about the Shoah. For many years, Rosa worked in tandem with Professor Boris Shapiro, a long-serving vice minister of health in the country. This leadership in tandem is very common in the region. Rosa Fish was the doer, who provided the vision and oversaw the day-to-day operations; Professor Shapiro was the public face, and a source of great pride given his standing in the general society. He also provided government access and connections when needed. Both were apolitical figures in the sense that they were not identified with any particular party or faction.

* * *

As noted earlier, most Jews in Kyrgyzstan live in Bishkek. However, Jews can be found in ten other locales throughout the country. I hesitate to speak of ten other "communities"; in many of these towns, there is only a handful of Jews, and in some there is only one. To give some perspective: Bishkek has

535 Hesed clients, almost half of the city's Jews. The population is heavily weighted toward the elderly, as many of the able-bodied young Jews have emigrated. Osh, the city with the next-largest concentration of Jews, has thirty-nine of them, of whom twenty-eight are elderly Hesed clients.

When the rioting spread earlier in the week, and then escalated into a full-scale revolution, we established immediate and ongoing contact with our sources in the community. There were no reported injuries among the Jewish population. Critically, we were told that services to elderly clients were not interrupted.

The Hesed communicates regularly with all of its clients. The normal concerns and fears that elderly elsewhere would experience in a situation like this were not as acute here; upheaval is a common occurrence in Kyrgyzstan. Fortunately, and perhaps for this reason, the Jewish community is very well organized: an estimated 82 percent of its members are involved and registered with the community, so monitoring their situation locally is made much easier. Neighbors are given lists of elderly shut-ins in close proximity, and either visit or call them regularly. Our staff often hears from their Kyrgyz neighbors about the Jews they visit and how much they admire the Jewish community and its concern for its own. One noted, "Jews know how to care for Jews. The rest of us, it seems, are always on our own."

Unlike in Russia and Ukraine, the Jews are not players in the general political arena. They are neither close to nor identified with the previous incumbents or those who have recently seized power. Therefore, they do not expect any change in their situation or feel particularly threatened by the change in government.

What follows are highlights of a trip to meet with the Jews of a small Kyrgyz town. I think that more than the dry descriptions above, the highlights give some insight into what it means to live as a Jew in a small town, in a country most of us have never heard of, in an environment that is so foreign to the ones with which Western Jews are familiar. While reading them, one is struck by the Jews' alienation from things Jewish, a condition born of many years of isolation from the Jewish world. One is also struck by the thought of what the connection to JDC – and by extension to the Jewish people – must have meant for those people when they first encountered it so unexpectedly. Several times a day this week, there have been calls from the Bishkek Hesed for updates on the situation of the Jews in Osh, Shopokov, Uzgen, and seven other cities and towns in the unstable region. In a way, this is the real concretization of Jewish peoplehood.

* * *

Osh is the second-largest city in Kyrgyzstan, with about four hundred thousand residents. Ninety percent of Kyrgyzstan is covered by high mountains, which are difficult (and, at certain times of the year, impossible) to cross. The simplest way to reach Osh from the capital of Kyrgyzstan is by plane.

Osh lies in the Fergana Valley, which stretches into Uzbekistan and neighboring Tajikistan. Most of the citizens of Osh are ethnically Uzbek, with roots in that neighboring, much larger country. The Uzbeks look down on the Tajiks as less educated, less cultured, and altogether less civilized.

The city was famous during Soviet times for its large factory, which produced pumps of all kinds. There were pumps for cars, for air, for water, for oil, and for coal mines. Over twenty thousand workers were employed by the city's one pump factory. It was what we would call a company town. When the Soviet Union collapsed, the pump factory closed down and the town of Osh was thrown into a depression. The vast majority of ethnic Russians who lived in Osh left for Russia; some Uzbeks returned to Uzbekistan, and the Tajiks and many other members of minority groups emigrated whenever they could. The poorer Kyrgyz had nowhere else to go and remained behind.

Among the residents of Osh in 1991 were twelve hundred Jews. They were not native to the area; all of them were refugees who had come at the outbreak of the Second World War. They came to Osh in different ways. Every one of them had a long story of wandering through different parts of the former Soviet Union until they reached Osh. Some had originally been evacuated to Siberia ahead of the Nazi blitzkrieg and, in time, moved south to Kyrgyzstan. Others had been evacuated with their factories, which were moved from Ukraine and reconstructed in Osh, beyond the reach of the Nazis. Still others arrived first to Uzbekistan, where the enormous number of evacuees from the western part of the country arrived with no assets, putting a tremendous burden on regions that had primitive infrastructure, or none at all. Housing was scarcely available. Food was hard to come by. Employment opportunities did not exist. The result was widespread civil unrest. Tens of thousands of recently arrived refugees camped near the central station of Tashkent because they had no place to go. Water was unavailable. Diseases spread easily. In their despair, they continued on to neighboring Kyrgyzstan and its capital and largest city, Frunze. The authorities there sent the Jews on to Osh.

When emigration became possible upon independence in 1991, many Jews left for Israel, but that option was available only to those who could prove their Jewish heritage. Many could not. They were descendants of evacuees who had fled the German advances two generations earlier with nothing more than the clothing on their backs. Their identity papers were left behind. With no evidence to establish their Jewish identities, they were essentially stranded in Osh.

The Borodoskis of Osh had no documents. At his aliyah interview, Yasha Borodoski was asked by the Israeli consul to say a few words in Yiddish. He was five years old when he, his mother, and his sister had fled from Kryvyi Rih in Ukraine. Borodoski knew no Yiddish words, so he and his Russian wife were not granted a visa. His daughter married a Jew from Uzbekistan, and she left for Israel. Borodoski remained in Osh.

In his younger days, he had been a physical-education teacher. His hobby was marathon running. He became Kyrgyzstan's champion marathon runner and always remained proud of his Jewish identity. He and his wife now live in what is essentially a one-room hut. Toilet facilities are in a nearby latrine, and they have electricity for an hour a day. They take care of a small garden where they grow their own vegetables. A few chickens roam over the garden and the small yard. They are "too old and tired" now to think of emigrating. They are not even interested in repairing the cracks in the walls and in the ceiling caused by an earthquake last January. Rainwater seepage is a regular occurrence.

Olga Yakubovna has a different story. Born a Jew, she is a qualified physician and worked in medicine until retirement. Now in her eighty-fifth year, she recalls the odyssey of her evacuation as a young girl from Belarus to the Urals, and from there on to Kazakhstan. An uncle appeared in Bishkek after the war and invited her to join him in Kyrgyzstan. As a qualified doctor, she was assigned to Osh by the government in Moscow to work in a clinic responsible for the surrounding region. She married an ethnic Tajik and had two sons, one of whom served in the navy. He was discharged from the navy after a traumatic service experience from which he emerged a broken man. Now fifty, he lives with her and does not communicate. Olga, now a widow, looks after her son, who has no one else to take care of him, and does her best to make him as comfortable as possible.

Today, thirty-nine identifying Jews remain in Osh. Their children married Uzbeks, Kyrgyz, Tajiks, or Russians. There is no organized Jewish life in Osh – no synagogue, no Sunday school, no Jewish society, no Jewish cemetery. In each case, their Jewish identity is anchored in an era in the hoary past. They remember their parents, and often their grandparents. They remember their difficult flight from their native towns in western Russia or Ukraine. It was not only a lifetime ago; it was a different life.

By war's end, all of them had rebuilt their lives in these new places among foreign peoples. They wanted to survive. To do so, they tried to forget their past, which was laden with too much pain. Even the good memories became painful reminders of a lost personal world of family and community. Today, they are adamant that life for them began only after the war.

In the vicinity of Osh, there are a dozen Jews isolated in different villages and small towns. They married local Kyrgyz, and their children grew up as other Kyrgyz village children did and, naturally, married local partners. Many of the children know nothing about their own family's history. If the children born after the war know that one of their parents was Jewish, they certainly know nothing about the content of that identity. One of the older women who met with us in Osh spoke of Babyn Yar, near Kyiv, where her family was killed. Another told us that the KGB had shot her parents for reasons unknown to her. Each one had a story to tell, and each story was different, but they were all tragic parts of a chapter of twentieth-century Jewish history from this part of the world.

None ever shared his or her personal Jewish memories with family members. Their Jewish experiences were frozen in time from decades earlier. To be a Jew for most of their adult lives was to be a target of discrimination and hatred. It was an unmitigated liability from which they were determined to shield their offspring.

Our visit and our meeting with twenty of the thirty-nine Jews of Osh stirred up old memories and somehow reconnected them temporarily with their Jewish past. For those few hours, a benign nostalgia infused their memories. Those sitting around the table were keen to hear about Israel, about other Jewish communities and, above all, about the Jewish organization, the Joint, that sent them food packages, supplied them with winter relief, provided some needed medications, and united them as Jews. More than sixty years after the war, they live in Osh, with sporadic electricity most of the year and without heat during many days in the winter. The packages of food by no means solve all their problems, but they do give them some relief. The candles included in the monthly packages mean that they do not have to sit in complete darkness. Wood or coal allocations provide some heat and cooking fuel. Medicines are provided all year round.

The visit of a JDC representative not only transported them to what little remained of their past in their memories but also encouraged them to speak to one another, to get to know other Jews who had shared similar fates, to find neighbors with whom they did not know they shared a basic component of identity.

Osh is by no means unique. The description of Osh would fit hundreds of other provincial communities where dispersed Jews found shelter and refuge during the war. The economic situation in those distant settlements is always far worse than in the capital or the larger cities. The unexpected and providential assistance provided by JDC is literally a godsend, as essential as it is welcome.

I want to emphasize one element of this piece: the Jewish connection. There must be hundreds, maybe thousands, of Oshes throughout the FSU, villages and towns basically shut off from the world, with small numbers of Jews in each. In every such place, there are Jews who suffered indescribable misfortunes as they fled the Nazis in search of safe harbors, hoping to find a piece of bread at a time when bread was scarce. Now, with most of them in the twilight years of their difficult lives, they have received a sign of kindness from fellow Jews, a ray of sunshine, a feeling of warmth, and a reminder that Jews are indeed tied to one another and also responsible for one another.

Many of them lived their lives identified as Jews, by a stamp on their internal passports if nowhere else. That identity may have had no meaning to them except this: It was generally a liability. It meant that they could not enter certain professions. They could not attend certain schools of higher learning. They were denied jobs or promotions.

Now, that same identity has been transformed from a liability into a privilege. No matter how physically isolated they may be, there is a community that reaches out to them in very difficult economic or political times, says, "We care about you" – and acts on it. For the first time in their lives, they consider the label "Jew" to be meaningful and beneficial.

Transnistria (March 17, 2006)

In the early 1990s, in the aftermath of the breakup of the USSR, a number of regions experienced tremendous turmoil. In many cases, ethnic or national antipathies erupted and developed into minor skirmishes, and in other cases into full-scale war. In most instances, the roots of the conflicts were anomalies inherent in the artificial drawing of boundaries; occasionally there were tribal rivalries dating back centuries. Sometimes, the hatred was the result of Soviet attempts to engineer societies by uprooting and relocating native peoples who presented real or imagined threats to the regime. Sometimes, the problems were the result of the caprice of some leader or bureaucrat who "gifted" territories from one republic to another, occasionally uniting under one administrative umbrella ethnic groups that despised one another and had violent histories between them.

Some of these battles were brief and have since been forgotten. Some places are in perpetual war mode, like Chechnya and the breakaway regions in Georgia. Others, like the Azerbaijan-Armenian struggle for hegemony over the enclave of Nagorno Karabakh, flare up from time to time, and then lie dormant for extended periods.

Recently, tensions resurfaced in the Prednestrovian Moldavian Republic, also known as Transnistria, a breakaway region in Moldova that lies on the banks of the Dniester River, wedged between Moldova and the western border of Ukraine. It is a "country" of about half a million people, with a Jewish population of about thirty-seven hundred. Most of these Jews are elderly and live in the Transnistrian capital, Tiraspol.

The region was the scene of a civil war in the early nineties. During Soviet times Transnistria was settled primarily by ethnic Russians, many of whom were military veterans. In the days of the Soviet Union, there was a significant

Red Army presence in a series of bases in this region protecting the country's southern flank. Enormous amounts of weaponry were stockpiled to support the armed forces, and many ethnic-Russian soldiers then retired there.

When the Soviet Union imploded, these Russians were not happy about having to transfer their allegiance to the newly independent Moldova to which it formally belonged or, for that matter, to Ukraine, with which it was contiguous. They did not share an ethnic identity with their new rulers in Chişinău. Nor a language. Nor a culture. In brief, they saw themselves as Russians and wanted no part of this new country Moldova. They wanted to remain under Russian rule, surrounded by Russian culture, and to continue to conduct their daily affairs in the Russian language. But because the territory was not geographically contiguous with Russia, this was not an option. Unhappy with this arrangement, they declared independence from Moldova in 1990 and fought a war with Moldova in 1992 to secure their independence.

The war was fought to a stalemate: the Moldovans vastly outnumbered those in the breakaway region, but the ordnance of the rebels gave them an insurmountable advantage. The conflict did not last long, but it did present a risk for the not-insignificant local Jewish communities in Bendery, Tiraspol, and some smaller cities.

JDC's rescue operation was based in Odesa, a few hours' bus ride away. With the help of a high-ranking Jewish officer in the local army who tipped off the leadership of the Jewish community regarding impending military moves, most of the community was temporarily relocated to Odesa until the fighting abated. Ultimately, some stayed in Odesa, some emigrated, and some returned to Transnistria. Since then, those Jewish communities have begun to rebuild.

The political situation today remains much as it was at the end of the conflict: Transnistria has become an independent enclave and does not recognize the government in Chişinău. It has its own president and a border with a fully manned guard post. It has its own customs service, currency, parliament, flag, postal service, and military. Its script is based on the Cyrillic alphabet, unlike Moldova's Latin script, and its foreign policy has a decidedly pro-Russian tilt.

Transnistrians live in a self-declared state that is not recognized as such by any member state of the United Nations, with one exception. Their status as an independent nation is recognized by a grand total of three other political entities: Russia and two breakaway regions of Georgia – Abkhazia and South Ossetia – themselves not recognized by any country other than Russia. Its economy is dominated by all sorts of sordid enterprises, including illicit trafficking in arms and a well-developed illicit narcotics industry.

Last week, tensions rose precipitously with Ukraine's announcement that it would no longer allow goods to be exported through its territories without proper licenses from the official government of Moldova, which the Transnistrian government does not recognize. The situation is severely complicated by the inherent tensions between Ukraine and Russia, which comes as close as any country to being Transnistria's (unofficial) patron.

My grandmother periodically asks, in response to newspaper headlines, "This is *their* problem" – meaning the local non-Jewish majority. "But what does it mean for the Yidden?"

As it happens, this is also a Jewish problem. Almost the entire elderly Jewish population in the region is dependent on JDC for its welfare. Pensions there are rarely paid, and people have no assets. To paint the picture as clearly as possible, this is a totally dysfunctional economy within Moldova, which is already the poorest country in Europe – and which has now sealed its borders.

We have some supplies available locally, and the professional head of the Tiraspol Jewish community has made an official request of the authorities that an exception to the restrictions on imports be made on humanitarian grounds for the people we support. The Transnistrian government's response to this request is pending. Meanwhile, our lawyer in Chişinău is studying the situation in Moldova, because even if the Tiraspol authorities grant a temporary waiver, it is not clear that the Moldovan authorities will agree to let humanitarian aid pass.

While this is a difficult situation, it is not unique. Abkhazia, a breakaway region from Georgia, also has a Jewish community, and there are isolated remnant Jewish communities in the northern Caucasus that are sandwiched between warring factions and suffer from it.

Today's FSU isn't all as pretty as a new JCC in St. Petersburg or a modern Hesed facility in Novosibirsk.

Kalmykia (November 4, 2011)

Each summer, we conduct a survey of all our offices, from which we produce a document called the "FSU Activity Report." It documents, in the form of a chart, all the locales in which we work in the FSU. In order for an area to be included on the list, there has to be some activity sponsored by JDC in that place. It can reflect any part of our work – the village in which there is a client who receives a food package on a regular basis, or a place from which someone engages in a distance-learning program. If someone there is touched in some way by a Jewish activity, the location is recorded in this report. As of August 31, 2011, there were 2,781 locales throughout the FSU where "something Jewish" took place. This weekly is about locale number 2,782.

Recently, I was on a working trip to our Rostov office in southern Russia. As an aside, the staff mentioned that they suspected that there are Jews in a neighboring Russian republic who are not yet connected to the Jewish world. I was a bit taken aback. It has been quite a few years since we entered new territory. The truth is, I thought we had made connections with Jews everywhere they are to be found across the expanse of the FSU. That is not to say that we reach every Jew in need, but we do reach every needy Jew of whom we know. And as far as I knew, we knew of needy Jews in every region in the FSU. Our tentacles extend into the FSU's most-distant and forbidding areas. There are places that cannot be reached during the winter months (which are defined very broadly) due to severe weather conditions, but our assistance does get in when conditions permit. There are areas that are extremely dangerous because of civil unrest, political instability, or ethnic strife, but we have found ways to provide goods and services to Jews who remain there.

Now I was learning of an entire region – in Russia no less – in which Jews reside, which has neither severe weather conditions nor security restrictions that would prevent access. A place with Jews in the FSU that, twenty years after we returned to the region, was entirely new to us. In fact, I had never even heard the name of the republic, nor of its capital. What follows is a bit of history of the region, and how we go about looking for Jews there in the second decade of the twenty-first century.

The republic is called Kalmykia, and its capital is Elista. It is unique, not only in the FSU, but in all of Europe, for reasons that will follow shortly. It is located in southern Russia, and its eastern border is on the shores of the

Caspian Sea. It is relatively small as Russian republics go, with a population of just under three hundred thousand. Approximately half of that number is made up of ethnic Kalmyks, for whom this is their homeland.

In and of itself, this is not surprising. But what is surprising is their religious background. This republic is the only territory in Europe in which the majority of inhabitants are followers of Tibetan Buddhism! In southern Russia!

So, before we get to the Jews, let us explore a little bit of the fascinating history of the region: The Kalmyks were a tribe that probably originated in Mongolia. Sometime in the seventeenth century they migrated to the area of the Volga River, most likely in search of land on which their cattle could graze. Their leaders cut a deal with the czar, who granted them political autonomy and pasture (probably at the expense of natives who were uprooted) in return for a promise that the Kalmyk army would protect Russia's southern flank for the czar. Both sides profited from the arrangement. Gradually, the majority of the tribe moved west and further south into today's Kalmykia.

During the October Revolution in 1917, many Kalmyks sided with the Whites against the Soviet Reds. To win their allegiance, Lenin promised them a large degree of autonomy under future Soviet rule. This promise was not made simply to win over the Kalmyks: It was given a great deal of publicity by the Bolsheviks in order to gain sympathy for their cause in the wider Asian and Buddhist world. A show of concern for Russian Buddhists had numerous geopolitical benefits for the new Bolshevik regime. A compromise on the issue of autonomy was a small price to pay for that international support.

The problem was that while some countries and international Buddhist leaders were bamboozled by the Soviet assurances, the local population was not. Loyalty remained with tribal leaders and was not transferred to Moscow. This was exactly the kind of thing that preoccupied Lenin's successor, and Stalin made the Kalmyks pay for it.

Through the twenties and early thirties, life was made increasingly difficult for the Buddhist population. Monasteries were severely taxed, eventually forcing them to close. Children were indoctrinated in Soviet schools and were denied access to a religious education. The local language was replaced by Russian, its vertical script by Cyrillic lettering. Most important, community leaders were exiled or executed. A forced collectivization resulted in repression of the small farmers and cattle producers, deepening the hatred for the central regime. Much of this resonates with those who are familiar with how the Jewish community was treated in that period.

During this time, the Jewish community in Kalmykia began to grow. Jews came in small numbers, primarily from Ukraine, to escape repression and famine. Many believed that, once distanced from large concentrations of Jews, they would be less conspicuous and thus less vulnerable to antisemitic campaigns. By the outbreak of the Second World War, there were an estimated fourteen hundred Jews in Kalmykia, most in the capital, Elista.

One of the three major thrusts of the German Wehrmacht's infiltration into the USSR in the summer of 1941 was in the south, via Rostov, in order to reach the oil fields farther east. When Rostov was overrun, most of the region around it fell to the Nazis as well (the advance in this area was, of course, halted at Stalingrad, today's Volgograd). This included Kalmykia in August of 1942. Many Kalmyks expressed their hatred for the Soviets by welcoming the Nazis, who subsequently ruled them in a benign manner. Toward the Jews, though, no mercy was shown. Almost all local Jews were killed during the brief period of Nazi control of the area between August and December 1942.

A year after recapturing Kalmykia, Stalin's regime meted out punishment to the Kalmyk people, accusing them of collaboration with the enemy during the war. The entire Kalmyk population was exiled to Siberia in the course of one night in 1943, with no advance warning. It was only in Khrushchev's time, in 1957, that the Kalmyks were allowed to return to their ancestral home. By this time most traces of their own culture had been obliterated, and they returned to find their homes occupied by other locals, their temples destroyed, and any vestige of their heritage wiped out.

There is a great deal more to note about the area, but all of this is really only background to our concern for the local Jews. Just one more point before moving on: From the breakup of the USSR until 2010, the republic was ruled with an iron fist by its president, the flamboyant and dictatorial Kirsan Ilyumzhinov. There is much to be told about that government's corruption and mismanagement. Suffice it to say that, by his own admission, he took his inspiration from Herbert Hoover, which is about all one needs to know about him. With a slight adjustment of the latter's commitment to his voters, the Kalmyk president promised, "A cell phone for every shepherd." Alas, that promise still awaits realization. The region is Russia's poorest.

In late August, members of our Rostov staff traveled to Elista in search of Jews. How does one carry out a mission like this? First, one determines that there are no other Jewish organizations, local or international, that have made contact with Jews there and could share their contacts. There were none. Next, one sets up, in advance of a visit, a series of meetings with people who might know of Jews.

Meetings were set up and held with the following:

- The chairperson of the local historical/cultural foundation in Elista
- A television reporter and two print journalists
- The editor of a local newspaper
- The head of the Council for World War II Veterans
- Staff in the local museum and library

All were very cooperative, and indeed, when they learned the nature of JDC's mission, they were quite enthusiastic, in fact, more enthusiastic than we had anticipated until we learned that the main thoroughfare in Elista carries the name of a Jewish physician. He was sent to the region to deal with an outbreak of typhoid before the war and retains an honored place in the Kalmykian historical narrative.

By the end of her three-day visit the JDC coordinator had made contact with fourteen Jewish families. Here is a sample:

1. Mikhail Kalist has been in Kalmykia since 1971. He was born and raised in Russia's Ural region and moved to Elista when he heard from a friend who preceded him there that the standard of living was high. This turned out not to be the case, but he had no means to return to his home and was doubtful that he could get official permission (required at the time) to go back. His situation is further complicated now because whatever family he has lives in Ukraine, which requires the costs of international travel, access to a different currency, etc. In short, he is aging and alone, with a limited pension, and stuck in Elista.

2. Gregory Goldberg, born 1926 in Odesa, was evacuated to Elista at the outbreak of the war and then moved again further east to Kazakhstan. Once there, he was drafted as a teenager. Eventually demobilized, he returned to Elista, where he thought the prospects of a Jew would be better than in Odesa. He is widowed and has three daughters, all of whom have state pensions that are below the minimum subsistence level set by the government, so he shares what he gets with them and their families. When asked if he knew of any other Jews, he responded most emphatically, "My brother Boris."

3. Boris Goldberg. Same early history. He is married, with a daughter who has three children and lives in the Ural region, a great distance away.

4. The Shayen family. They have a young daughter who has severe neurological problems and would benefit from some outside assistance. Medical care in this field is severely limited in the entire republic.

Most of the Jews who were contacted readily admitted to being Jews, and were anxious to meet the JDC representative, even before they knew of any entitlements. With the exception of the two brothers, they all lived in a "Jewish vacuum," unaware of any other Jews in their surroundings and not connected to any Jews elsewhere.

The JDC staffer is convinced that she reached only a small number of the Jews in the region. She has submitted a plan for her next steps, a plan that includes using mass media to connect with more Jews. The first step will be an article in the local press and an interview with the Rostov Hesed director on the local (Elista) television station. Social networks on the Russian internet will play a key role.

Postscript: Three years later, I had the opportunity to visit Elista to gather material for a project we were doing on our operations in hard-to-reach communities. I spent a great deal of time with the Goldberg brothers, separately, at their request. Gregory reminisced about his Jewish past. He recalled with nostalgia and warmth his family's holiday observances. His Yiddish was still fluent, though a bit rusty. He follows the news from the Middle East and dreams of visiting Israel. All of this is in stark contrast to his brother Boris.

Boris is a throwback to a previous era. As far as he is concerned, in his little corner of the world, he still lives in the USSR. He is a proud Communist. In fact, he longs for Stalin, a personal hero. He made a career in the Red Army and views his Jewish identity as a "meaningless accident of birth." He was adamant that he never personally encountered antisemitism. Of the Jewish people and the State of Israel he says, "It all means nothing to me." For two hours I talked with this man who shared nothing in common with me, a fact he repeated throughout our conversation. There was little personal chemistry. There was certainly no shared Jewish experience. Although this was certainly not rare in the FSU, most Jews above a certain age can relate in some way to their Jewish identity, even if only by recalling long-gone family members or holiday experiences, as his brother did. Not Boris.

On the way out of his apartment I saw his military uniform hanging on a hook by the door. It was full of medals. As a way of departing on a positive note, I pointed to one medal at random and asked him to explain why it was awarded to him. The Red Army was the premier Soviet institution, and I wanted to give Boris the opportunity to feed his pride, to tell this foreigner how he had contributed to the system that he so valued, and how it in turn valued his contribution. I was totally unprepared for what came next. As a reminder, I had spent the previous two hours attempting to find some vestige of Jewish identity in this man, all of which had come to naught.

"So, tell me about this medal," I said.

"I received it from the assistant to General Zhukov [the architect of the Soviet victory over the Nazis]. I led my unit in the Red Army in the liberation of Auschwitz, and I was the second soldier of the liberating army to enter the camp."

And in the previous two hours he had no "Jewish experiences" to share!

Mogilev (March 17, 2006)

Mogilev is a regional capital in Belarus. Once the heart of the Pale of Settlement, it is now home to some forty-two hundred Jews. Recently, the local rabbi went into business with a local bakery to bake kosher bread and sell it in local supermarkets. They started with thirty kilograms (sixty-six pounds) a day in October and were up to double that amount by late February. The packaging on each loaf labeled the bread as kosher. And then the complaints started pouring in to the local authorities, to the factory that produced the bread, and finally in the form of letters to the local newspaper. The newspaper, in the best tradition of muckraking journalism, sent one of its reporters to investigate.

The article that follows begins by quoting a Mrs. S., who writes from extensive experience, a point that will be eminently clear to anyone who reads what she has to say. Mrs. S. points out that "it is insulting to see such bread, i.e., kosher bread, on the shops' shelves." She reminds readers that, "it is a *well-known* fact [emphasis added] that one of the ingredients of such products was the blood of a sacrificial animal." (Note that she is enlightened enough to realize that it is animal blood, and not human blood, as many of her intellectual predecessors once claimed.) She goes on to acknowledge that this is no longer the case, but she warns us, her loyal readers, that "there is no guarantee that this will not be reinstituted." She also shares, from her vast knowledge, a bit about the history of yeast, saying that, originally, yeast was grown on human bones. (It is not clear from the article how this is relevant to kosher bread, but perhaps I am missing a point.)

The reader is then treated to the assessment of a reporter from this large-circulation daily. He opens by reassuring us that he is not an antisemite but does quote a local priest who anonymously tells him that those who buy any kind of kosher food are automatically paying a tax, which goes for support of the synagogue.

The reporter concludes by offering his own opinion that the baking of such bread should be enjoined, not because he is an antisemite, or against Judaism, but because there are a lot of different religions in Belarus, "and what if each decided to produce their own 'cult' products?"

Indeed! Belarus, Europe, 2006!

Orsha (January 2, 2009)

Orsha is a town in Belarus. For many years, it had a particular resonance for anyone familiar with the Jewish history of that part of the world. A visit to Orsha now reveals nothing of its glorious past. But perhaps a brief description of its environment and of its illustrious past compared to its current predicament will add perspective and context to the history of Jews in this region.

As with many cities in this area, a native of that town might have been a citizen of numerous countries during the course of a lifetime without ever changing his or her address. In a radius of several dozen miles, one could reach towns with names that are long forgotten to most Jews, but which once were spoken of in many Jewish circles with a reverence normally reserved for holy cities.

Nineteen miles to the west is Volozhin, which was always a small town; perhaps that is why it was chosen by Reb Chaim, a student of the Gaon of Vilna, to be the seat of his yeshivah. In the nineteenth century, the Volozhin Yeshivah was at the top of the "Ivy League" of the yeshivah world. Many of the great Ashkenazic rabbis of the nineteenth century were alumni of that yeshivah. Commentaries on the Bible and Talmud that were produced there are still studied today. The yeshivah building still stands. It is not even a campus. It looks to be little more than four walls. When we think of comparable institutions throughout the world, we conjure up visions of grand facilities. Not Volozhin. It's a singularly unimpressive architectural structure, which in its own way is a statement of the value Jewish tradition placed on knowledge over physical beauty.

The yeshivah's impact was not limited to the religious world. Many of the leaders of the Haskalah movement, which strove to create a secular Jewish culture, started their intellectual searches in Volozhin. The poet laureate of the Jewish people, Chaim Nachman Bialik, is probably the most famous of these intellectuals, but he is by no means the only example.

Traveling further west from Orsha, one comes to Radin. There, in the early twentieth century, one could find the authoritative codifier of Jewish law in that period, a rabbi known as the Chafetz Chaim. In addition to his works in the area of Jewish religious ritual, he was interested in promoting ethical behavior – which he did by promulgating laws governing our actions and through personal example. He also wrote a treatise on gossip that we could all learn from today. His material support came from a grocery store that he owned in town but which he kept open only two days a week so as not to compete unfairly with other groceries nearby that were not run by luminaries and therefore were not able to attract as many customers.

There were other towns in the vicinity of Orsha, each with its own claim to Jewish fame. This part of the world pulsated with Jewish life for hundreds of years and produced numerous Jewish scholars and poets. All the nearby towns were predominantly Jewish before the war, and almost all the inhabitants marked time by the Jewish calendar. Yiddish was the lingua franca for Jews and non-Jews alike. Market days always included Thursdays so the residents could prepare for Shabbat. And so on.

What follows is a description of Jewish life in Orsha today. It could easily apply to Mir, Radin, or any of the other villages and hamlets in the area that were once centers of Jewish life.

To my mind, you can read what follows in one of two ways. It is infused with the pain of the contemporary predicament. Places that once hosted Jewish scholarship are now bereft of any learning. The Jews who remain in Orsha are victims of the twentieth century – ignorant of Jewish texts and of the beauty of Jewish living. A Jewish wedding, a Pesach Seder, a Yiddish poem – all are alien to people living where once all these things informed daily life.

But there is another way to read the description that follows, that is, not to be depressed by comparing it to what once was, but to read it with a sense of wonder that despite it all – despite the Stalinist purges, the Nazi occupation, and the attempts by the Communists to obliterate any vestige of Jewish life – Jews are still here. They are here, and they are determined not only to keep the flame of Jewish life alive, but to nurture it to the extent they are able. Orsha – and Radin and Mir and various other cities that were once Jewish to their core – will never again witness the rich Jewish life they once hosted. That is gone from these sites forever. But these locales are seeing something equally noble in its own way. The prospects for a real Jewish renaissance in these places with virtually no Jews are nonexistent, but the remaining Jews are determined not to let those dim prospects rule their lives. They gather together on Shabbat and on Jewish holidays; they have Jewish discussions in Jewish social settings, in defiance of the despair that is only natural. Each tiny remnant of a Jewish community is its own statement about the eternal nature of Jewish existence. The Jews living there may be uneducated about Jewish practices, and they may know little about the history and culture to which their ancestors laid claim and to which they contributed so much, but they are fiercely proud, and that pride drives them to persevere where others would long ago have given up. They know they will not renew, but they are determined to preserve as much as they can for as long as they can.

Orsha now has a community of about seven hundred Jews, descendants of returning Shoah survivors who at the beginning of World War II were evacuated to the eastern parts of the Soviet Union or to Siberia, beyond the clutches of the Nazi invaders. Not all evacuees survived the unbearable conditions of life during the war. Hunger was rampant. Clothing was inadequate, and medicines were in short supply. The lives of civilians could be sacrificed; nothing was spared to ensure that the Red Army could resist the Germans.

Those who did survive came back to their places of origin hoping to find Jewish communities similar to what they had known before the war. Included among the returning Jews were evacuees who fled eastward in advance of the Nazi juggernaut in 1941, Jews who spent the war in the forests fighting with the partisans, demobilized Red Army veterans, and Jews who were from other towns who thought that the opportunity for employment in Orsha was greater than where they had roots.

There were four thousand Jews in Orsha before the war. This was 70 percent of the total population of the town. These demographics were common in the region; in some towns, the Jewish population was as high as 90 percent. Every community had its Jewish schools and welfare societies, its synagogues, its scholars, its writers, its musicians.

The vast majority of the prewar population did not return, however. They were murdered by the occupying armies and by the extermination units that accompanied the advancing German forces. In the wake of the war, Orsha's Jewish population was just 10 percent of its prewar size.

The system of extermination of Jews was similar in all the shtetls. The first directive of the Germans upon their arrival was to set up Jewish ghettos, to squeeze the Jews into a few streets. The next step was to murder the potential leaders of resistance: intellectuals, doctors, lawyers, and the rabbis – anyone who might object to the destruction of Jewish life. The final step was to lead the remaining Jews into the woods, where hirelings from the local non-Jewish population or people brought in from other occupied regions operated the machine guns. The Germans stood behind them, overseeing the mass murders of the Jews. There was no lack of informers among the local population to cooperate with the Germans and reveal the Jews' hiding places in return for a few coins. Gentile neighbors betrayed Jews, often families that had lived next door to one another for multiple generations.

Today's leadership of the Jewish community of Orsha is trying hard not only to take care of the needy, but also to maintain Jewish life. A small hut serves as the "community center." A dozen people attend Shabbat morning services. No one among them knows how to read the Hebrew prayers or to conduct a Shabbat prayer service. They read part of the prayers in Russian, taking turns to each read a paragraph. In the corner of the room where they meet stands a cupboard, and in it lie two Torah scrolls.

"They are there to remind all of us what a synagogue used to contain," a community member explains. "At the conclusion of the service, we sit around the table and enjoy a small glass of vodka with cookies or black bread."

None of the Jewish residents observes Jewish traditions, nor do most recall them in any detail. But Jewish life has not been completely wiped out in Orsha; they insist on having a weekly Shabbat service. The young people come on Friday evening and play music, sing, and sometimes hear a talk on "tradition" or Jewish history, or a story from the Bible. Some elderly people who remain are supremely aware of what was once here. They have memories and a strong desire to keep a Jewish spark alive. They have no Jewish education and little background, but they are determined that they will not be the last link in the Jewish chain in Orsha. They will do what they can and try to pass on to the next generation what little they know.

Music is part of their life. They have a small orchestra, and the president of the community, a physician by profession, is also an accomplished musician. He has organized a music group that performs regularly, as well as a small choir, a children's orchestra, and an Israeli dance group. They have performed in small Jewish towns throughout Belarus that once were homes to vibrant Jewish communities that left their marks on Jewish history – places like Orsha, Mogilev, Borisov, Bobroisk, Grodno, Gomel, Pinsk, and Vitebsk. These are remnant communities, where little remains of the Jewish life that once existed in these places. And yet, these small communities are determined to resist extinction. It is a story as old as the Jewish people itself, and no less inspirational.

CHAPTER 5

Identity

A Jewish Artifact (January 15, 2002)

At a recent training seminar for local Jewish communal professionals, one of the issues discussed was their *identities* as Jewish professionals in their respective communities, and how that affected their work. Each was asked by the trainer to bring one Jewish artifact from his or her home.

The report by the session leader was quite extraordinary. Maxim brought a prayer shawl, a tallit, that had been in his family since the eighteenth century, hidden for many of those years. Yasha brought four 78-RPM records of his father singing Yiddish songs.

Masha brought a pair of earrings in the shape of a Star of David, which had been owned by her grandmother. She told the following story: Her grandmother lived in Minsk and was shot in the street by the Nazis in the winter of 1942. The rest of the family could not reach the body before it was carted away. In 1952, a non-Jewish neighbor of Masha's grandmother tracked her down. She had taken the earrings from the body while it lay in the street and only ten years later felt comfortable returning them to the family.

While the above stories were moving, I was most touched by one woman who said she felt deeply ashamed by the request to bring a Jewish artifact. Vicka realized that she had nothing to bring. There were no articles of Judaica in her home. She agonized for several days over how to respond. Of course, she realized that coming empty-handed would be understood; after all, everyone above a certain age knew how scarce Judaica was in the USSR. But she felt challenged by the request and believed it was a reasonable expectation of a Jewish professional. After this short introduction to the group, she reached into her bag and pulled out a set of candlesticks for the group to see, which she had purchased in the market in anticipation of this last class.

This was one proud lady. Her parting words exemplify the desire to be a part of the renewal of Jewish life in today's former Soviet Union: "I owned no Jewish items. I am going from here to give these candlesticks to my daughter. She will never say that about herself."

The Notebook (February 7, 2004, and October 1, 2004)

Birobidjan is a city in Russia's Far East, designated by Stalin as a Jewish homeland (which qualified as an "autonomous region" within the USSR) in the late 1920s. Jews were recognized as a national group in the Soviet Union but had no specific area to claim as their own. The Zionist proposal for a homeland in Palestine was ideologically unacceptable in Soviet orthodoxy. Instead, Birobidjan was set aside as a "Jewish autonomous region." The stated goal was to populate it with Jews who would then be like other nations, with a tie to specific territory.

The place was not without its obvious drawbacks. It was far from an urban setting. The weather made it particularly unappealing – extremely cold in the winter and hot, humid, and mosquito infested in the summer. In the end, it developed into a "Jewish autonomous region" that in fact attracted very few Jews.

On a recent visit to Birobidjan, I was given a notebook. On its cover is one word, handwritten in Russian. After deciphering the handwriting, it becomes clear that the word is transliterated from the Hebrew. It says *Vayikra*. Open the notebook and find, in a very deliberate Russian script, words squeezed closely together to conserve space.

Vayikra is the Hebrew term for Leviticus, the third book of the Bible. What I was handed was one notebook of a set of five, which together make up the five books of the Pentateuch, of the Torah.

The background: Inna, a twenty-two-year-old Jewish woman from a poor family in Birobidjan, was caught one night in a cold rainstorm. She ducked into the first public building she passed for shelter. She heard a crowd on an upper floor and decided to investigate. She climbed a set of stairs and happened upon a lecture, and thought it was a good way to spend the time while she dried off. Gradually she became absorbed in the subject matter, which was not familiar to her at all. The lecturer was clearly speaking about a work of literature of profound importance. Inna was totally unfamiliar with it, but she was intrigued. To her regret she had to leave before the lecture concluded.

At home that night she told her mother about her encounter at the lecture. As she began to share the content of what she'd heard, her mother broke out in a smile. "The book you are referencing is the Bible. And it has special meaning for us. Your father and I never shared this with you for a number of reasons that you may never understand: We, and therefore you and your brother as well, are Jews. This is 'our book.'"

It turned out that the building into which Inna had gone for shelter that rain-swept night was a JCC, unmarked as such for security reasons. The lecture she'd heard was the first in a series on adult Jewish literacy.

Inna was stunned and determined to read the book and claim it for her own. But getting a copy was not so simple. Even if she could get hold of a copy of the Bible, photocopying at the time was an extravagance a student her age could not afford.

For the next seven months, several times a week, Inna sat in the library of the JCC from the end of her school day until the library closed at 10 p.m. and copied by hand every single page of the first five books of the Bible. The volume I have is a copy of Leviticus, the third work she completed.

Local Interpretation (May 30, 2003)

A study group of Jewish artists and writers was recently formed in one of the JCCs we established in Moscow. In Russian society, leading lights in the arts have a special status. They are almost universally revered, which made this collection of Jews in these fields – and their interest in exploring Jewish themes – all the more meaningful. They meet together regularly to study Jewish texts and, in a sense, to reclaim them. By design, they do not have a teacher; they want to understand the text on their own terms. The hope, of course, is that, ultimately, they will incorporate the results of their study into their respective fields.

Recently they invited a member of our staff with a strong background in Jewish texts to one of their meetings. They had some issues they wished to clarify and asked him to come by for an informal chat. He later related that they presented their commentary on the biblical story of Cain and Abel. Many Jewish commentaries try to understand why the former killed the latter. Some tie the motive to the apparent divine preference for the victim's sacrifice of an animal over Cain's offering of agricultural produce. There are many more possible explanations.

These Russian Jewish intellectuals studied the text in depth and asserted that the motive was not jealousy but was rooted in misunderstanding. Cain saw the preference given to Abel's sacrifice of a creature, and he took the next step. If a creature is preferred, and an animal is a good choice, then a "higher level" creature, a human being, would be preferable. Therefore, the murder of Abel was really an attempt to appease, and not anger, God. And then they elaborated on this position by bringing proofs from other biblical narratives, such as the command to Abraham to sacrifice Isaac.

I bring this example not to endorse this commentary – not that there's anything inherently wrong with it – but rather to show how the creation of an indigenous Jewish culture in the FSU is progressing and how that culture is struggling to understand and interpret texts in light of their own experiences, where, for example, so much murder was merely a misguided attempt to please figures of authority.

Pieces of Identity (July 1, 2005)

How does one go about planning a communal institution in an environment in which planning is a word not used in polite company? In a society in which "five-year plans" based on falsehoods and individual whims rather than on data determined the direction of everything from careers to budget allocations to diets, from what was grown and where, to the fortunes of cities and regions, planning is dismissed as valueless by almost everyone.

Those involved in determining the nature of Yesod, the future JCC in St. Petersburg, were not prepared to concede to the cynics. They insisted on a comprehensive planning process that was data driven and informed by an understanding of Jewish identity of St. Petersburg Jewry. They commissioned a study by a prominent Russian Jewish sociologist to get a better picture of the Jewish population of St. Petersburg. Who are they? What do they want from Jewish life? What is the nature and composition of their Jewish identity? Their findings present a window not only into that community, but also into certain segments of FSU Jewry. The study was based on a sample of 1,050

Jews. I will not present a full analysis of the data, but some highlights follow, in some instances conflating questions and possible choices:

1. Respondents were asked which of the following three points is most important in order to consider a person Jewish: pride in one's nationality, defending the honor and dignity of one's people, or preserving the memory of the Shoah. In what is termed part of the "middle generation" (40- to 49-year-olds), defending dignity and remembering the Shoah ranked higher in importance than national pride. In all age cohorts, the Shoah response scored very high. It is only in the last fifteen years that the Shoah has been a subject for discussion at all among citizens who came of age in the Soviet era. Before then, it was swallowed up in the larger issue of the sacrifices in the Great Patriotic War of all Soviet Peoples – the singularity of Jewish suffering was nowhere mentioned. Thus, the role of collective memory as a key part of Jewish identity is critical. Commemorations of events in Jewish history become a central theme in communal life, together with exhibits, as well as lectures on the determination of Jews to survive despite repeated efforts to annihilate them.

2. A desire for further knowledge about Jewish history and tradition also scored high, although history far outstripped tradition as a topic for study.

3. Jewish observance was not considered important by the majority of respondents. They were asked about the role of circumcision, kashrut, and Shabbat in Jewish identity. Are any of these a sine qua non for Jewish identity? The answer was a resounding no. One fascinating finding: of the three rituals mentioned, Shabbat was the one they found most compelling and valuable.

4. Finally, the question of intermarriage was raised. Here, the vast majority of respondents said it did not matter one way or the other with respect to Jewish identity if a Jew married a Jew or a non-Jew.

It is clear that there is a keen desire to be Jewish, but Jewish identity here takes a form that is different from what we are accustomed to in the West. Jewish identity in the FSU is rooted in a desire to encounter Judaism intellectually.

There is no religious component to their Jewish identity, and while the ethnic component is downplayed, an identity rooted in Jewish nationalism is very strong. It speaks to a need to identify usable parts of the Jewish past and to build programs around them.

Conflicting Identities (April 4, 2003)

The starting point for JDC's work with any Jewish community around the world is an attempt to understand what it means to be a Jew in that country. The object is not to talk about identity as measured in the study I referred to earlier. Here, I want to raise a more concrete issue: How do profoundly conflicting identities affect individuals? What do you experience in a very real sense, moment to moment?

In downtown Kyiv, there is a statue of Bogdan Chmelnitzki, the national liberator who led Ukrainian peasants into battle against the Polish occupiers of seventeenth-century Ukraine, in an uprising that ultimately resulted in one of the only periods of freedom and independence in the country's history, albeit short-lived. He is a national hero, the subject of epic poems and legends. His statue watches over the government of the once-again independent Ukraine and is meant to inspire all Ukrainians and instill in them national pride. The statue, incidentally, stands at an intersection where the Ukrainian Court of Appeals once sat, the court in which Mendel Beilis was tried in the twentieth century's first great blood libel, a trial immortalized in Bernard Malamud's novel *The Fixer*.

Not coincidentally, this great liberator is also remembered in Jewish lore as one of the most vicious antisemites in history. During the course of his "war of liberation," he led his bands in rape, pillaging, and the murder of any Jews who were unfortunate enough to find themselves in his path. The impact was so traumatic that, to this day, there are Jews who observe fast days in commemoration of that period, and liturgical poems remembering the martyrs are incorporated into many contemporary prayer books.

What does a Ukrainian Jew feel walking by that statue? How does one reconcile these conflicting identities – one that vilifies a sworn enemy, and one that elevates him to the status of national hero?

Let's suppose that this same Jew is inured to it. He walks past this statue every day and does not see the conflict inherent in it for him. The Chmelnitzki events were in the distant past, and he may not even be aware of them. But what if a similar conflict confronts him today and both elements of the conflict are from his lifetime?

When German forces marched into Ukraine in 1941, they were welcomed by many as liberators from the hated Bolsheviks. Many Ukrainians were still alive who remembered an independent Ukraine some twenty years earlier. Their experiment in national independence had been brought to an abrupt end with the victory of the Bolsheviks in the Russian Civil War and the incorporation of Ukraine into the USSR.

The invading Nazi army was welcomed by many Ukrainian nationalists as the force that would free them from the Communist yoke, and its troops were hailed in friendship rather than seen as occupiers. That welcome lasted for a few years and ran the gamut from cheers and invitations into homes to collaboration with the SS, including in the killing of Jews, who were seen as the prime supporters of the Communist regime.

Metropolitan Archbishop Andrei Sheptytsky was a high-ranking cleric in the Ukrainian Uniate Church during the Second World War. He was, in effect, the archbishop of the Lviv region in Ukraine, an area with fluid borders that have shifted throughout history with the victories and defeats of different ruling powers. At various times it has been part of the Russian Empire, under Polish control, or part of an independent Ukraine.

Metropolitan Sheptytsky was a Ukrainian patriot. For him, the Bolshevik entry into Lviv after the 1919 Ukrainian Civil War was an unmitigated disaster: The atheist regime in Moscow was bent on suppressing the church and erasing any memory of Ukrainian independence. He fought the masters in Moscow both aggressively and passively in any way that he could, which endeared him to his flock.

The Metropolitan was also close to many Jews. The Lviv region had an extremely large Jewish population – there were villages in the region that were more than 40 percent Jewish. This was the heart of the Pale of Settlement of czarist times. When stories are told about non-Jews in that part of the world who spoke fluent Yiddish in order to engage in commerce with Jewish merchants, this is the region frequently referenced.

Metropolitan Sheptytsky was among those who opened his doors willingly to the Germans. Finally, the yoke of the Soviet oppressors would be lifted. At the same time, he worked to save Jews from the fate that awaited them with the Germans. He hid Jews and urged his followers to do the same. He collaborated with the Nazis in their attempts to establish hegemony in the region by expelling the hated Soviets, and at the same time risked his life to save Jews and encouraged his parishioners to risk theirs.

Hero or enemy? Do his efforts to save Jews overshadow his support for the Nazi regime, or was that support to be considered so determinative of his legacy that nothing else he did could mitigate it? Yad Vashem, Israel's Holocaust Remembrance Center, has taken a strong position – that to place him in the same category with righteous gentiles who saved Jews, and who need no asterisks next to their names, would be blasphemy. His support of the Nazi regime is therefore the defining element of his persona, according to this view.

Tekuma, the local Holocaust studies foundation in Ukraine, founded with the help of JDC, recently held a symposium in western Ukraine on the Sheptytsky issue entitled, "The Dilemma of Humanistic Choice under the Conditions of a Totalitarian Regime." The text was about how Sheptytsky should be treated by history. The subtext was a community of contemporary Jews struggling with the issue of dual identity when a traditional understanding of those two identities, Ukrainian and Jewish, seemed to be contradictory, at least in the last few centuries. What does it mean to be a citizen of a country whose people have a long legacy of antisemitism? Does teaching the Ukrainian citizenry at large about the Shoah foster an us-versus-them mentality, which forces the Jew to acknowledge that he is forever doomed to be an outsider there? Can the Jew and his neighbor agree on who the liberator was and who the occupier was? Is their shared history, by definition, something that will drive a wedge between this minority and majority?

We can pontificate from our positions of comfort and argue the merits of Yad Vashem's position, knowing that the implications of either are of no more than passing academic interest to us. We advance a position and then go about our business. For the Ukrainian Jews with whom we work, however, taking a stand in this debate is a statement about who they are and how they see themselves. This is neither theoretical nor academic; it can influence how they see their neighbors, what their curriculum must look like in school, for whom they vote in elections, and, ultimately, how they define themselves.

JDC initially supported Tekuma because of its potential to redress a historic wrong: the erasing of the Shoah from Ukrainian history. According to Soviet history, 27 million Soviet citizens were killed in the war. Period. There is no basis for singling out the Jewish experience. With the passage of time, though, that experience has become a prism through which contemporary Jewish identity is discussed and debated. These debates have attracted young Jews and intellectuals and have stimulated their involvement in Jewish life.

The questions that surface in the Sheptytsky debate arise repeatedly with respect to Jewish identity in many places in this part of the world. Most of the countries that were freed from the Soviet yoke in the 1990s are now searching for national narratives around which their citizens can rally. They look for heroes who can serve as role models to their citizens and inspire patriotic sentiments. This is common in most countries, but the challenges in this region are a bit different.

Many of these now-independent countries experienced short periods of independence even before the Soviet period. Their founding myths are often based on patriots and rabid nationalists, who are appropriate, to their thinking, as role models. Stepan Bandera and Symon Petliura are two such heroes for Ukraine: They inspired armed bands that took to the forests to resist Soviet domination in Ukraine. Both were Ukrainian nationalists, no question, and both were accused of being antisemites. What does that say about the Ukrainian nation? And what does it say about the possibility for Ukrainian Jews to have a hyphenated identity? Do you build a national mythology on these kinds of characters? And if you do so, for lack of alternatives, how can Jewish citizens be expected to identify with a nation that raises to the level of national heroes people who butchered Jews as a matter of course? Obviously Sheptytsky is not to be equated with Bogdan Chmelnitzki or others of his ilk, but he can be said, in a sense, to represent a similar problem: finding the proper historical context in which to render moral judgment on figures of Ukrainian history whose legacies are complex and difficult to reconcile. And, of course, Bandera, Petliura, and Chmelnitzki present the additional problem of how to reconcile Jewish and Ukrainian identities.

Fast forward to Ukraine of the twenty-first century. Like many countries forced to examine their past after the breakup of the USSR, Ukraine has embarked on a process of national reconciliation. So begins a period of rewriting its history. Heroes become villains as liberation becomes occupation in retrospect. The vaunted Red Army, once the harbinger of salvation from Nazi occupation, is now understood by Ukrainian nationalists to have been an occupying force. President Yushchenko is spearheading this drive to effect national reconciliation, to redefine the Ukraine nationalists of the Second World War as freedom fighters without delegitimizing the efforts of Red Army veterans.

All fine and good. If successful, this reconciliation will help avert the potential breakup of Ukraine, a prospect that regularly surfaces, and a potential rift between the country's nationalist West and its Russian-leaning East. But where does this leave the Jews?

Many elderly Jews whom we encounter, who have so little to begin with, take great pride in their wartime contributions. We've seen them in every city we visit in the FSU, decked out in the finest clothes they own, dripping with medals. But now those they fought are being granted legitimacy. Worse, those who murdered their relatives are becoming part of the national narrative. How does one then see oneself? Can you be a proud Ukrainian Jew – that is, proud of both parts of that title at the same time? Is there an inherent contradiction, mutual incompatibility? And if so, which part of their identity is forced to compromise?

The purpose of raising this question here is not to give an answer, but to share the dilemma, for if we do not understand it, we cannot address the Jewish element of it.

Subbotniks (September 22, 2006)

All of us are aware of the joke about two Jews and three opinions, and its various forms. We are a stiff-necked people – and a contentious one at that.

Often, those debates are kept within the family, and they stimulate a creative tension that brings dynamism and inventiveness to Jewish life. Occasionally, though, these debates grow into something much larger, and eventually lead to a schism between the normative Jewish community and those advocating a new or different path. This aspect of Jewish history has always interested me: Why are some changes and innovations adapted to and assimilated into normative Jewish life, while others precipitate separation from the Jewish community and result in a schism? Why does a revolutionary movement like Chasidism, a rebellion against established norms and the leadership of the time, continue to be part of the Jewish narrative, while the followers of Jesus break away or are pushed into forming another religion? Of course, historians can give numerous answers to this question, but my experience has been that there are more schisms than answers. What follows is one such schism and our connection to it in the FSU.

Russian history is full of groups that broke away from the Jewish mainstream over the last four hundred years or, alternatively, who came close to the Jewish people without ever fully casting their lot with them through conversion. The latter even warrant a title: they are called "Judaizers" in the literature. These are defined as people who, without being Jews, follow parts of the Jewish religion, or claim to be Jews, despite rejection of this claim by contemporary Jewish authorities. They may practice circumcision on the eighth day, aspects of kashrut or Shabbat, and the like.

The group under discussion in this weekly briefing is the Subbotniks. Historically, they are a rural, peasant group from eastern Russia who adopted Jewish practices. Their name, interestingly, points to their roots: They observe Shabbat on Saturday, which in a Russian context immediately connects them with Jews. Hence their name, which comes from the Russian word for Saturday.

There are an estimated ten thousand Subbotniks still living in the FSU, although many are in small, hard-to-reach enclaves. This is a result of the persecution to which they were subjected, which led to forced dispersion in the late nineteenth century. In general, there is little intramarriage, and there is not much hope for their continued existence as a distinct group. Interestingly, though, the assimilation trend works both ways. While many are absorbed into FSU cultures, there are also examples of families that have moved to Israel over the past century. In fact, there are rumors that the family of one of the chiefs of staff of the Israel Defense Forces was Subbotnik before its arrival in Israel.

The town of Sevan, Armenia, has thirty thousand inhabitants, of whom thirteen are Subbotniks, down from about two thousand in the town in the 1920s. Three are men and ten are women; all are eighty years old or close to it. They do not practice kashrut or circumcision, but they were, until recently, in possession of two Torah scrolls, one of which was transferred to the capital,

Yerevan, and is used in the (Jewish) synagogue there. The Subbotniks of Yerevan have no synagogue today: the Soviet authorities treated them as Jews and confiscated their synagogue in the mid-1930s.

Recently, one of the surviving members of the community was interviewed. "We lead a simple life," he said, "but life has become very expensive. Without the aid of the Jewish community, we would have a very rough time. Our pensions are meager, not enough to cover utilities." The article goes on to point out that "the Armenia office of Hesed Avraham, sponsored by the Joint, periodically provides the Subbotniks with food packages."

One issue that arises repeatedly when looking at groups like this is whether they are authentic Jews, or at least close enough to be eligible for support from those donating to Jewish causes. JDC does not determine Jewishness. Instead, we rely on the standards established by the local Jewish community in which we work.

In some regions of the FSU, local communities abide by standards established due to external events. For example, there is a remnant Karaite community in the Crimea and Baltic regions. Part of a group that separated itself from Rabbinic Judaism in the Middle Ages, they accept the authority of the Written Torah, but not that of the Oral Law. During the Nazi occupation, the Karaites generally succeeded in convincing the Nazi authorities that they belonged to a discrete religious group and had no connection to the Jewish people. In this way, they averted deportation and murder. As a consequence, in the postwar period, many Jewish communities in those regions did not consider Karaites to be members.

There is no analogous situation for the Subbotniks, as they did not live in occupied territory. Local Jewish communities do not shun them, however, and they have been allowed to make aliyah, as Jews, hence the appearance of about a score of them on the Hesed rolls in Russia.

A fascinating piece of Jewish (or quasi-Jewish) history, soon to disappear.

Giving Back (March 17, 2006)

Kamianske is a city in eastern Ukraine. Two years ago, JDC helped the community purchase an apartment that would serve as a base for community activities. In the ensuing two years, the community, using its own devices, expanded the size of the property by buying two neighboring apartments. It asked for contributions from members of the community.

Last Tuesday, a woman came to the community center and handed over an envelope containing two hundred hryvna (about forty dollars). She is a Hesed client and told the secretary, "I am not a wealthy woman. In fact, this is all the savings I have. But my daily needs are taken care of. To be honest, I was saving this for one thing: I am alone in the world. I have no family, and it is very important to me that I receive a proper Jewish burial next to my parents when I die. Since there is no one to pay for it, I have saved this money for my own funeral. But when I heard that the Jewish community needed money, that was more important." Then she added with a wink, "Take this money. My funeral will have to wait."

Community Responsibility (September 7 and 14, 2007)

Supreme Court Justice Potter Stewart's famous comment about pornography is equally applicable in many instances to community development: "It is difficult to define (and, in the case of community development, I would add, 'to measure'), but I know it when I see it."

I want to share with you an event that happened recently in southern Russia that, to my mind, is eloquent testimony to the fact that a group of Jews in one city can now be called a community. An event they recently put together demonstrated that they understand one of the central tenets of community life, and that is the community's responsibility for its members.

The event took place in Volgograd, a city that lies on the Volga River, from which it derives its name. It is one of thousands of city names in the FSU that mean little to foreigners. It is a municipality like any other, anywhere in Russia. But in fact, anyone with a passing knowledge of World War II is familiar with the circumstances under which the city became infamous under its previous moniker, Stalingrad. The Battle of Stalingrad is generally considered to be the turning point of the war. The German defeat there was a harbinger of the ultimate downfall of the Third Reich.

In 1961, the city's name was officially changed to Volgograd. Its name prior to the change was judged inappropriate, given the changes in Soviet society at the time. There is a community of volunteers in Volgograd whose task it is to find the remains of Soviet soldiers who fell in defense of the city.

The devastation was tremendous and in the aftermath of the war, for ideological reasons, Stalin insisted on rebuilding the city as quickly as possible. Human remains to this day are scattered around the area and are periodically uncovered.

In April 2007, a set of remains was discovered on a building site, and with them a dog tag identifying the body as that of one Naum Isaakovich Dunaevsky. A search in the Red Army archives revealed that an eighteen-year-old soldier from Bashkiria, Russia, was reported missing in the Battle of Stalingrad. His data card had "Jew" entered as his nationality.

The members of the volunteer group started to look for his relatives in Russia and beyond, but their search turned up nothing. They were about to bury the remains in a military cemetery when one of the activists decided, on a lark, to call a Jewish welfare organization he had read about in the local paper and see if they were interested in becoming involved. Not only did the Hesed agree to become involved, but its directorate immediately assumed responsibility for burying the remains.

It was decided to reinter the body on June 22, the anniversary of the beginning of the Nazi invasion in 1941. It was further decided that this was to be a Jewish community-wide commemoration, and indeed the Jewish community turned out in force: Almost three thousand people came out for the ceremony in a city with four thousand Jews.

The Hesed board committed to raising the money needed to create a fitting monument to Dunaevsky and other anonymous Jews killed in the battle, whose burial places were not known. The community was further determined to raise all the necessary funds locally, as this was their responsibility, and theirs alone.

The old Jewish cemetery of the city, long out of use, was opened for this occasion. The students of the local Jewish school spent the week before the ceremony learning about the Jewish contribution to the Red Army victory.

The ceremony was brief but poignant. A member of the community currently serving in the Russian army recited the ritual mourning prayer, the Kaddish, in uniform. Among those present, most had spent their formative years in the USSR. For several generations, the Red Army uniform represented an empire dedicated to the obliteration of Jewish life. Its presence at a Jewish event now electrified the crowd.

Children laid down wreaths and pictures they had drawn. Finally, the chairman of the board of the Hesed, Vladimir Paikin, spoke. Much to everyone's surprise, he revealed that his own brother had been drafted to fight in the war and had not returned. To this day, the family does not know his fate.

Perhaps most moving were his final words in tribute to the fallen soldier. "This soldier died not only for Russia but for the Jewish people. Therefore, we Jews have a unique moral debt to this boy and his Jewish comrades."

This kind of public outpouring and declaration was inconceivable just a few years ago.

A Two-Way Street (August 1, 2008)

This is a story from a former colleague of ours, Dr. Seymour Epstein (aka Epi):

> While in Khabarovsk a year ago, I met a young woman who had taught herself Hebrew and was now teaching in the local Sunday school. She told me about a fascinating Jewish book that she had found hidden in the pages of a prayer book that JDC sent to Khabarovsk. Thinking that somehow a mysterious manuscript had slipped into one of our shipments, I asked her about the book. She said that she couldn't believe that such a rich collection of ethical values existed in Jewish life, and that the name of this esoteric volume, which she was sure I had never heard of, was *The Ethics of the Fathers*, from the Mishnah. It almost hurt to inform the woman that literate Jews had been studying this book for generations.
>
> I suddenly realized how significant this Jewish revival is in the FSU, not only for "them," but also for *us*. We, who take such books for granted, have neglected Jewish letters so much that our children and grandchildren often no longer can read works like these in the original. These Jews of the former Soviet Union, the new limb of the Jewish people, may yet bring us back to Hebrew, the Bible, Jewish history, and a new Zionist dream. Their enthusiasm for the things we have forgotten is real Jewish continuity. Who is helping whom?

Ethnic Divides (June 5, 2009)

We all know that FSU countries are troubled societies. Many of these problems could be expected in countries that emerged from the breakup of the USSR. Societies had to be reconstructed, economies created almost from scratch, and political cultures formed de novo. Healthy civic society, as that concept is understood in the West, did not exist. The Jewish population in each country is not insulated from the turmoil these societies are undergoing.

But these countries face another challenge, in which the Jews are bystanders, sometimes courted by one side or the other. This struggle is often titanic, and its fallout affects everyone. Most of the FSU countries are thought to be ethnically homogenous, but few actually are. Some cases of heterogeneity are well known, and lethal. Beslan and Chechnya in Russia are two examples: Muslim and Russian Orthodox populations have a tenuous coexistence in these regions and many proximate to them. Occasionally, there are violent flare-ups, with devastating results. Often the rivalries and hatred don't spill over into violence but still have a negative impact on social development.

The roots of these problems can be traced back to Soviet policy regarding ethnic groups within the empire. The central government made monumental efforts to ensure sizable ethnic Russian populations in all regions, with the hope that this would offset any competing loyalties to local ethnic or national groups. There were often financial incentives for ethnic Russians to settle outside of the Russian Republic, and Russian university graduates were often assigned jobs in other republics in order to ensure a Russian majority, or at least a significant minority. Population transfers were a common method for ensuring that all regions contained populations of ethnic Russians who were loyal to Russian national identity and to Moscow. The effect of this was to dilute any national or ethnic loyalties of the non-Russian populations and thereby ensure political stability in the USSR. No attention was paid to ensuring integration or to resolving disputes between the groups.

The negative consequences of this became most apparent when the USSR dissolved. Some of the countries that were formed from the ashes of the Soviet Union were controlled by minority populations. For example, Kazakhstan, one of the largest post-Soviet states, has an ethnic-Russian majority, making Kazakhs a minority in their own country. This means that the majority of the population, or a very significant minority, generally cannot speak the national language and, in some cases, is relegated to second-class status within the country. In most places, Russian was the official language during the Soviet period, no matter what the predominant nationality was. For example, in Azerbaijan, government and educational institutions generally operated in Russian. The indigenous population used the national language among themselves and transmitted this to succeeding generations, but most citizens knew and spoke Russian and conducted their official affairs in Russian. Ethnic Russians saw no reason to learn a second, local language, which was not a hindrance for them until the breakup of the USSR, when the local language was formally adopted by the newly established country as the only official language. In each successor country, the local language gradually took precedence over Russian, and ethnic Russians were at a loss. Often, requirements are put in place, such as fluency in the local language, that make it difficult for these Russian residents to acquire citizenship in countries that were formed on territory in which their families have lived for several generations.

Local Jewish populations often reflect these differences and are accorded the same status as the larger ethnic groups with which they are identified. Many educated Russian Jews with skills needed in far-flung republics of the empire were resettled in these regions by the Soviet government. Like their Russian counterparts already resident in these republics, they had little to do with the local populations. They spoke Russian, had been educated in Russian, and identified with Russian culture.

In a place like Uzbekistan, there were also indigenous Jews whose roots in the region extended back hundreds of years. These Jews were Uzbeks. They spoke the local language, they interacted with their Uzbek neighbors, and they felt most comfortable in Uzbek settings. They had, and have, far more in common with Uzbek society than they do with the Russian Jews who live in the same region.

Until 1991, all shared Soviet citizenship and certain common experiences, e.g., army service. After 1991, Uzbeks became the dominant group in the country, and the divide between the Russian and Uzbek Jews in the region persisted.

There are places in which we work where there is little interaction among Jewish populations that identify with different ethnic groups. Jews from Russia in Georgia have little to do with native Georgian Jews. They don't share a language, they study at different schools, and they often have different national loyalties, which can be a particular problem when Russia and Georgia go to war. It took a yeoman's effort to get the two groups to cooperate on a Hesed program.

These problems are not limited to the east. In Moldova, the ethnic divide can spill over into the Jewish community, with Russian speakers on one side and Romanian speakers on the other. Debates raged about the kinds of food to serve in the soup kitchen, the language of programming in the JCC and family camps, and, of course, from which group community professionals and lay leaders would be chosen. Even a small Jewish museum established by some members of the community was controversial. The divisions over how to tell the history of the Soviet period and the government's traditional treatment of the Jews became a fault line that reflected larger political differences. Jews with Russian backgrounds pushed for a more benign assessment of Moscow's behavior, while local Jews identified with the oppressed of the national group.

We Need More of Them (May 8, 2009)

Kolkhoz was the Russian term for a communal settlement. Stalin was keen to resettle much of the population on kolkhozes around the USSR as a way of eliminating private property, and the cost involved to achieve this was of no consequence to him. Jews, who were generally shopkeepers and owned small businesses, were targets of the new regime to be collectivized in the immediate post-revolution period because they were engaged in quintessentially capitalist behavior. In the 1920s, Agro-Joint attempted to train these capitalists to become "productive members" of collective agricultural settlements, and thereby prevent them from being singled out by Stalin's regime. The process of moving these Jews from business to agriculture proved to be quite difficult.

In keeping with Jewish tradition, even this painful chapter was mined for its humor: The kolkhoz chairman addresses the membership at a meeting and begins by telling them that there are two issues on the agenda:

1. Should the kolkhoz begin to raise rabbits?
2. Should the Jew Yakobovitch be allowed to emigrate?

One of the members asks permission to speak. "I'd like to address the second issue. I say let him go. It will be good for us: When he leaves, he'll leave us his car. We can turn his house into a storage facility. And since he can't take the contents of his bank account out of the country – we will inherit it."

No sooner does he finish than a comrade of his asks to speak. "I want to relate this to the first issue. If this is all true, why are we considering raising rabbits? We should raise Jews."

Alive and Well (March 12, 2010)

They say that a picture is worth a thousand words. I want to test that, but by going in reverse. I want to describe a photograph that I have in front of me as I write. The photo is of poor quality and dates from the early 1920s.

At first glance, the picture appears to document some sort of large gathering. There are several dozen people marching in a parade formation, with a large box in the middle of the assemblage. The parade route is lined with several hundred more people on either side who are observing the goings-on.

If one studies the picture carefully, one can make out what appear to be large masks of distorted human faces held on poles at the head of the march. These are a key indicator of what is happening. At the rear of the procession are two large candles. These are typical of a funeral procession in some Slavic countries at that time, and there are regions where traditional funerals are still conducted in this manner today.

Therefore, we can assume that the procession is a funeral. A second, closer look at the marching group shows that the box they are holding is in the shape of a coffin. The pieces all fit neatly together except for one item: The "coffin" has a covering, and on it is Cyrillic writing. With a magnifying glass in hand, the letters can be made out. They spell the word "Shabbat" in Russian.

This is, indeed, a photograph of a funeral procession or, to be more precise, a mock funeral. It is from the early 1920s. The marchers are Jews who are demonstrating their allegiance to the relatively new Soviet regime. The particularity of Jewish identity stands in stark contrast to the universal values this new regime is trying to inculcate in its citizens. To be an identifying Jew was to be particularistic in the face of the universalism being touted, to remain loyal to the old and discredited in the face of the new promises of the workers' society, and to be superstitious and religious when rationalism and atheism were the new shibboleths. These Soviet Jews felt a need to publicly demonstrate the transfer of their loyalty from the Jewish people, symbolized by "Shabbat" written on the coffin, to the Politburo and its minions. What better way to do that than to bury their past in a coffin representing one of the gifts of the Jewish people to humanity, the notion of a weekly day of rest.

The picture is particularly poignant in light of the work going on in the Jewish community during the last few years. Over and over again, we are witness to a desire on the part of young Jews not only to reconnect with their past, but to do so publicly. As we approach Passover, this is particularly worthy of note. Several large cities have billboards advertising the sale of matzot. On the Internet, Jews are creating social networks of and for Jews and are making the existence of such networks known all over social media. Young Jews are taking over restaurants to hold events for themselves and their Jewish friends, and several cities host Jewish salons, holiday celebrations, or simply Jewish cultural experiences, including concerts, movies, and talks about Jewish-themed books. Their pride in their Jewish identity is an impetus for them to almost flaunt it publicly.

While they are not aware of this picture specifically and are unfamiliar, to a large degree, with what it represents, they are its counterpoint. Whereas some Jews in early Soviet times needed to demonstrate publicly that their Jewish identity was dead, many young Jews today in the FSU are attracted to JCCs and public Jewish programs and wish to publicize their identity for all to see.

The other major difference between the reality reflected in the picture and today's reality on the Russian-speaking street is this: In the 1920s, the Soviet identity could not coexist with the Jewish identity. The old identity needed to be jettisoned to make room for the Soviet one. Today, many young Jews live comfortably with their Jewish and Russian identities. This is in marked contrast to many of their Ukrainian counterparts as described earlier. They enjoy Russian culture, eat Russian foods, and participate in Russian civic life. They often view political developments worldwide through a Russian lens. At the same time, they see their Jewish identity as one that enriches rather than competes. They celebrate Jewish holidays with their contemporaries in Jewish homes or in Jewish settings, and they belong to Jewish clubs and attend Jewish cultural events. Increasingly, they volunteer in Jewish organizations and put their children into formal and informal Jewish educational frameworks in order to develop that aspect of their identity as well.

So the value of this picture is really in its contemporary negation: In the 1920s, the forbears of many of today's young Jews needed to show not only that they could be *Homo sovieticus*, but that they could be better models of that species than their neighbors. Many lived sordid lives under the czars, and the new Soviet regime represented for them an opportunity for equality and achievement, of which Jews before them in that region had not even dared dream. Over the years this vision evaporated, and the dream turned into a nightmare for many.

The recent outdoor Festival of Jewish Culture in Odesa, sponsored by the Beit Grand JCC (founded by JDC), is the contemporary refutation of the picture I described above. It is a public celebration of Jewish pride, with booths promoting Jewish tradition in the city's main square, Jewish-themed books on sale on the main business thoroughfare of the city, along with loud-speakers blasting Hebrew songs and an estimated fifteen thousand people in attendance, including government officials.

Resistance by the Book (September 9, 2011)

On December 31, 1991, the flag featuring the hammer and sickle was low-ered from the tallest building in Moscow's Kremlin and immediately replaced with the blue, red, and white striped flag of the newly independent Russian Federation.

Subsequently, numerous books and articles appeared, attempting to explain how it came to be that the USSR simply collapsed, an event that few had predicted. Today, with our years of experience in the field, the question is turned on its head. It is hard to believe, given the rot, that the USSR lasted as long as it did. But the best and the brightest, with the most sophisticated tools at their disposal, had no inkling prior to 1991 of what was to come.

The explanations vary. Some attribute the collapse to the inherent diffi-culties in central planning for a country of that size and diversity, others to an economic system that discouraged initiative, and still others to a political sys-tem that could not keep such dissimilar populations united under its thumb. Other reasons include technological revolutions that hindered the state's abil-ity to control information, an arms race that bankrupted a tottering system, and more. In fact, each book and every article that I have come across dealing with these events has its own explanations, or variations on a theme.

I dare not venture a theory of my own. However, I do want to propose a way of thinking about this issue that differs in very substantive ways from what is proposed by most pundits. Most of the theories concentrate on the macro explanations. They look to political, economic, and social "systems" for the roots of the collapse. Most, if not all, ignore the individuals who make up those systems. They ignore what is, to my mind, the larger issue, which is how individual citizens contributed to the downfall of the USSR in their own, often furtive, way. Seen another way, was the USSR ever the monolithic society and state that generations understood it to be? Were the dissidents like Sakharov, the Jewish refusenik movement, Solzhenitsyn, and others really the exceptions to the rule in an otherwise solid society marching in lockstep to the tune set by a strong central government? Or was this a society rife with dissidence and nonconformity that were not conspicuous but were more prevalent than the regime recognized and was prepared to allow?

Recently, I received a copy of a beautifully handwritten Hebrew manuscript. It comprises some 150 pages and is very pleasing to the eye. The manuscript is a siddur, a prayer book for weekdays and Shabbat. Under other circumstances, and without knowing any of the background, one might think that this was a commissioned piece – that an artist had been asked to create a unique prayer book for use on some special occasion. However, when I was given the copy of the siddur, I was told a bit about the provenance of the original, and its history speaks to the issue raised above.

Photo credit: JDC

Handwritten Siddur, by Naum Suponitsky

The person who created this siddur did not do so as an act of defiance. Indeed, as you will read, it was more for purposes of preservation than for protest. But, in its own way, and despite what the scribe may have felt at the time, it was an act that defied the government to which he was subject. Multiply these individual acts by the millions, and perhaps the implosion of the USSR begins to look a bit different. Perhaps it collapsed because it did not rest on a firm foundation. The slightest challenge and the enterprise simply crumbled. Here is the story of the siddur.

In many respects, Naum Suponitsky was an ordinary Soviet citizen. He grew up in a shtetl near Dnepropetrovsk (later, Dnipro) in the early years of the twentieth century. His was a religious family, a religious home, part of a tightly knit Jewish community steeped in faith and in tradition.

Russia's Communist Revolution in 1917 changed all that. Gradually, but inexorably, the country's new Soviet rulers dismantled Naum's Jewish life, as it did those of millions of others. Physically, Naum survived.

We don't know how Naum came to terms with the Soviet Union's destruction of the Jewish world around him. Details of this period of his life have been lost. All we know is that he remained in his native village for many years. He married a woman named Vicka, and together they had four children.

With the outbreak of the Great Patriotic War, as it is known to this day in the former Soviet Union, Naum was drafted into the Red Army, leaving his wife, his children, and all his worldly possessions behind. He was sent to the front lines, where he served with distinction. At war's end he returned to the shtetl only to learn that his wife and children had been murdered.

On hearing this news, he set off to find his sister who he had heard had moved to Leningrad. There he discovered that, in fact, not all of his family had perished. Two of his daughters and his sister had been employed at the famous Kirov tractor plant in the city and were evacuated eastward when the Soviets dismantled much of the factory and moved it, complete with its workforce, to Chelyabinsk in the Ural Mountains, beyond the grasp of the invading Nazi army.

So Naum went east and was reunited with what remained of his family. Chelyabinsk became his new home. And, like his daughters and sisters, he also found a job at the tractor plant. He was, to all appearances, an ordinary Soviet citizen.

An ordinary Soviet citizen, only more so. In fact, he was a model Soviet citizen. He was a war veteran who now worked at the Kirov tractor plant, a bastion of Soviet proletarianism, founded in the city where the revolution began. And Naum wasn't just any employee. His job was to sing in the plant's theater choir and thereby to inspire his fellow workers with the revolutionary zeal they needed to achieve greater and greater productivity.

And yet, appearances were deceptive. Because for all of Citizen Naum's Communist conformity, the *pintele Yid*, the Jewish spark, lived. In his soul, he remained a committed and believing Jew.

It seems that throughout his adult life Naum knowingly put everything he held dear at risk. Long after the synagogues were closed and religion outlawed, he secretly engaged in a prohibited activity: He prayed.

Perhaps he had kept a hidden siddur. Perhaps, when he was drafted, he left it behind in his village, where it was lost or destroyed. Or perhaps he secretly took it with him when he joined the Red Army but either lost it or found that its pages had disintegrated after decades of daily use. Again, we'll never know.

What seems fairly certain is that, years later, he was left without a siddur and was afraid he would forget the prayers and lose this act of faith that sustained him. He also knew that it would be impossible to find another siddur in Stalin's Chelyabinsk.

Which is why this ordinary man did something quite extraordinary. He took the matter into his own hands – literally – by writing out the siddur in a notebook. Painstakingly, using Hebrew block letters with full and complete vowels, he transcribed the entire siddur. And from then until his death in 1982 he would return to his handwritten manuscript on a daily basis. Silently. Secretly.

Such was the oppressive nature of Soviet rule that Naum feared telling anyone about it. When his grandchildren asked about the notebook with its strange characters, he told them he was reading a book in the Ukrainian language. They accepted the explanation without question; in the Soviet Union you didn't ask too many questions. Like countless others, his grandchildren had no inkling that they were Jewish.

After Naum died, the family kept the notebook siddur in his honor, but its real meaning remained a mystery to his family.

Years passed. The Soviet Union collapsed, and Jews were again free to be Jews. But still Naum's family remained unaware of the meaning of his legacy – until his daughter found herself growing old and needing more help than her family could provide. She turned to the Chelyabinsk Hesed, and then explained to her children that she had turned to this Jewish organization because she was Jewish…and so were they.

Naum's granddaughter, Marina, began to explore her previously unknown heritage and took the notebook to the Jewish school where she had started sending her children. The astonishing truth was finally known.

Naum never lived to see the fall of the Soviet Union or the freeing of the Jewish spirit from the bonds of Communism. But his Jewish spirit must surely be rejoicing that his granddaughter Marina works at Chelyabinsk's Yevreski Dom, the local Jewish community center founded by JDC; that she helps to educate the city's Jewish children; and that her children are being raised to be proud Jews, as part of their people, at one with a heritage they can explore and express in ways he could not.

The creation of this siddur was the extraordinary act of an ordinary man. For Naum Suponitsky *was* just an ordinary man; one who survived oppression and persecution and protected his family from knowledge that could have destroyed them. But he never forgot. Through the siddur that he so lovingly wrote, he left a legacy in the form of a mystery that his descendants would unravel when the time was right.

That time is now. Many thousands of Jews can now be Jewish because many thousands of people like Naum, each in his or her own way, refused to succumb. They may have been persecuted, exiled, starved, and abused, and their bodies punished, but they were masters of their own souls. This siddur is eloquent testimony to their unyielding commitment to maintaining a connection to the Jewish people against incredible odds.

This "notebook siddur" is a reminder of the indomitability of the Jewish spirit. It is Naum Suponitsky's legacy to us all.

To return to the question posed earlier, I don't know what caused the USSR's collapse. But I am sure that a contributing factor, a significant one at that, was the Naums throughout the years – outwardly conforming, but unwilling to be broken from within. Each resisting in his or her own way, until larger, external forces created the conditions for the collapse of their prison.

In this case, resistance by a book. How uniquely Jewish!

Aliyah Libraries (June 12, 2009)

When JDC first reentered the USSR in the late 1980s, we were faced with a tremendous challenge: We did not know where to begin. Put aside for a moment the budget challenge of suddenly coping with a prospective program for an estimated 2.5 million Jews, when JDC's worldwide budget was already fully allocated. Perhaps even more daunting, we were already expending several million dollars on Jewish communities in countries like Hungary and Romania, communities that were dwarfed in size by the number of Soviet Jews. Extrapolating the amount needed from what we did in those countries to what would have been needed for a JDC program in the USSR would have required a tripling of JDC's worldwide budget at the time, a budget that already exhausted what we understood to be our fundraising capacity.

But even before we struggled with that issue, we needed to determine how we would begin a program in the Soviet Union. The needs were tremendous, and the political situation was developing at breakneck speed. We needed to make a decision, and fast. No one knew how long the "opening," as it was being characterized at the time, would last. How to begin?

Would we start with Jewish schools, which were just beginning to form, in the hopes of educating a population that had received no Jewish education for generations? Would we begin by seeking to provide a safety net for elderly Jews who had inadequate pensions and medical care, and were vulnerable in ways that were simply astounding to those new to the Soviet reality? Should we look to create institutions that would form the foundations of Jewish communities, an initial step toward the goal of nurturing self-sufficient communities that would be able to meet the needs of their members within a generation?

After much thought, study, and discussion (all done in an intense, hurried framework), and following a series of exploratory trips, we decided on a program that eventually turned out to be an inspired choice. During the dark years, JDC was a primary supporter of something called the "Aliyah Library."

Books on Jewish themes and of Jewish interest were translated from their original languages – generally Hebrew or English – into Russian. In various ways, for several decades, these books were transported into the Soviet Union and distributed to Jews interested in countering Soviet efforts to obliterate all traces of Jewish culture or knowledge. By the time JDC returned to the USSR, some nine hundred titles were available through this operation; they ranged from the Bible to Golda Meir's biography to Leon Uris's *Exodus*.

We decided that our first program would be setting up Jewish libraries in the nascent Jewish communities that were being formed as the USSR gradually imploded. A group of Jews in each city had to commit to finding a space and a person to run the library. In turn, JDC would train that person in how to use the library as a program tool, including story hours for children, book clubs, and resources for holiday celebrations, and would send in a complete set of Russian-language books on Jewish themes – basically, the inventory of the Aliyah Library.

We thought that this would be an appropriate way to start. A library of circulating books allowed Jews who were not yet comfortable identifying publicly as Jews or attending public Jewish programs to educate themselves with books in the privacy of their own apartments. Whatever these Jews might have lost in terms of their Jewish identities and Jewish literacy, a quintessentially Jewish trait stayed with them – the thirst for knowledge. They were readers, so books were an effective educational tool. And if the "opening" was terminated and the borders of the USSR once again closed, a significant number of the books already sent in would remain and could be circulated furtively.

In retrospect, the program succeeded beyond our expectations. Twenty years later, there were still Jewish libraries in some communities. The books may have been replaced over the years, but the libraries themselves were the foundation of an institution that still exists. They still serve as a resource for nurturing identity.

In addition to the reasons enumerated above, I want to add one personal reason why this initial programming calling card was so effective, and it is an ideological reason: this program was a kind of mission statement for JDC in its subsequent work in the FSU, a clear declaration of our purpose and goals for our work with post-Soviet Jewry.

I have a vivid memory of a childhood visit with my parents to Mexico City, where my father had once studied. One interaction I had with my parents during that trip remained with me my whole life, and later provided context for this library decision. We had just been inside Mexico City's largest cathedral. It is an imposing structure, and all the more so if you have never encountered anything so cavernous. It overwhelms the senses. It is visually magnificent. A distinct smell of incense pervades the edifice. There is an organ that literally can be felt as much as heard.

I remember asking my father something like, "How come we don't have anything like this?" I was comparing this cathedral to the synagogues I knew from that time – the one in which I was raised, that of my grandparents, and those of uncles and aunts. They were composed of four walls, maybe some stained glass, and some worn furniture. You could call them anything you wished, but "monumental" or "majestic" were not the words that would come to mind. Why was it that others had such impressive buildings, compared to what I had become accustomed to in the synagogues of my childhood?

In retrospect, the question invited an answer that touched on many dimensions of comparative religion. But at that age, anything more than a few simple words would have been lost on me. The answer I received made an impression on me deep enough to remain with me to this day. My father said to me, "For Jews, books are our cathedrals."

* * *

On Jews and books, one more anecdote: Several days after the end of hostilities between Russia and Georgia in 2008, I paid a working visit to a small Georgian town on the front lines in order to learn the needs of the local Jewish community. At the end of a long day of meetings, my hosts took me to the center of town, where the fighting had been fierce. We stood opposite an enormous apartment building several stories high and two city blocks long. The entire wall of the building had been shorn off by Russian shelling and, from where we stood, we could see into every apartment that faced the street – over 110 in all. Each looked identical: a kitchen with a stove and a refrigerator to the right, and a living room to the left. Even the furniture that we could see from the street was all similar – not surprising given that there was only one furniture manufacturer in that part of the country.

My hosts pointed out something I'd missed as a casual observer: Every apartment was exactly the same, except for five sprinkled throughout the building. Each of these five apartments had one additional item in the salon – a large bookcase filled with books. It was a distinctive addition to each of these five apartments and appeared only in these.

Each apartment belonged to one of the five Jewish families in the building.

Novy God (November 18, 2002)

Here is an issue germane to our FSU work, but with Israel as its point of departure. Haifa is a city known for the diversity of its population. There are many expressions of this. One of the more interesting is a recent proposal brought before the Haifa municipal council by an immigrant from the FSU. He notes that Haifa, in recognition of its multicultural population, has an annual festival called "Holiday of Holidays." This community-wide celebration, held in a valley just outside the city, began in 1994, when Chanukah, Ramadan, and Christmas all fell in December. The proposal recently tabled in the city council is to include a fourth winter holiday called Novy God – the Russian New Year holiday, the observance of which, according to the proposal, is devoid of conventional religious content. It is asking, in effect, to recognize the presence of a large, secular Russian population by incorporating the secular Russian New Year holiday into the city's festivities.

This request represents a profound philosophical revolution. One journalist wrote that "it portrays secularism not only as the absence of religion, but as a faith which demands recognition." For the Russian immigrants, it is an effort to preserve a part of the cultural life they've imported with them.

This holiday has some of the trappings we would recognize as connected to Christmas: a Grandfather Frost similar to Santa Claus, decorated trees in homes, etc. A new cultural reality is being formed by Russian Jews who are comfortable with both apples and honey on Rosh Hashanah and decorated fir trees at home in December. They are being neither defiant nor nostalgic. This is who they are.

An immigrant in Haifa commented on this issue as it reflects on Jewish identity. She decried the efforts to formally acknowledge the "Russian Christmas," as she called it, although not on religious grounds. "What you consider a Jew and what I consider one, isn't the same at all. If a Buddhist from Thailand were to come and convert to Judaism, for you he would be a Jew. For me, never. A Jew to me is education, upbringing, a way of thinking, language. It has nothing to do with religion. That was the distinction made in Russia. We have to conform to Jewish life culturally in order to be considered authentic Jews."

The challenge for JDC is how to address this issue in the FSU as we help recreate Jewish communal life. What are the boundaries of cultural events, for example, in a JCC? What is the most appropriate way for JDC to contribute to the renewal of a minority culture while recognizing the part the majority culture plays in the lives of the FSU's Jews?

Can the lighting of the Chanukah menorah, for example, coexist comfortably with a December family dinner in honor of the (non-Jewish, though essentially secular) holiday? Or for that matter, can Kol Nidrei be recited in the same venue that will later host Grandfather Frost during the winter holiday? Is it appropriate for the Kharkiv JCC to have a decorated tree in its lobby in December? To what extent can these cultures coexist, and at what point does the existence of one threaten the other?

At one level, the simple answer is that local mores should determine the direction. We may understand these symbols and rituals as Christian, but if the Jews of the FSU view them as secular cultural symbols and see no contradiction with their emerging Jewish identity, so be it. But things are not quite that simple. In the quest to assist FSU Jewry in creating or recreating an indigenous Jewish culture, are there parameters that should limit our participation, or JDC as a source of funding, at least until their knowledge base is sufficient to make knowledgeable choices? If the answer is yes, how is that to be done without being paternalistic and imperialistic?

We don't always define our internal struggles in this way, but as we work to foster Jewish renewal, it is a leitmotif that informs much of our work. The question of what we do and how comes only at the end of the process. First, we have to understand the "why." Our work with Hillels, JCCs, and other renewal operations requires us to give serious thought to what is authentically and legitimately Jewish in a pluralistic context.

Forsaking a Synagogue (February 27, 2009)

Melitopol is a city in eastern Ukraine, several hours by car from the regional capital of Kharkiv. The local Jewish community of between four and five thousand Jews works closely with JDC. There is a Hesed in town, and all of the community leaders and professionals have participated in JDC training programs. The community is very strong and has some wonderful Jewish culture and education.

Recently, through various connections with the local authorities, a building that had formerly served the community as a synagogue was returned. The community asked the local JDC representative to come, together with a rabbi, and work with community leaders to plan the building's future. The two guests arrived and were immediately taken to the community's new acquisition. There was no doubt from the outside that this had once been a synagogue. In addition to an upper window graced with a Star of David, the building conforms to typical synagogue architecture in the region from the first quarter of the last century.

Opposite the synagogue was another building, with a sign designating it as the municipal bathhouse. It was clear that this building had once housed the community *mikveh*. Its transformation into a bathhouse during Soviet times was therefore a natural one.

The two guests entered the former synagogue to find it totally dark inside. During the Communist era, it had been requisitioned from the Jews and used to smelt silver. The walls and ceiling were blackened by the soot from the ovens used to heat the metal. It was not an easy sight to behold. The synagogue had clearly once been a magnificent building, and pictures indicate that the internal design had been quite beautiful.

The modest delegation – by now, some fifteen people – proceeded down a staircase into the basement of the building. It was small, or in the parlance of real estate brokers, intimate. It could comfortably hold thirty people; any additional person would be a squeeze. This was the *beit midrash*, where daily prayers were once held.

"Can we make this into the prayer hall?" asked the community president. It was clear to the locals that they would not need a large amount of space to accommodate people coming to pray – this size seemed just right. But the space was in a state of tremendous disrepair: there was no floor, the walls were seriously pockmarked, and the ceiling was rotted.

Just as the question was asked, one of our colleagues in the delegation looked out of a small basement window and noticed that the building next door appeared, at least from the outside, to be in much better shape.

He was told that that building housed the municipality's night school. A member of the group, Rabbi Meir Schlesinger, shared his hunch with those present, and indeed one of the elderly people confirmed that that building had once been the school belonging to the community, the local Talmud Torah. The community's president volunteered that the municipality had offered to return that building as well.

After a short visit and conversation, it was established that part of the former synagogue required about seventy thousand dollars to repair and make functional as a prayer hall. The school building needed much less work to make it fit for the same purpose. Rabbi Schlesinger thought that given the needs of the community and the fact that budgets were tight, the priority should be supporting people – welfare, renewal activities, education, etc. The school should be refashioned into a synagogue, and there would be much-needed money left over for these activities, even as an appropriate place to pray was made available. For now, the investment in the previous synagogue building seemed not to make sense.

As far as he was concerned, Rabbi Schlesinger had fulfilled his task. But one factor had not been considered. A woman, advanced in years, approached him, clearly very agitated. As he described it later, "She had fire in her eyes." Her Yiddish was fluent: "What kind of rabbi are you, and from Israel no less? This is the way a rabbi speaks? For dozens of years, I have been waiting for the day that I can pray in the same spot my *bubbe* (grandmother) once prayed, in the same synagogue. Indeed, in the same spot. I never stopped hoping that God would answer that prayer. In the hardest times, those bastards took so much from us, but I held onto that prayer. And now you tell me I should pray in the classrooms of a night school? This is what we waited for all these years?"

Here then, was the dilemma: No one had seventy thousand dollars to invest in that synagogue building. And even if that amount was available, weren't there more important concerns for Ukrainian Jewry today than a beautiful synagogue in Melitopol? This, at a time when there are unmet needs for the elderly and unfunded education and outreach programs for youth. How can an investment in a building, to satisfy the nostalgic yearnings of some, be justified?

As Rabbi Schlesinger pointed out to us, "I was devoid of sentiment at that moment. Here was the choice: cold and calculating need versus sentiment. There wasn't a question in my mind. Until that woman harangued me."

The woman was not religious by any stretch of the imagination, but this was not an issue of religion. It was an issue of roots, of identity, of passion, and of connectedness, values no less important to Jewish survival than education. She was desperate to connect to the Jewish people, her family, here and now, and back through the ages.

To her and many others, this wasn't an issue of dollars and cents, or even strategic priorities. This wasn't just any building; it was the possibility of a dream fulfilled, exactly the kind of dream we deal with in the FSU on a daily basis, a dream of redressing a sin against the Jewish people – forced assimilation over five generations.

I have no doubt that the recommendation and ultimate decision to renovate the school property for the prayer hall was correct. But one cannot witness this scene, or hear it described, and remain absolutely sure. The pathos and passion of this woman have to touch us if we are to take our mission seriously. The decision, justified though it may have been, was not an easy one.

Assimilation (March 4, 2003)

There is a general lesson that FSU Jewry has taught the Jewish world since the collapse of the USSR: In the years prior to the breakup, nearly all observers believed that Soviet Jewry was essentially lost to the Jewish people. There were those who wanted to emigrate; many of them became refuseniks and spent long periods trying to escape the Soviets' clutches. But they were a very small minority. The others were lost, or to use the more common term, they had assimilated. It is commonly understood that assimilation has a finality to it. Once assimilated, the individual has left the community, and the understanding is that one can append to this sentence the words "never to return again."

FSU Jewry and, in general, the Jewries of what was once the Eastern Bloc have introduced a new notion into the consciousness of the contemporary Jewish world: a post-assimilation Jewish community. This was a community that had assimilated. For several generations, there were no Jewish educational settings, there was no communal life but for a few moribund synagogues, and the community's leadership had been eliminated. And now this community has returned to the Jewish people in great numbers, a phenomenon unprecedented in Jewish history.

As I write these lines, I am reminded of an experience I had at the outset of my career in 1986, in a different place. At the time I saw it as an isolated incident. In retrospect, particularly after encounters with these Jews and their history, I understand it to have been a portent of things to come. The place was Zagreb, then the second-largest city of Yugoslavia, later the capital of independent Croatia. As the JDC representative responsible for our programming in the country, I was invited to be a guest of the community at what was to be a special event with far-reaching implications. JDC had worked with the community for decades, and its members were therefore insistent that JDC have a presence at this event.

The gathering was to dedicate a new kindergarten in the Jewish community. An event like that, of course, is always reason for celebration. But this was something different. There were few Jewish kindergartens in the Communist Bloc, and it certainly had been a long time since a new one had been opened. Little did I realize how significant this was.

The ceremony was very moving, and most of the members of that thousand-strong community participated. I noticed out of the corner of my eye a woman who had cried throughout the proceedings. There was something peculiar about the depth of her response, so I approached her, introduced myself, and asked what this dedication meant to her. Her name was Sima, and she told me that she had been the director of the last Jewish kindergarten in Zagreb:

Before the war, there were 72,000 Jews in Yugoslavia, of whom 60,000 were murdered. Of the remaining 12,000, half went to Israel and half remained here. Those who remained were committed to the new regime, the new life that Communism promised us. We knew that we were Jews, but there was little content to that identity. We wanted to maintain social connections. We reconstructed a Jewish community but did not give it much substance. There was no Jewish educational setting. There were no synagogues that functioned. There was no educated leadership. We needed a national identity like our neighbors had, but it was not terribly significant for us. Almost all members of the community married non-Jewish spouses and raised their children without exposure to anything Jewish.

We established a kindergarten more out of nostalgia than anything else. There was no real effort at any level to pass on a Jewish identity to the next generation. By the early 1960s, it was basically all over. We closed the kindergarten for lack of interest. And when we did that, we assumed, not that a chapter had closed on Yugoslav Jewry, but that the whole book was closed. This was the end. With no tools or mechanisms to pass on an appreciation of Jewish life, the love of the Jewish people, or any sort of Jewish identity, the closing of the kindergarten meant the eventual end of Yugoslav Jewry.

Today, I participated in the dedication of a Jewish kindergarten. More than a generation later, Jewish life is not extinct, contrary to what all of us believed. This is not due to an influx of foreign Jews from other places. Our children and grandchildren have defied all prognostications about assimilation, and they have returned. Against all odds. No one looked at us and believed that Jewish continuity was possible. And to be frank, neither did we.

Yom Hashoah (May 1, 2009)

When they learned that I would be away from family and Israel on Yom Hashoah (Holocaust Memorial Day), my children were distressed. It was to be the first time in many years that I would not be with my family at the Yom Hashoah commemoration at Yad Vashem. They wondered aloud what it would be like, marking this day so far away – in Ukraine, no less. For them, Yom Hashoah is almost a uniquely Israeli experience. We live in a country in which the profile of survivors is prominent, and the legacy of the Shoah is ubiquitous, so that marking it elsewhere almost borders on the sacrilegious. The official Yad Vashem ceremony is carefully choreographed and tremendously moving, and it is witnessed by most Israelis on television as it happens. The day has its own rituals, including a siren during which the entire country stops to stand at attention, special television and radio shows, and other rituals of reflection. The message of the day is enveloping in a way that can only happen in Israel. Would my being abroad mean that the day would pass virtually unnoticed? It certainly seemed that it would be diminished in meaning.

While I am the first to acknowledge the special significance of observing Yom Hashoah in a sovereign Jewish state, my children had nothing to fear on my behalf. I was at the Yom Hashoah commemoration held in the largest park in Dnipro in eastern Ukraine, adjacent to the city's university, at midday. There were scores of people strolling through the grounds on that fine spring day. Unaware of the day's importance to their Jewish neighbors, they were initially oblivious to the gathering of the Jewish community at a small monument, which marked the site where ten thousand Jews had been slaughtered in 1941. To the extent that place contributes to meaning, we were where we needed to be.

The ceremony was extremely moving in its simplicity. There were survivors present – not just Shoah survivors, but actual survivors of the mass slaughter at that site. Occasional passersby stopped to inquire about what was going on, and they were informed in a quiet and respectful way by some of the young people who had volunteered for that role and had been trained for it. But the ceremony was very much an internal one for the community.

All this is by way of background to what was most moving and meaningful. Six candles were lit, each by a survivor accompanied by a Hillel student or a graduate of Metzudah, a training program we run for young community activists. The presence of both ends of the generational spectrum was powerful, as was the lighting of the fourth candle. The young part of the duo was a fourteen-year-old girl, Irina Zarchenko, who had serious developmental issues and was confined to a wheelchair. With tears streaming down her face, she was pushed up the small hill by her survivor grandfather. Together they lit the candle.

As a Jew, and as "an imperfect human specimen" (in Nazi terminology), Irina would have been a prime victim of the mass murder at that site sixty-eight years ago. Today, she is an active participant in the Tikvah program for special needs children at the Dnipro JCC. Her presence at the ceremony and her participation in it were not the result of her being singled out in any way. She was a participant, like all of her peers who were present. She was treated with the same dignity as all the others who lit candles. She was a young Jew, fully integrated into her Jewish community, which is committed to addressing her needs through the various institutions that JDC was instrumental in setting up. The value placed on every individual by the Jewish community stood in stark contrast to the history of that place and ultimately gave that ceremony a meaning it might not have had anywhere else in the world at that moment. It was the Jewish Community of Dnipro, whose existence was a difficult thing to imagine a few short years ago, that, through Irina's participation in it, made this event so meaningful.

I witnessed several other things that week, none so emotionally wrenching, but each with its own significance. In Zaporizhzhia, a town of some fifteen thousand Jews an hour from Dnipro, we had a three-hour encounter with some graduates of a program for young communal leaders. We studied with them, and then we broke up into smaller groups for more intimate discussions about topics with which they had been grappling in their course of study: the Jewish values that need to inform fundraising, how to engage middle-aged Jews in community life, and several other topics that would be familiar to those who care about Jewish communal life, anywhere in the world.

I was part of a group that discussed the common ground of Jewish identity. That is, if you have a room full of Jews with varying degrees of religious commitment, including those who have none, and people who define themselves as Zionists, ethnic Jews, etc., with all that diversity, what ultimately unites? The subject was intriguing, and I looked forward to the opportunity to hear what these young Jews, from an environment so different from the ones to which we are accustomed, would say. I expected differences but did not expect what I encountered.

One young man began a tirade against assimilation and spoke about how it has to be fought in an uncompromising way. It was his contention that not enough resources are being employed to combat this threat, which he considered to be the biggest challenge facing Jews in our generation, and that concessions made to engage the assimilated only serve to dilute the essence of

Jewish peoplehood. And so on. He spoke for ten full minutes. He was passionate. Even though I disagreed with some of what he said, I was impressed with the way he structured his arguments and how committed he was to his beliefs. I couldn't help wondering, as I listened, how some of those present would respond, knowing that by most measures they were all products of assimilated backgrounds.

At one point I was called out for an urgent phone call, and on the way back in, I met the JCC director. I asked her for a thumbnail sketch of the background of this young man. She said that his name was Vitali, he was a stalwart of the Jewish community, and he had exhibited expansive leadership abilities. "He also takes time to study Jewish history," she said, "and he is a talented teacher, which he does while getting his PhD in linguistics."

It doesn't get much better than this, I thought to myself. So you can imagine the impact of her next sentences: "I wish he would give us more time. He's with us five days a week. His mother is Jewish, and his father is Armenian. So, the other two days a week he is a leader in the local Armenian community. He runs a youth program for them and is vice president of their community."

Identity and Its Idiosyncrasies (May 1, 2009)

I recently had a conversation with a young woman who directs the JCC in Dnipro. We talked about a host of issues, both personal and work oriented. At one point she mentioned that she has made her life in Ukraine and expects to remain there to serve the Jewish community. She was a very impressive young woman, and part of the growing cadre of Jewish communal professionals we are seeking to develop through training programs and mentoring.

She told me that her parents live in Ashkelon, on Israel's Mediterranean coast, and have been there for about eight years. "We speak regularly. My parents are always calling me and asking for explanations about Jewish traditions they are encountering in Israel. Imagine how ironic that is. My parents in Israel call me in Ukraine to have *me* explain Jewish practice and tradition to *them* in the Jewish state."

Agitprop Updated (May 1, 2009)

By its very nature, a Hesed deals with Jews who spent their formative years under Communist rule. Anyone who has ever visited Communist countries knows that propaganda played a major role in trying to keep the population loyal. The term for this kind of political propaganda is agitprop. Statues of Lenin were everywhere. Large hammers and sickles adorned all public buildings, and banners caught your eye wherever you turned. They were hung from rooftops and bridges, and even on schoolbags, and each had a pithy slogan – or, at least, whoever dreamed them up thought they were pithy.

I was reminded of these when I visited the Hesed in Zaporizhzhia and saw a large banner bearing a slogan taken from Communist times. The latter part read, "is always with you." The writing was bold – black on a red background, a classic Communist-era banner. At one time it would have been, "Lenin is always with you." Later they replaced him with "Stalin," and at an even later time, when they were downplaying the cult of personality, the slogan was, "The party is always with you." This slogan clearly resonated with people of a certain age, and it was reassuring to them in a way that most of us today find a bit bizarre. But the banners had meaning, and a value we cannot necessarily understand.

Now to the banner in the Hesed: It reads, in the same bold lettering on a red background, "The Joint is always with you." Communist agitprop, updated?

* * *

On the way to the airport to begin the long trip home I spoke on the phone to one of the local Chabad rabbis, who had called to tell me the following story: Several weeks earlier, he had been summoned to the office of the city's mayor. Until that point, the rabbi and the mayor had enjoyed a warm relationship. Through the years, the rabbi had hosted numerous foreign groups who had come to see the developments of Jewish life in the city. He always took them to meet top municipal officials, who encouraged the foreigners to invest in the city. In return for these opportunities, municipal officials often ruled favorably on the rabbi's requests for assistance. They gave him a building for his school, provided transportation for its students, and made warehouse space available for the storage of matzah.

Now, the mayor was quite angry with the rabbi. He recounted all that the municipality had done for him and stressed that this was in return for introductions to important visitors from abroad whom the rabbi hosted. The rabbi related to me on the phone that as the mayor continued, he (the rabbi) was increasingly perplexed about what he had done wrong. Finally, the mayor got to the point: "My people report to me that on a railroad trestle just outside of town, your students have hung a banner welcoming a clearly important guest. I know nothing about this."

When the rabbi gave him a baffled look the mayor elaborated: "The banner says, 'We welcome the Mashiach (the Messiah).' Why haven't you informed me of the details of his arrival and set up a meeting?"

The Meaning of Jewish (October 16, 2009)

In a recent meeting of senior JDC staff, several of us were asked to present our notion of what the term "Jewish" means in the context of the name of the American *Jewish* Joint Distribution Committee. Many organizations incorporate that word in their name. For organizations with political agendas, political issues with a Jewish dimension are in their bailiwick. Religious organizations use the term in their mission statements, informed by a specific ideology that provides the lens through which they view Jewish life. And so on.

What about the Joint? The problem of definition is not unique to us, but given what we do, it is not easy to borrow the definitions others have created and superimpose them on our work plans. And the stakes are high. How we understand Jewishness, and how that drives our work, will make some people eligible for services that will potentially prolong their lives, will give some families access to better education and quality social and cultural programs, and more.

I want to be careful with the words I choose here. I am not talking about how JDC defines who is a Jew. That definition is not ours to make; our policy is to leave it up to the communities in which we work. The goal is to understand what makes us a Jewish organization, and how that organizational identity must be reflected in the programs we choose to support, the communities in which we choose to work, the values that guide us, who will represent us.

I cannot say my thoughts on this are fully fleshed out. But I want to share what I spoke about in the six minutes allotted to me at that meeting, perhaps as a way of stimulating further conversation on the subject.

First, let me recount two anecdotes that nudged me in the direction I chose. The first took place at the very outset of our work in the FSU. It is the story of Victoria, who was mentioned in the preface. I was with three other people, and we were in Leningrad to inaugurate a program for delivering wheelchairs to indigent elderly Jews who were housebound without this equipment. These chairs enabled them to move beyond the four walls of their apartments, often after years of essentially being imprisoned there.

At the end of a long day of delivering wheelchairs, we came to the apartment of an elderly woman who was clearly suspicious when she opened the door a bit for us to identify ourselves. We had been given her name and told she was a needy Jewish widow with little income who could not walk unassisted. We told her who we were and why we had come. She could not understand why anyone would bring her something and not insist on something in return. She was further baffled by the Jewish part of the explanation for our visit. Finally, the local social worker convinced her that our motives were good, and she invited us into her apartment. After a brief chat, she opened up a bit and articulated the source of her surprise that we would help her.

"Of course, I was born a Jew. We spoke Yiddish at home, and, before the revolution, we led a traditional Jewish lifestyle. But I want to be honest with you. From the time I was able to think on my own, I rejected any identification with the Jewish people. I was a Communist my whole life and remain one even now. I practice no Jewish rituals. I have no special affinity for other Jews. I have no more interest in the State of Israel than I do in Kenya. I take no pride in the accomplishments of my fellow Jews, and I socialize with people without any regard for their nationality or identification."

As her explanations continued, we could see that she was increasingly bewildered that we were not moved by them, even as we listened intently to her explanation of how she saw herself. The wheelchair remained in its packaging in the center of her salon. Our explanation, that we represent a Jewish community that wants to help Jews in need, irrespective of their personal history, personal belief system, ideology, etc., was simply incomprehensible to her.

The second story here is of the publication of what later became known as The JDC Talmud. It refers to the specific edition of the Talmud published by JDC in cooperation with the US occupation forces in Munich and Heidelberg in 1948. A group of rabbis who survived the Shoah and were now in displaced persons (DP) camps run by JDC and the American army were interested in resuming their study and teaching of Talmud. There were almost no extant copies of the Talmud to be found anywhere in Europe after the war. They approached the chief Jewish chaplain of the United States Armed Forces in Europe at the time, a rabbi named Philip Bernstein, who immediately committed to trying to help publish sets of the Talmud for them to study and teach.

The stumbling blocks were enormous. This happened soon after the end of the war. Paper was rationed. Few printing presses survived massive destruction at the war's end. Publication of this multivolume work required considerable financial resources and a large staff to oversee the operation. Both were in short supply. Access to paper and printing presses was controlled by the American army. Moreover, and perhaps most important of all, the challenges facing those trying to rehabilitate the survivors physically required so much that it was hard to make this any kind of priority.

The director of JDC's European operations, Dr. Joe Schwartz, accompanied Earl Harrison, President Truman's special representative, on a 1946 mission to the DP camps to report back to the president on the needs of the survivors. A delegation of rabbis presented a proposal for printing the Talmud. At the same time, Rabbi Bernstein began to impress upon General Lucius Clay and the man he was to succeed as military commander in the German theater, General Joseph McNarney, the need for publication of the Talmud. Clay and McNarney acquiesced to Rabbi Bernstein's lobbying. Harrison agreed, as well, and saw this as consistent with Truman's position that the care of the Jewish survivors was both a moral and political responsibility of the United States and was a demonstration of America's moral revulsion at what happened in Europe during the previous years. The U.S. administration went one step further: it required the German government to help financially underwrite the publication of the Talmud. That left one party that had to commit: JDC.

With so much funding required for the survivors' physical rehabilitation, it could not have been an easy ask. At its peak during this period, the Joint provided service to about 250,000 Jewish DPs. It ran 114 schools and kindergartens, 24 hospitals and clinics in Germany and Austria, and provided clothing for the survivors. In addition, meals were provided every day for those 250,000 people. It was an enterprise of unprecedented scale for an NGO at that time, and all was based on JDC fundraising in the United States. Any project like the Talmud publication would divert much-needed resources from the provision of basic needs.

Did anything not contributing directly to the material welfare of these people justify diverting resources? The decision was not merely a budgetary one. The amount of money needed could easily be translated into the cost of meals or the equivalent amount needed for antibiotics and the like. And that was painful.

But JDC's board was convinced and allocated the sums asked of it. A distinction between body and soul may have theological significance, but in this instance it was artificial. The mission for JDC was to rehabilitate these Jews; doing so required an acknowledgment that the spiritual devastation caused by the Shoah also needed to be rectified. To reconstruct Jewish life did not only mean to physically rehabilitate Jews, it was also to help them find meaning once again in the face of the evil they had experienced during the previous years.

The title page of the Talmud is decidedly not subtle in confirming this. The lithograph that frames it is of barbed wire and an image shows two prisoners picking up a corpse in a death camp, with a verse from Psalms that speaks of the devastation. But the barbed wire leads up to palm trees which point the eye to a scene of Jerusalem, bathed in the glow of a shining sun, labeled: "From bondage to redemption."

I have never seen the protocols of the JDC board meeting at which the decision was taken to approve the publication of the Talmud. We can only imagine that the vote was preceded by a passionate debate, with both sides marshaling compelling arguments. In many senses, it must have been a discussion of life and death. But we do know that the final decision was to allocate the money, a not-insignificant sum. In the days before designated giving, this money came at the expense of material support. It was a courageous decision.

* * *

While not necessarily referencing that decision of almost seventy years ago, the same dilemma has repeatedly faced those charged with determining JDC's direction since that time. We confront it every day in the FSU. Yes, one can argue that much of our money is designated by donors for specific program categories. But early on, JDC leadership committed to a dual approach. It was beyond dispute that the needs of the poor and vulnerable had to be addressed and that we would never have enough resources to meet this challenge. Over and over, we have shown how many who need our help do not yet receive it. At the same time, it was made clear that community development in all of its component forms – education, leadership development, and the like – were to be an integral part of our FSU program. To respond to physical needs was essential. To invest in issues like identity and spiritual growth was no less important. At some level, resources to the one are diverted from the other, at least partially. But future generations will judge the value and success of our FSU efforts based on the extent to which viable communities are established, and not on the number of food packages distributed or home care hours offered.

There is a tension between these things. Getting the balance right is not easy, and perhaps not even achievable. But it is a tension we have chosen to struggle with rather than abandon. If the decision by the JDC board after the war had been *not* to finance the Talmud, the whole enterprise would probably have been forgotten. And, if uncovered years later, I doubt that any but a few would have criticized it, given the state of the survivors. But that was not what the JDC board chose to do.

I could go on about this story, but I want instead to return to the point of this weekly briefing: the question of the meaning of the word *Jewish* in the name "American Jewish Joint Distribution Committee." My understanding can be reduced to three *w*'s: whoever, wherever, whatever.

Whoever: JDC supports Jews in need. Period. Regardless of their convictions, affiliations, or ideologies. Their personal political stances are irrelevant (and some of the Jews we have supported have personally held odious political convictions by any standard). If a Jew is in need, he or she is entitled to JDC's assistance. It may not make sense, nor may it be politically correct as these things are judged, but that is a cornerstone of the JDC credo. A woman who has intentionally cut herself off from the Jewish people for her entire life and who now does not have the resources to live in dignity is, by virtue of her birth, no less entitled to JDC support than Jews who have lived lives of Jewish commitment and are now facing similar straits.

Wherever: Jews may live in places that are not hospitable to Jews. We may wish them to emigrate to safer shores. We may think they are endangering themselves or their loved ones by staying put. We may be absolutely convinced that their continued presence in a particular place will lead to the disappearance of their offspring from the Jewish people. No matter. Their decisions are to be respected. Jews, wherever they may be, are entitled to JDC assistance if they need it.

Whatever: JDC's understanding of its role is rooted in the Jewish understanding of the human being. We each have physical needs; about this there is no argument. But our spiritual needs are no less important. Whether that need for spiritual enrichment is addressed by a visit to a synagogue or to a JCC, by hearing the blowing of a shofar or by attending a Jewish cultural event, JDC responds to Jewish needs – their very real and valid spiritual needs among them. Medicine for the elderly in the FSU is absolutely essential for them. We contend that campus Hillel plays no less important a role in the lives of younger Jews during their university years. Just as there are needs for individual Jews, there are needs for the Jewish people. Both are part and parcel of JDC's responsibility.

Through my years in JDC, I have come to believe that the approach embodied in these three *w*'s has created the mystique around the JDC name and contributed to the awe in which it is held by Jews who have benefited from its help during the last ninety-five years. For many of them – and I have witnessed this on numerous occasions – the name Joint has come to refer to more than an organization. It is an idea, the crystallization of the concept of mutual responsibility among the Jewish people. This makes the case for the centrality of "Jewish" in the full and proper name of the organization: The American Jewish Joint Distribution Committee.

Epilogue

At a JDC forum in 2014, I reflected on my twenty-two years directing the FSU program for JDC. It was an incredible period in my life, in no small part because it coincided with wholly unexpected, dramatic changes in the plight of a very significant number of Jews and, by extension, of the Jewish people.

What follows is the talk I gave on that occasion. It is not meant to be a comprehensive record of JDC's work in that area during this period. We will leave that task to historians. It is, instead, a reflection on this period from someone who lived it, and who will be eternally grateful for the privilege he was given to direct this program on JDC's behalf:

* * *

Masha was born in Kyiv in 1980. She was born in the USSR into a Jewish family. When JDC first returned to the Soviet Union in the late eighties, into Masha's world, it was clear to all that to be a Jew was to be burdened with an albatross. You were labeled a Jew – it was stamped in your internal passport. That stamp was one of limitations. It meant that there were schools you could not attend; entire faculties of universities were either wholly off-limits or subject to quotas. You couldn't pursue certain careers, and you were imprisoned in this country – your chances of leaving, should you so desire, were slim.

Your heritage was a black hole. The Shoah didn't exist in Soviet texts or in Soviet consciousness. According to Soviet textbooks, Masha's uncles, killed at Babyn Yar, were victims because they were Communists. The fact that they were Jewish was not relevant.

Israel was a far-off country, unreachable, mentioned sporadically in the media, always in a negative light. Zionism, imperialism, and anti-Soviet were the words that accompanied each mention of Israel. It was a pariah state. A Jewish state. And you, as a Jew, were willy-nilly connected to it.

Masha's parents had no Jewish community to which to turn for Jewish education, for Jewish culture, or for support if they suffered some sort of setback. There were no Jewish ceremonies. Bar or bat mitzvah and Jewish weddings were poisonous superstitions and a threat to Communist ideology and therefore weren't allowed. No Jewish books were printed. No lectures with Jewish content.

Jewish leadership? Here and there were rabbis, appointed and supervised by the state. Jewish organizational life was forbidden, so leadership and leaders were alien terms.

That was the USSR JDC came to in the late eighties. A Jewish wasteland. To say there was nothing there would be incorrect. There were refuseniks, towering in courage but small in number. They hand-copied Jewish texts and studied them. They produced Jewish music, surreptitiously imprinted in their homes on vinyl records and passed around among trusted friends. They held seminars and meetings. They protested, as did we on their behalf. But the numbers were small.

Most Jews were like Masha: vaguely aware of being Jewish, supremely aware of the liabilities of the stamp that labeled her Yevreika, a Jew, on line 5 of her internal passport.

Six of us from JDC came to the USSR in 1989. We traveled around individually, gathering information and impressions. Meeting, talking, networking. As a reminder, this was before mobile phones. No Internet. No fax. International phone calls had to be ordered seventy-two hours in advance and could only last up to twelve minutes. No local offices or local staff. You had to actually make appointments and interact with real human beings sitting opposite you.

The scale and scope were unprecedented for JDC in the modern era. The largest Jewish community in which we worked at the time was Hungary, with an estimated 100,000 Jews. The estimated number of Jews in the USSR was more than twenty times that. An overnight train could take you from one end of Romania to another, from the capital to the most remote outpost of Jews. From Moscow to Vladivostok was a twelve-day train ride, round the clock.

Wherever we touched, we found rot. Many apartments were uninhabitable. Pensions inadequate. Medicine scarce. No places for Jews to gather. No Jewish programs. No Jewish communities. No visions for Jewish communal life. No elder statesmen and only a handful of Passover Seders.

And yet, something was happening to Soviet Jewry in 1989. This sleeping giant was stirring. Perestroika provided a window of opportunity. A Hebrew teachers' association was established in Kharkiv. A volunteer Jewish welfare society was established by a young, retired woman in Tashkent. A Sunday school for children was opened in Minsk. In Zhitomir, help was provided for an autistic child in a Jewish family from Jewish doctors and nurses after their workday.

This brings me to my first question: How did it all come about?

Tallinn, Estonia. The week before Rosh Hashanah, 1990. Still in the USSR, I learned a lesson that I carry with me to this day and that has informed my work and the work of our entire staff, and that begins to answer my question of how it all happened. I met with an activist in the Jewish community who told me that he was establishing a Jewish school the week following the holiday. I felt that, as someone who knew something about Jewish education, I could be of some assistance. Advice could be given for free. "Who will be the teachers?" I asked.

"I don't know yet," he responded.

"What textbooks will you use?"

"We don't have any yet."

"Where is the curriculum from?"

"Haven't gotten one yet."

I'm not an expert in Jewish education, but I do know something, and I was willing to share that knowledge with him. "In my opinion, with no teachers, no curriculum, and no texts, you really can't open a school."

His answer was given respectfully, but it touched my very core in a profound and lasting way, and it taught me a lesson that is the foundation of my work even today: "I have forty Jewish children who, after so many years, can now learn what it means to be a Jew. They want to learn. Should I deny them that privilege because I don't have teachers, or textbooks, or a curriculum? After so many generations, when we finally can, I should say, 'Not yet'?"

The school indeed opened the following week, with sixty-three students. By December it had over 230. Almost singlehandedly, he made it happen.

Herein lies the lesson: It all comes down to people. You can create programs. You can fund, invest, and train. You can decide what needs to be taught. You can build the buildings that will host it all. All of that is necessary for the renaissance of FSU Jewry. But it is not sufficient. The critical factor, for which there is no substitute, is people.

Consider these Jews, three or four generations distanced from all things Jewish. Targets of forced assimilation for more than seventy years. Pushed to give up anything that set them apart. Beaten down, humiliated as Jews, discriminated against, targeted for oppression. Without Jewish community, without Jewish education, without positive Jewish experiences, without Jewish leadership. The objects of derision and scorn. Watching poets and writers and doctors and actors murdered because they were Jews. Mocked at school by teachers and fellow students for their names or their noses. Reading about their people in the media in the most unflattering of terms. Knowing that any expression of Jewish life would turn them into pariahs.

Yet, when they could reconnect with Jewish life, they did. How was that possible? To put it another way, we all know that assimilation is inexorable. Assimilate, and you are gone; you are no longer part of your group. Any sociologist will tell you that is a given. Yet, here is a post-assimilation Jewish community – Jews coming back. They showed us that there is Jewish life after assimilation. They taught us that it's a mistake to understand assimilation as a final step. To give up on these Jews, or any Jew anywhere who has undergone a process of assimilation, is a mistake. They taught us that.

And so, the meta-mission of JDC in the FSU was born. With all that we do, and in every one of the places we operate, we have one goal that supersedes all others: to reclaim Jews for the Jewish people. To take these Jews – who never had a Jewish conversation, never gave a ruble to charity, never sang a Jewish song or learned a Hebrew letter, and who didn't know the difference between Moses and Maimonides –and reclaim these Jews for our people.

We do this so that when a Jew in the FSU declares her identity, she says she is a doctor, a pianist, a wife, a mother, a daughter, a resident of Chelyabinsk… and a Jew. Somewhere in that calling card, and in some form – ethnic, cultural, national, religious, whatever – she is also a Jew, and proud of it.

From the first day of our return to that region, that mission in the FSU – to reclaim Jews for the Jewish people – has not wavered.

I have spent my professional career haunted by a story I heard years ago at a convention of an Israel advocacy organization. A speaker related that he had met an elderly gentleman who filled his days volunteering on Israel's behalf. He would do anything he was asked, and the speaker was curious why. The older man said that he had been a soldier in World War II and was with US troops when they liberated a concentration camp. As he drove into the camp, he saw an inmate and approached him. The inmate saw his name tag and asked in Yiddish if the soldier was Jewish. Expecting a warm hug and gratitude as a liberator, the soldier said that yes, he was Jewish.

The inmate slapped him, said, "*Zu shpayt!*" (You're too late!), and walked away. These many years later, the former soldier said that he volunteered for Israel as much as he could because he never wanted to be too late again.

We could not be too late for these Jews, and the Joint didn't wait. We moved. We planned. In those early days, we didn't have the funds and didn't know where they would come from. But we knew that history would never forgive us if we hesitated.

Where are we now? Where is Masha, now in her early thirties, and where are her children with respect to Jewish life? Almost three decades after JDC returned, where do things stand?

A new generation has grown up for whom a Jewish identity is a given. There is no ambivalence. There is no liability. It's natural to call yourself a Jew. There is an entire generation that has been exposed to the beauty of Jewish life. Consider the Jewish kindergarten that JDC established in Chișinău, where little Misha and Sasha welcome Shabbat on Friday afternoon with singing and smiles. This is something their grandparents never imagined. They've gone with their parents and siblings to Jewish family camps, a kind of laboratory of Jewish life where they live and learn with other Jews in an intensive setting for two weeks each summer. They have older siblings in Hillel, who bring Seders and Shabbat into their homes.

Young Jews visit elderly shut-ins in the Hesed system. They hear stories of Jews during the war and Jewish life before it. They've learned Jewish values like mutual responsibility and an obligation to care for the vulnerable. They learned that each Jew is responsible, one for another – not from textbooks or lectures, but by seeing the Hesed provide home care for the bedbound, and food and medicine for the indigent. Not only where it's convenient, for neighbors and friends, but where the obstacles are overwhelming – to twenty-four hundred cities and towns and hamlets throughout the FSU, in the heat of the Kazakh summer, in air filled with mosquitoes, and over tundra in the heart of a Siberian winter.

If an elderly Jew is in need, he or she will be helped, wherever and whenever. Not because JDC insists on it, but because the locals who run the Hesed now see it as their Jewish responsibility. The Soviet state ignored this needy person, and there was no one else. The state simply didn't give a damn. The Jewish people do. Today, anywhere in the FSU, the Jewish community, through the Hesed system, provides the safety net. It is almost unfathomable.

Jews in the FSU today are big brothers and big sisters for young Jews at risk in single-parent families or with special needs. Jewish community centers are second homes for these young Jews after school, on weekends, and during vacations. JCC directors use a Jewish lexicon. They speak of inclusiveness and pluralism. Their governance is based on accountability and transparency, against all odds in that environment.

These Jews haven't grown up in Jewish communities as we know them. But they've grown up in places in which there is now Jewish infrastructure, physical and human. There are local Jews – people trained as engineers in Odesa and teachers in Chişinău – who've left the security of those fields and who now work as Jewish communal professionals. They direct welfare programs and community centers with budgets in the millions of dollars and scores of staff and are responsible for the welfare and well-being of young and old.

There are Jews who live longer and who live significantly better lives, and people who are proud Jews because of those professionals – not professionals sent in from Boston or Ramat Gan, as we did twenty years ago, but local Jewish professionals who have dedicated their own lives to serving the Jewish people. They've been empowered to do this. There is now a cohort of young Jews eager to contribute, young Jews who are passionate about Jewish life, who are talented and committed and driven, and who will someday head their Jewish communities – communities not based on need and entitlement, but on initiative and independence.

There is much work left to be done in the FSU. There is much to be done, and it will be done.

I want to conclude by coming back to a question I raised earlier. There is much to consider about programs and budgets and procedures. About strategies and tactics. About programs and challenges. The one thing that can't be fully explained is: Where did it all come from? Despite all the reasons for pessimism and despair about the fate of the Jews of the former Soviet Union, after generations of persecution and assimilation, how have they come so far since their shackles were removed little more than one generation ago? This renaissance – how was it possible?

I can only offer one explanation, which for more than a century has informed the work of this magnificent organization. It comes from a verse taken from the first biblical Book of Samuel (15:29):

נצח ישראל לא ישקר

"There is an eternity to the Jewish people."

Afterword

Today, from a distance of several decades, it is difficult to comprehend how the rest of the world looked at the Soviet empire before its implosion and its ultimate collapse in December 1991. It was an imposing and intimidating entity. It had a large army, nuclear weapons, near-total control of the lives of its citizens – their education, their exposure to media, how, and even where, they led their lives. Of course, in retrospect we know that this behemoth was rotting from within and could not continue to exist as conceived at the time, but that is not what most of the world saw or experienced in encounters with the USSR. Few saw anything but the strength and control that the Soviet Union projected. Certainly, the prospect of disintegration seemed highly implausible.

As a consequence, it would be fair to say that there was little planning for a post-Soviet reality. When the collapse did come, it was so sudden and so comprehensive that there were few plans in place for how to proceed. Governments, international business conglomerates, and even most think tanks dealing with the Soviet Union had never considered such a scenario. The unimaginable had happened.

The organized Jewish world was no exception. There are several parts in this book that deal with the implications of the need to improvise due to the absence of a road map on how to move forward, or even lessons that could be learned from similar situations elsewhere, and at different times. The Soviet collapse was rapid and profound, and the Jewish world had no experience with the opportunities it now faced to reclaim otherwise "lost" Jews, certainly not in this scope and on this scale.

My JDC colleagues and I began to meet to map out our strategy for operations in the final days of the USSR and the early days of a post-Soviet reality. There was one question that hovered over all of our discussions, and was referenced repeatedly as ideas were mooted for how to proceed: What if this window of opportunity slams shut? What if there is backsliding, and a return to a Soviet-type model?

The question was neither theoretical nor inconsequential. On one level, we knew that we might create and propose programs that would require a significant initial investment and then might be shut down before their goals were realized. That was certainly a risk, but there was a general consensus that it was one worth taking given the potential rewards. But that approach had its limits. For example, while we understood that most viable Jewish communities around the world had a physical address of their own to host offices, meetings, events, exhibitions, etc., we could not responsibly invest in physical space given what we saw as the tenuous nature of the political changes at the time. That would be too large an investment to lose. Taking risks had its limits.

And there was an even more consequential risk that we needed to weigh in light of the prospect of a possible Soviet reincarnation: A Jewish community requires people – lay and professional leaders, educators and social workers, rabbis and administrators, and more. Whether the list in any given city was long or short, the fact was that there was no such thing as a Jewish communal professional in the USSR (with the notable exception of a handful of rabbis appointed by, and beholden to, Soviet authorities). In the new, post-Soviet reality, anyone who filled one of these roles had to leave his or her secure employment, or even a profession that was previously acceptable to the regime, and join this fledgling enterprise of Jewish communal life. What if the Soviet Union *was* reconstituted? Or even if some of its component political entities, now independent, reverted back to the antisemitism endemic to the Soviet Union? To what extent were our efforts potentially putting local people whom we recruited at risk?

Gradually those fears began to fade. To be frank, I became uncharacteristically complacent. I knew that history does not proceed in a straight line, nor in a predictable direction. As an eyewitness to the collapse of the "impregnable" Soviet empire, that much was clear. I also knew that an entity like the USSR does not become transformed overnight, even if it has unraveled, into an open, liberal, and tolerant society fully embracing the values and rights of those it long oppressed. But in my travels around the FSU, I became convinced that there would be no return of the Soviet system, certainly not as it had been. The citizens of the various successor states wanted change. That change might be incremental, but its direction was clear. It would not be consistent across the region, it would not uproot all that was problematic, but the limitations of the previous system were increasingly clear. The specifics of the future may have been shrouded in mystery, but my colleagues and I did not consider the prospect of a resurrection of all that was repudiated with the Soviet collapse in December 1991. The arc of Soviet history and its aftermath bent in another direction.

The descriptions, narratives, and stories in this book were initially meant to be a testimony to what the beginnings of FSU Jewish communities looked like decades on. A visitor to a vibrant Jewish community center in one of the FSU cities decades hence would understand how the center was created, both its original purpose and the challenges to be surmounted in establishing it.

How did local Jewish communities come to realize their responsibility for those who lived on the margins of these communities? Embedded in this book are at least some considerations.

Who are these Jews who now occupy leadership roles in Jewish communities? What were their roots? What was the process they underwent to create, or to reclaim, their Jewish identities? This book was meant to share the stories of some of these people.

How was it that when the shackles were removed, post-Soviet Jewry was able to create communities, despite the efforts of the Soviet regime to force assimilation on them over decades and generations? What was the vision that drove the predecessors of the current community leadership, and how and why over time did these visions change and adapt? The narrative in these pages was meant to give some answers to those questions.

These are some of the insights this book has tried to articulate and share. It was to give a sense of the foundations of what was expected to develop into flourishing, dynamic, and inspirational Jewish communities in what was for generations a Jewish desert. It was to be a look back to the foundations of the new era of post-Soviet Jewry. In brief, to encapsulate the early years of a Jewry reborn. That was the original purpose of this collection.

Then came February 24, 2022, and the Russian incursion into Ukraine.

That date is a demarcation point for everyone in the region and beyond. As these lines are written, no one knows what the outcome of the current hostilities will be, but one thing is clear with respect to the Jewish story in the post-Soviet era: a new chapter has opened. For the Jewish narrative of the post-Soviet period there will always be a time before February 24, 2022, and the time after that day. That is true for the Jews of Ukraine, but it is by no means limited to them.

All of FSU Jewry has been impacted by the events of that fateful day and its aftermath. Myriad Jews are being uprooted, or are moving on their own, to safer regions within their own country, or beyond. There are cities that have been physically decimated and that are bereft of residents, who have been killed or have fled. The Jewish renaissance has left few traces in these places. There are Jewish communities that have shrunk considerably in size, and while they may survive the war, the communities themselves will be forever changed. At the same time there are cities and towns beyond the war zone that have welcomed Jewish refugees, sometimes in numbers that strain their ability to cope. What this means for their future is unclear. Will the recent arrivals stay or move on?

The impact of the Russian incursion is even felt widely in the cultural space, as the use of Russian language, and the exposure to Russian writers, playwrights, poets, and others takes on political overtones far beyond the confines of the Russian Republic.

There are families that have been profoundly divided by different understandings of the causes and justifications of the war. Jews have suffered along with their neighbors. And Jewish communities have not been spared. In some places, efforts will be made to resurrect Jewish communal life. Without prejudging the success or failure of these efforts, one thing is clear: what will be built, or rebuilt, will be different from what existed on February 23, 2022. Life in many places throughout the FSU, and certainly Jewish communal life, will not be the same as it was prior to the Russian incursion.

There is one thing, though, that I will venture to predict that is a lesson drawn from the narrative in this book. The creation of Jewish communities and the revival of Jewish life in the early years of the post-Soviet era relied to a great extent on the assistance of world Jewry. That assistance came in the form of both personal and financial investments. There were mistakes made along the way – in fact, many. There were expectations that were unrealistic, and paths followed that led nowhere. But all of these were overshadowed by the successes: the leaders who were trained, the organizations that were formed, and the institutions that were created. All of this was in the service of the nascent Jewish community, and all on a scale and in a time frame never seen before in Jewish history.

In Soviet times a Jewish identity was often a liability. Over the last three decades, the nature of that identity has been transformed from a liability into a source of pride for many. As a consequence, one development stands out, and that is the shifting dynamic in the relationship between world Jewry and its post-Soviet counterpart. The early days of this enterprise were marked by the efforts of those who came from abroad to do the work. "Partnership" was rooted in a "we give and you receive" formula.

Very soon, the balance began to shift. As post-Soviet Jewry matured, it proved to be passionate, creative, capable, proud, and committed to the communities it formed. The Jewish communities that were created were not copies of what existed elsewhere. Instead, these newly formed communities were products of the unique vision and circumstances that marked *their* Jewish identity. They were shaped by their own history and culture. I have no doubt that this Jewry, reborn over the decades following the Soviet collapse, will determine its fate and the course of its history.

And that is the true miracle of its rebirth.

Glossary

ahavat Yisrael (Hebrew). Love of the Jewish people.

britot milah (Hebrew). Plural of *brit*, used to refer to the covenant marked by circumcision of Jewish males on the eighth day after birth. See Leviticus 12:3.

challot (Hebrew). Braided Shabbat loaves.

chanukiot (Hebrew). Plural of chanukiah, the candelabrum lit on each of the eight nights of Chanukah.

glasnost (Russian). "Openness." Policy instituted by Soviet leader Mikhail Gorbachev in the late 1980s to encourage limited political and economic reform. See also *perestroika*.

Great Patriotic War. The Soviet/Russian name for World War II.

groggers (Yiddish). Noisemakers used to blot out the name of the wicked villain Haman during the reading of the biblical Book of Esther on the holiday of Purim.

Haggadot (Hebrew). Plural of Haggadah, the text read on Passover commemorating the exodus from Egypt.

Hesed (Hebrew). Literally, "kindness." A social service delivery system established by the Joint in the former Soviet Union. At its peak, it provided essential goods and services to 240,000 elderly Jews in need.

Kaddish (Hebrew). A prayer in praise of God, recited by mourners and leaders of prayer services.

mezuzah (Hebrew). A brief selection of biblical texts appended to doorposts, as commanded in Deuteronomy 6:9.

mikveh (Hebrew). Ritual bath.

mohel (Hebrew). Ritual circumciser.

NKVD. The Soviet secret police, a forerunner of the KGB.

perestroika (Russian). "Restructuring." Policy instituted by Soviet leader Mikhail Gorbachev in the late 1980s to encourage limited political and economic reform. See also *glasnost*.

refusenik. A term used to characterize Jews during the Soviet period whose request to receive a visa to emigrate was denied (refused) by Soviet authorities.

repressed. In the Soviet context, a term that refers to individuals tried for infractions, real or fabricated, that generally led to internal exile.

shofarot (Hebrew). Plural of shofar, a ram's horn blown on Rosh Hashanah and various other significant occasions.

shtetl (Yiddish). Small town or village in prewar Eastern Europe with a significant Jewish population.

siddur (Hebrew). Jewish prayer book.

tefillin (Hebrew). Phylacteries. Weekday morning prayer accoutrements, referred to in Deuteronomy 6:8.

USSR. The Union of Soviet Socialist Republics, the Soviet Union. The Communist-ruled country established in Russia following the Bolshevik Revolution of October 1917, it ultimately encompassed fifteen republics spanning ten time zones. After World War II, the USSR became the world's second superpower and the West's Cold War enemy, before collapsing in 1991.

Warsaw Pact. Military alliance of the Soviet Union and the Communist-ruled countries of Central and Eastern Europe that were its semi-autonomous satellites.

Index

numbers in italics indicate photos

The Former Soviet Union